Credits

Authors
Stoyan Stefanov
Kumar Chetan Sharma

Reviewers
Kumar Chetan Sharma
Alex R. Young

Acquisition Editors
Martin Bell
Jonathan Titmus

Lead Technical Editor
Arun Nadar

Technical Editors
Prasad Dalvi
Mausam Kothari
Worrell Lewis
Amit Ramadas

Project Coordinator
Leena Purkait

Proofreaders
Paul Hindle
Linda Morris

Indexer
Rekha Nair

Graphics
Ronak Dhruv

Production Coordinator
Arvindkumar Gupta

Cover Work
Arvindkumar Gupta

D0204296

About the Authors

Stoyan Stefanov is a Facebook engineer, author, and speaker. He talks regularly about web development topics at conferences and his blog `www.phpied.com`, and also runs a number of other sites, including `JSPatterns.com`—a site dedicated to exploring JavaScript patterns. Previously at Yahoo!, Stoyan was the architect of YSlow 2.0 and creator of the image optimization tool Smush.it.

A "citizen of the world", Stoyan was born and raised in Bulgaria, but is also a Canadian citizen, currently residing in Los Angeles, California. In his offline moments, he enjoys playing the guitar, taking flying lessons, and spending time at the Santa Monica beaches with his family.

I'd like to dedicate this book to my wife Eva and my daughters Zlatina and Nathalie. Thank you for your patience, support, and encouragement.

To my reviewers who volunteered their time reviewing drafts of this book and whom I deeply respect and look up to: a big thank you for your invaluable inputs.

Kumar Chetan Sharma studied to be an electronics engineer and has always wanted to build an ultimate sound system. He then, by chance, got a part time job as a trainee HTML guy. From there he picked up CSS and JavaScript and there was no looking back. It was the time when JavaScript was used to validate forms or create fancy DHTML effects and IE6 was the only browser the world knew. He has been developing web applications since then, using LAMP stack. He has worked on white label social networking applications to web control panels for telecom and networked electrical charger infrastructures. He currently works as a frontend engineer for Yahoo! Search.

About the Reviewer

Alex R. Young is an engineering graduate with over 10 years of web and mobile industry experience.

He's the editor-in-chief of DailyJS, and writes regularly about all things JavaScript. He has also worked for major multinational corporations, including Thomson Reuters, and is currently writing a book about Node.

www.PacktPub.com

Support files, eBooks, discount offers and more

You might want to visit `www.PacktPub.com` for support files and downloads related to your book.

Did you know that Packt offers eBook versions of every book published, with PDF and ePub files available? You can upgrade to the eBook version at `www.PacktPub.com` and as a print book customer, you are entitled to a discount on the eBook copy. Get in touch with us at `service@packtpub.com` for more details.

At `www.PacktPub.com`, you can also read a collection of free technical articles, sign up for a range of free newsletters and receive exclusive discounts and offers on Packt books and eBooks.

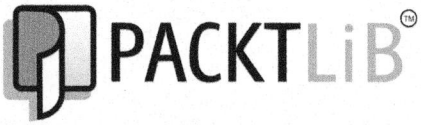

`http://PacktLib.PacktPub.com`

Do you need instant solutions to your IT questions? PacktLib is Packt's online digital book library. Here, you can access, read and search across Packt's entire library of books.

Why Subscribe?

- Fully searchable across every book published by Packt
- Copy and paste, print and bookmark content
- On demand and accessible via web browser

Free Access for Packt account holders

If you have an account with Packt at `www.PacktPub.com`, you can use this to access PacktLib today and view nine entirely free books. Simply use your login credentials for immediate access.

Table of Contents

Preface **1**

Chapter 1: Object-oriented JavaScript **7**

A bit of history **8**

Browser wars and renaissance 9

The present 10

The future 11

ECMAScript 5 **12**

Object-oriented programming **12**

Objects 13

Classes 13

Encapsulation 14

Aggregation 15

Inheritance 15

Polymorphism 16

OOP summary **16**

Setting up your training environment **17**

WebKit's Web Inspector 17

JavaScriptCore on a Mac 18

More consoles 19

Summary **20**

Chapter 2: Primitive Data Types, Arrays, Loops, and Conditions **21**

Variables **21**

Variables are case sensitive 23

Operators **24**

Primitive data types **28**

Finding out the value type – the typeof operator 28

Numbers 29

Octal and hexadecimal numbers 29

Exponent literals 30
Infinity 31
NaN 32
Strings **33**
String conversions 34
Special strings 35
Booleans **36**
Logical operators **37**
Operator precedence 39
Lazy evaluation 40
Comparison **41**
Undefined and null 43
Primitive data types recap **44**
Arrays **45**
Adding/updating array elements 46
Deleting elements 47
Arrays of arrays 47
Conditions and loops **48**
The if condition 49
The else clause 49
Code blocks **50**
Checking if a variable exists 51
Alternative if syntax 53
Switch **54**
Loops **56**
While loops 56
Do-while loops 57
For loops 57
For-in loops 60
Comments **61**
Summary **61**
Exercises **62**
Chapter 3: Functions **63**
What is a function? **64**
Calling a function 64
Parameters 65
Predefined functions 66
parseInt() 67
parseFloat() 68
isNaN() 69
isFinite() 70
eval() 71

Scope of variables **72**
Variable hoisting 74
Functions are data **75**
Anonymous functions 76
Callback functions 77
Callback examples 78
Immediate functions 80
Inner (private) functions 81
Functions that return functions 82
Function, rewrite thyself! 83
Closures **85**
Scope chain 85
Breaking the chain with a closure 86
Closure #1 88
Closure #2 88
A definition and closure #3 89
Closures in a loop 90
Getter/setter 92
Iterator 93
Summary **94**
Exercises **95**
Chapter 4: Objects **97**
From arrays to objects **97**
Elements, properties, methods, and members 99
Hashes and associative arrays 100
Accessing an object's properties 100
Calling an object's methods 102
Altering properties/methods 102
Using the this value 104
Constructor functions 104
The global object 105
The constructor property 107
The instanceof operator 108
Functions that return objects 108
Passing objects 109
Comparing objects 110
Objects in the WebKit console 111
console.log 112
Built-in objects **112**
Object 113

Array 114
A few array methods 117
Function 118
Properties of function objects 120
Methods of function objects 121
The arguments object revisited 123
Inferring object types 124
Boolean 125
Number 126
String 127
A few methods of string objects 129
Math 132
Date 134
Methods to work with date objects 136
RegExp 138
Properties of RegExp objects 139
Methods of RegExp objects 140
String methods that accept regular expressions as arguments 141
search() and match() 141
replace() 142
Replace callbacks 142
split() 144
Passing a string when a RegExp is expected 144
Error objects 145
Summary 148
Exercises 149
Chapter 5: Prototype 153
The prototype property 154
Adding methods and properties using the prototype 154
Using the prototype's methods and properties 155
Own properties versus prototype properties 156
Overwriting a prototype's property with an own property 157
Enumerating properties 159
isPrototypeOf() 162
The secret __proto__ link 163
Augmenting built-in objects 164
Augmenting built-in objects – discussion 165
Prototype gotchas 166
Summary 169
Exercises 169

Chapter 6: Inheritance **171**
Prototype chaining **171**
Prototype chaining example 172
Moving shared properties to the prototype 175
Inheriting the prototype only **177**
A temporary constructor – new F() 179
Uber – access to the parent from a child object **181**
Isolating the inheritance part into a function **182**
Copying properties **184**
Heads-up when copying by reference **186**
Objects inherit from objects **188**
Deep copy **190**
object() **192**
Using a mix of prototypal inheritance and copying properties **193**
Multiple inheritance **195**
Mixins 197
Parasitic inheritance **197**
Borrowing a constructor **198**
Borrow a constructor and copy its prototype 200
Summary **201**
Case study – drawing shapes **205**
Analysis 205
Implementation 206
Testing 210
Exercises **211**
Chapter 7: The Browser Environment **213**
Including JavaScript in an HTML page **213**
BOM and DOM – an overview **214**
BOM **215**
The window object revisited 215
window.navigator 216
Your console is a cheat sheet 217
window.location 217
window.history 218
window.frames 219
window.screen 221
window.open()/close() 222
window.moveTo() and window.resizeTo() 222
window.alert(), window.prompt(), and window.confirm() 223
window.setTimeout() and window.setInterval() 225

window.document 226
DOM 227
Core DOM and HTML DOM 229
Accessing DOM nodes 230
The document node 231
documentElement 232
Child nodes 233
Attributes 234
Accessing the content inside a tag 234
DOM access shortcuts 235
Siblings, body, first, and last child 237
Walk the DOM 239
Modifying DOM nodes 239
Modifying styles 240
Fun with forms 240
Creating new nodes 242
DOM-only method 243
cloneNode() 243
insertBefore() 244
Removing nodes 245
HTML-only DOM objects 247
Primitive ways to access the document 247
document.write() 248
Cookies, title, referrer, domain 249
Events 250
Inline HTML attributes 251
Element Properties 251
DOM event listeners 252
Capturing and bubbling 253
Stop propagation 255
Prevent default behavior 257
Cross-browser event listeners 258
Types of events 259
XMLHttpRequest 260
Sending the request 261
Processing the response 262
Creating XMLHttpRequest objects in IE prior to Version 7 263
A is for Asynchronous 264
X is for XML 264
An example 265
Summary 267
Exercises 268

Chapter 8: Coding and Design Patterns **271**
Coding patterns **272**
Separating behavior 272
Content 272
Presentation 273
Behavior 273
Example of separating behavior 274
Asynchronous JavaScript loading 275
Namespaces 275
An Object as a namespace 275
Namespaced constructors 276
A namespace() method 277
Init-time branching 278
Lazy definition 279
Configuration object 280
Private properties and methods 282
Privileged methods 283
Private functions as public methods 284
Immediate functions 285
Modules 286
Chaining 287
JSON 288
Design patterns **289**
Singleton 290
Singleton 2 290
Global variable 291
Property of the Constructor 291
In a private property 292
Factory 292
Decorator 294
Decorating a Christmas tree 295
Observer 296
Summary **299**
Appendix A: Reserved Words **301**
Keywords **301**
Future reserved words **302**
Previously reserved words **303**
Appendix B: Built-in Functions **305**

Appendix C: Built-in Objects **309**
Object **309**
Members of the Object constructor 310
The Object.prototype members 310
ECMAScript 5 additions to Object 312
Array **318**
The Array.prototype members 319
ECMAScript 5 additions to Array 322
Function **325**
The Function.prototype members 326
ECMAScript 5 additions to a function 327
Boolean **327**
Number **327**
Members of the Number constructor 328
The Number.prototype members 329
String **329**
Members of the String constructor 330
The String.prototype members 331
ECMAScript 5 additions to String 333
Date **333**
Members of the Date constructor 334
The Date.prototype members 335
ECMAScript 5 additions to Date 338
Math **339**
Members of the Math object 339
RegExp **341**
The RegExp.prototype members 341
Error objects **343**
The Error.prototype members 343
JSON **343**
Members of the JSON object 344
Appendix D: Regular Expressions **347**
Index **353**

Preface

This is the second edition of the highly rated book *Object-Oriented JavaScript* by *Stoyan Stefanov, Packt Publishing*. After the release of the first edition, in the last five years, JavaScript has moved from being mostly used in browsers for client-side technologies to being used even on server side. This edition explores the "language side" of JavaScript. The stress is on the standards part of the language. The book talks about ECMA Script, Object-Oriented JS, patterns, prototypal inheritance, and design patterns.

The book doesn't assume any prior knowledge of JavaScript and works from the ground up to give you a thorough understanding of the language. People who know the language will still find it useful and informative. Exercises at the end of the chapters help you assess your understanding.

What this book covers

Chapter 1, Object-oriented JavaScript, talks briefly about the history, present, and future of JavaScript, and then moves on to explore the basics of object-oriented programming (OOP) in general. You then learn how to set up your training environment (Firebug) in order to dive into the language on your own, using the book examples as a base.

Chapter 2, Primitive Data Types, Arrays, Loops, and Conditions, discusses the language basics: variables, data types, primitive data types, arrays, loops, and conditionals.

Chapter 3, Functions, covers functions that JavaScript uses, and here you learn to master them all. You also learn about the scope of variables and JavaScript's built-in functions. An interesting, but often misunderstood feature of the language—closures—is demystified at the end of the chapter.

Chapter 4, Objects, talks about objects, how to work with properties and methods, and the various ways to create your objects. This chapter also talks about built-in objects such as Array, Function, Boolean, Number, and String.

Chapter 5, Prototype, is dedicated to the all-important concept of prototypes in JavaScript. It also explains how prototype chain works, `hasOwnProperty()`, and some gotchas of prototypes.

Chapter 6, Inheritance, discusses how inheritance works. This chapter also talks about a method to create subclasses like other classic languages.

Chapter 7, The Browser Environment, is dedicated to browsers. This chapter also covers BOM (Browser Object Model), DOM (W3C's Document Object Model), browser events, and AJAX.

Chapter 8, Coding and Design Patterns, dives into various unique JavaScript coding patterns, as well as several language-independent design patterns, translated to JavaScript from the Book of Four, the most influential work of software design patterns. The chapter also discusses JSON.

Appendix A, Reserved Words, lists the reserved words in JavaScript.

Appendix B, Built-in Functions, is a reference of built-in JavaScript functions together with sample uses.

Appendix C, Built-in Objects, is a reference that provides details and examples of the use of every method and property of every built-in object in JavaScript.

Appendix D, Regular Expressions, is a regular expressions pattern reference.

Appendix E, Answers to Exercise Questions, has solutions for all the exercises mentioned at the end of the chapters.

You can download this Appendix from `http://www.packtpub.com/sites/default/files/downloads/3127OT_Answers_to_Exercise_Questions.pdf`.

What you need for this book

You need a modern browser—Google Chrome or Firefox are recommended—and an optional Node.js setup. The latest version of Firefox comes with web developer tools, but Firebug is highly recommended. To edit JavaScript you can use any text editor of your choice.

Who this book is for

This book is for anyone who is starting to learn JavaScript or who knows JavaScript but isn't very good at the object-oriented part of it.

Conventions

In this book, you will find a number of styles of text that distinguish between different kinds of information. Here are some examples of these styles, and an explanation of their meaning.

Code words in text are shown as follows: "If you want to be sure, you can check the `cancellable` property of the event object".

A block of code will be set as follows:

```
var a;
var thisIsAVariable;
var _and_this_too;
var mix12three;
```

When we wish to draw your attention to an output of a code block, the relevant lines or items will be shown in bold:

```
> var case_matters = 'lower';
> var CASE_MATTERS = 'upper';
> case_matters;
"lower"

> CASE_MATTERS;
"upper"
```

Any command-line input or output is written as follows:

```
alias jsc='/System/Library/Frameworks/JavaScriptCore.framework/Versions/
Current/Resources/jsc'
```

New terms and **important words** are introduced in a bold-type font. Words that you see on the screen, in menus or dialog boxes for example, appear in our text like this: "If the user clicks on **Cancel**, the `preventDefault()` method is called".

Warnings or important notes appear in a box like this.

Tips and tricks appear like this.

Reader feedback

Feedback from our readers is always welcome. Let us know what you think about this book—what you liked or may have disliked. Reader feedback is important for us to develop titles that you really get the most out of.

To send us general feedback, simply send an e-mail to `feedback@packtpub.com`, and mention the book title via the subject of your message.

If there is a topic that you have expertise in and you are interested in either writing or contributing to a book, see our author guide on `www.packtpub.com/authors`.

Customer support

Now that you are the proud owner of a Packt book, we have a number of things to help you to get the most from your purchase.

Errata

Although we have taken every care to ensure the accuracy of our content, mistakes do happen. If you find a mistake in one of our books—maybe a mistake in the text or the code—we would be grateful if you would report this to us. By doing so, you can save other readers from frustration and help us improve subsequent versions of this book. If you find any errata, please report them by visiting `http://www.packtpub.com/submit-errata`, selecting your book, clicking on the **errata submission form** link, and entering the details of your errata. Once your errata are verified, your submission will be accepted and the errata will be uploaded on our website, or added to any list of existing errata, under the Errata section of that title. Any existing errata can be viewed by selecting your title from `http://www.packtpub.com/support`.

Piracy

Piracy of copyright material on the Internet is an ongoing problem across all media. At Packt, we take the protection of our copyright and licenses very seriously. If you come across any illegal copies of our works, in any form, on the Internet, please provide us with the location address or website name immediately so that we can pursue a remedy.

Please contact us at `copyright@packtpub.com` with a link to the suspected pirated material.

We appreciate your help in protecting our authors, and our ability to bring you valuable content.

Questions

You can contact us at `questions@packtpub.com` if you are having a problem with any aspect of the book, and we will do our best to address it.

1

Object-oriented JavaScript

Ever since the early days of the Web, there has been a need for more dynamic and responsive interfaces. While it's OK to read static HTML pages of text and even better when they are beautifully presented with the help of CSS, it's much more fun to engage with applications in our browsers, such as e-mail, calendars, banking, shopping, drawing, playing games, and text editing. All that is possible thanks to JavaScript, the programming language of the Web. JavaScript started with simple one-liners embedded in HTML, but is now used in much more sophisticated ways. Developers leverage the object-oriented nature of the language to build scalable code architectures made up of reusable pieces.

If you look at the past and present buzzwords in web development—DHTML, Ajax, Web 2.0, HTML5—they all essentially mean HTML, CSS, and JavaScript. HTML for *content*, CSS for *presentation*, and JavaScript for *behavior*. In other words, JavaScript is the glue that makes everything work together so that we can build rich web applications.

But that's not all, JavaScript can be used for more than just the Web.

JavaScript programs run inside a host environment. The web browser is the most common environment, but it's not the only one. Using JavaScript, you can create all kinds of widgets, application extensions, and other pieces of software, as you'll see in a bit. Taking the time to learn JavaScript is a smart investment; you learn one language and can then write all kinds of different applications running on multiple platforms, including mobile and server-side applications. These days, it's safe to say that JavaScript is everywhere.

This book starts from zero, and does not assume any prior programming knowledge other than some basic understanding of HTML. Although there is one chapter dedicated to the web browser environment, the rest of the book is about JavaScript in general, so it's applicable to all environments.

Let's start with the following:

- A brief introduction to the story behind JavaScript
- The basic concepts you'll encounter in discussions on object-oriented programming

A bit of history

Initially, the Web was not much more than just a number of scientific publications in the form of static HTML documents connected together with hyperlinks. Believe it or not, there was a time when there was no way to put an image in a page. But that soon changed. As the Web grew in popularity and size, the webmasters who were creating HTML pages felt they needed something more. They wanted to create richer user interactions, mainly driven by the desire to save server roundtrips for simple tasks such as form validation. Two options came up: Java applets and LiveScript, a language conceived by Brendan Eich at Netscape in 1995 and later included in the Netscape 2.0 browser under the name of JavaScript.

The applets didn't quite catch on, but JavaScript did. The ability to use short code snippets embedded in HTML documents and alter otherwise static elements of a web page was embraced by the webmaster community. Soon, the competing browser vendor Microsoft shipped Internet Explorer (IE) 3.0 with JScript, which was a reverse engineered version of JavaScript plus some IE-specific features. Eventually, there was an effort to standardize the various implementations of the language, and this is how ECMAScript was born. **ECMA (European Computer Manufacturers Association)** created the standard called ECMA-262, which describes the core parts of the JavaScript programming language without browser and web page-specific features.

You can think of JavaScript as a term that encompasses three pieces:

- **ECMAScript**—the core language—variables, functions, loops, and so on. This part is independent of the browser and this language can be used in many other environments.
- **Document Object Model (DOM)**, which provides ways to work with HTML and XML documents. Initially, JavaScript provided limited access to what's scriptable on the page, mainly forms, links, and images. Later it was expanded to make all elements scriptable. This lead to the creation of the DOM standard by the **World Wide Web Consortium (W3C)** as a language-independent (no longer tied to JavaScript) way to manipulate structured documents.

- **Browser Object Model (BOM)**, which is a set of objects related to the browser environment and was never part of any standard until HTML5 started standardizing some of the common objects that exist across browsers.

While there is one chapter in the book dedicated to the browser, the DOM, and the BOM, most of the book describes the core language and teaches you skills you can use in any environment where JavaScript programs run.

Browser wars and renaissance

For better or for worse, JavaScript's instant popularity happened during the period of the Browser Wars I (approximately 1996 to 2001). Those were the times during the initial Internet boom when the two major browser vendors—Netscape and Microsoft—were competing for market share. Both were constantly adding more bells and whistles to their browsers and their versions of JavaScript, DOM, and BOM, which naturally led to many inconsistencies. While adding more features, the browser vendors were falling behind on providing proper development and debugging tools and adequate documentation. Often, development was a pain; you would write a script while testing in one browser, and once you're done with development, you test in the other browser, only to find that your script simply fails for no apparent reason and the best you can get is a cryptic error message like "Operation aborted".

Inconsistent implementations, missing documentation, and no appropriate tools painted JavaScript in such a light that many programmers simply refused to bother with it.

On the other hand, developers who did try to experiment with JavaScript got a little carried away adding too many special effects to their pages without much regard of how usable the end results were. Developers were eager to make use of every new possibility the browsers provided and ended up "enhancing" their web pages with things like animations in the status bar, flashing colors, blinking texts, objects stalking your mouse cursor, and many other "innovations" that actually hurt the user experience. These various ways to abuse JavaScript are now mostly gone, but they were one of the reasons why the language got some bad reputation. Many "serious" programmers dismissed JavaScript as nothing but a toy for designers to play around with, and dismissed it as a language unsuitable for serious applications. The JavaScript backlash caused some web projects to completely ban any client-side programming and trust only their predictable and tightly controlled server. And really, why would you double the time to deliver a finished product and then spend additional time debugging problems with the different browsers?

Everything changed in the years following the end of the Browser Wars I. A number of events reshaped the web development landscape in a positive way. Some of them are given as follows:

- Microsoft won the war with the introduction of IE6, the best browser at the time, and for many years they stopped developing Internet Explorer. This allowed time for other browsers to catch up and even surpass IE's capabilities.
- The movement for web standards was embraced by developers and browser vendors alike. Naturally, developers didn't like having to code everything two (or more) times to account for browsers' differences; therefore, they liked the idea of having agreed-upon standards that everyone would follow.
- Developers and technologies matured and more people started caring about things like usability, progressive enhancement techniques, and accessibility. Tools such as Firebug made developers much more productive and the development less of a pain.

In this healthier environment, developers started finding out new and better ways to use the instruments that were already available. After the public release of applications such as Gmail and Google Maps, which were rich on client-side programming, it became clear that JavaScript is a mature, unique in certain ways, and powerful prototypal object-oriented language. The best example of its rediscovery was the wide adoption of the functionality provided by the `XMLHttpRequest` object, which was once an IE-only innovation, but was then implemented by most other browsers. `XMLHttpRequest` allows JavaScript to make HTTP requests and get fresh content from the server in order to update some parts of a page without a full page reload. Due to the wide use of `XMLHttpRequest`, a new breed of desktop-like web applications, dubbed *Ajax* applications, was born.

The present

An interesting thing about JavaScript is that it always runs inside a *host environment*. The web browser is just one of the available hosts. JavaScript can also run on the server, on the desktop, and on mobile devices. Today, you can use JavaScript to do all of the following:

- Create rich and powerful web applications (the kind of applications that run inside the web browser). Additions to HTML5 such as application cache, client-side storage, and databases make browser programming more and more powerful for both online and offline applications.
- Write server-side code using .NET or `Node.js`, as well as code that can run using Rhino (a JavaScript engine written in Java).

- Make mobile applications; you can create apps for iPhone, Android, and other phones and tablets entirely in JavaScript using PhoneGap or Titanium. Additionally, apps for Firefox OS for mobile phones are entirely in JavaScript, HTML, and CSS.
- Create rich media applications (Flash, Flex) using ActionScript, which is based on ECMAScript.
- Write command-line tools and scripts that automate administrative tasks on your desktop using Windows Scripting Host or WebKit's JavaScript Core available on all Macs.
- Write extensions and plugins for a plethora of desktop applications, such as Dreamweaver, Photoshop, and most other browsers.
- Create cross operating system desktop applications using Mozilla's XULRunner or Adobe Air.
- Create desktop widgets using Yahoo! widgets or Mac Dashboard widgets. Interestingly, Yahoo! widgets can also run on your TV.

This is by no means an exhaustive list. JavaScript started inside web pages, but today it's safe to say it is practically everywhere. In addition, browser vendors now use speed as a competitive advantage and are racing to create the fastest JavaScript engines, which is great for both users and developers and opens doors for even more powerful uses of JavaScript in new areas such as image, audio, and video processing, and games development.

The future

We can only speculate what the future will be, but it's quite certain that it will include JavaScript. For quite some time, JavaScript may have been underestimated and underused (or maybe overused in the wrong ways), but every day we witness new applications of the language in much more interesting and creative ways. It all started with simple one liners, often embedded in HTML tag attributes (such as `onclick)`. Nowadays, developers ship sophisticated, well designed and architected, and extensible applications and libraries, often supporting multiple platforms with a single codebase. JavaScript is indeed taken seriously and developers are starting to rediscover and enjoy its unique features more and more.

Once listed in the "nice-to-have" sections of job postings, today, the knowledge of JavaScript is often a deciding factor when it comes to hiring web developers. Common job interview questions you can hear today include: "Is JavaScript an object-oriented language? Good. Now how do you implement inheritance in JavaScript?" After reading this book, you'll be prepared to ace your JavaScript job interview and even impress your interviewers with some bits that, maybe, they didn't know.

ECMAScript 5

Revision 3 of ECMAScript is the one you can take for granted to be implemented in all browsers and environments. Revision 4 was skipped and revision 5 (let's call it ES5 for short) was officially accepted in December 2009.

ES5 introduces some new objects and properties and also the so-called "strict mode". Strict mode is a subset of the language that excludes deprecated features. The strict mode is opt-in and not required, meaning that if you want your code to run in the strict mode, you declare your intention using (once per function, or once for the whole program) the following string:

```
"use strict";
```

This is just a JavaScript string, and it's OK to have strings floating around unassigned to any variable. As a result, older browsers that don't "speak" ES5 will simply ignore it, so this strict mode is backwards compatible and won't break older browsers.

In future versions, strict mode is likely to become the default or the only mode. For the time being, it's optional.

For backwards compatibility, all the examples in this book work in ES3, but at the same time, all the code in the book is written so that it will run without warnings in ES5's strict mode. Additionally, any ES5-specific parts will be clearly marked. *Appendix C, Built-in Objects,* lists the new additions to ES5 in detail.

Object-oriented programming

Before diving into JavaScript, let's take a moment to review what people mean when they say "object-oriented", and what the main features of this programming style are. Here's a list of concepts that are most often used when talking about **object-oriented programming** (OOP):

- Object, method, and property
- Class
- Encapsulation
- Aggregation
- Reusability/inheritance
- Polymorphism

Let's take a closer look into each one of these concepts. If you're new to the object-oriented programming lingo, these concepts might sound too theoretical, and you might have trouble grasping them or remembering them from one reading. Don't worry, it does take a few tries, and the subject could be a little dry at a conceptual level. But, we'll look at plenty of code examples further on in the book, and you'll see that things are much simpler in practice.

Objects

As the name object-oriented suggests, objects are important. An object is a representation of a "thing" (someone or something), and this representation is expressed with the help of a programming language. The thing can be anything—a real-life object, or a more convoluted concept. Taking a common object like a cat for example, you can see that it has certain characteristics (color, name, weight, and so on) and can perform some actions (meow, sleep, hide, escape, and so on). The characteristics of the object are called *properties* in OOP-speak, and the actions are called *methods*.

There is also an analogy with the spoken language:

- Objects are most often named using nouns (book, person, and so on)
- Methods are verbs (read, run, and so on)
- Values of the properties are adjectives

Take the sentence "The black cat sleeps on the mat". "The cat" (a noun) is the object, "black" (adjective) is the value of the `color` property, and "sleep" (a verb) is an action, or a method in OOP. For the sake of the analogy, we can go a step further and say that "on the mat " specifies something about the action "sleep", so it's acting as a parameter passed to the `sleep` method.

Classes

In real life, similar objects can be grouped based on some criteria. A hummingbird and an eagle are both birds, so they can be classified as belonging to some made up `Birds` class. In OOP, a class is a blueprint, or a recipe for an object. Another name for "object" is "instance", so we say that the eagle is one concrete instance of the general class `Birds`. You can create different objects using the same class, because a class is just a template, while the objects are concrete instances based on the template.

There's a difference between JavaScript and the "classic" OO languages such as C++ and Java. You should be aware right from the start that in JavaScript, there are no classes; everything is based on objects. JavaScript has the notion of prototypes, which are also objects (we'll discuss them later in detail). In a classic OO language, you'd say something like "create me a new object called Bob, which is of *class* Person". In a prototypal OO language, you'd say, "I'm going to take this *object* called Bob's dad that I have lying around (on the couch in front of the TV?) and reuse it as a *prototype* for a new object that I'll call Bob".

Encapsulation

Encapsulation is another OOP-related concept, which illustrates the fact that an object contains (encapsulates) both:

- Data (stored in properties)
- The means to do something with the data (using methods)

One other term that goes together with encapsulation is information hiding. This is a rather broad term and can mean different things, but let's see what people usually mean when they use it in the context of OOP.

Imagine an object, say, an MP3 player. You, as the user of the object, are given some interface to work with, such as buttons, display, and so on. You use the interface in order to get the object to do something useful for you, like play a song. How exactly the device is working on the inside, you don't know, and, most often, don't care. In other words, the implementation of the interface is hidden from you. The same thing happens in OOP when your code uses an object by calling its methods. It doesn't matter if you coded the object yourself or it came from some third-party library; your code doesn't need to know how the methods work internally. In compiled languages, you can't actually read the code that makes an object work. In JavaScript, because it's an interpreted language, you can see the source code, but the concept is still the same—you work with the object's interface, without worrying about its implementation.

Another aspect of information hiding is the visibility of methods and properties. In some languages, objects can have `public`, `private`, and `protected` methods and properties. This categorization defines the level of access the users of the object have. For example, only the methods of the same object have access to the `private` methods, while anyone has access to the `public` ones. In JavaScript, all methods and properties are `public`, but we'll see that there are ways to protect the data inside an object and achieve privacy.

Aggregation

Combining several objects into a new one is known as **aggregation** or **composition**. It's a powerful way to separate a problem into smaller and more manageable parts (divide and conquer). When a problem scope is so complex that it's impossible to think about it at a detailed level in its entirety, you can separate the problem into several smaller areas, and possibly then separate each of these into even smaller chunks. This allows you to think about the problem on several levels of abstraction.

Take, for example, a personal computer. It's a complex object. You cannot think about all the things that need to happen when you start your computer. But, you can abstract the problem saying that you need to initialize all the separate objects that your `Computer` object consists of – the `Monitor` object, the `Mouse` object, the `Keyboard` object, and so on. Then, you can dive deeper into each of the sub-objects. This way, you're composing complex objects by assembling reusable parts.

To use another analogy, a `Book` object can contain (aggregate) one or more `Author` objects, a `Publisher` object, several `Chapter` objects, a `TOC` (table of contents), and so on.

Inheritance

Inheritance is an elegant way to reuse existing code. For example, you can have a generic object, `Person`, which has properties such as `name` and `date_of_birth`, and which also implements the functionality `walk`, `talk`, `sleep`, and `eat`. Then, you figure out that you need another object called `Programmer`. You could re-implement all the methods and properties that `Person` has, but it would be smarter to just say that `Programmer` inherits `Person`, and save yourself some work. The `Programmer` object only needs to implement more-specific functionality, such as the `writeCode` method, while reusing all of the `Person` object's functionality.

In classical OOP, classes inherit from other classes, but in JavaScript, since there are no classes, objects inherit from other objects.

When an object inherits from another object, it usually adds new methods to the inherited ones, thus extending the old object. Often, the following phrases can be used interchangeably: "B inherits from A" and "B extends A". Also, the object that inherits can pick one or more methods and redefine them, customizing them for its own needs. This way, the interface stays the same, the method name is the same, but when called on the new object, the method behaves differently. This way of redefining how an inherited method works is known as **overriding**.

Polymorphism

In the preceding example, a `Programmer` object inherited all of the methods of the parent `Person` object. This means that both objects provide a `talk` method, among others. Now imagine that somewhere in your code there's a variable called `Bob`, and it just so happens that you don't know if `Bob` is a `Person` object or a `Programmer` object. You can still call the `talk` method on the `Bob` object and the code will work. This ability to call the same method on different objects and have each of them respond in their own way is called **polymorphism**.

OOP summary

Here's a quick table summarizing the concepts discussed so far:

Feature	Illustrates concept
Bob is a man (an object).	Objects
Bob's date of birth is June 1, 1980, gender: male, and hair: black.	Properties
Bob can eat, sleep, drink, dream, talk, and calculate his own age.	Methods
Bob is an instance of the `Programmer` class.	Class (in classical OOP)
Bob is based on another object, called `Programmer`.	Prototype (in prototypal OOP)
Bob holds data (such as `birth_date`) and methods that work with the data (such as `calculateAge()`).	Encapsulation
You don't need to know how the calculation method works internally. The object might have some private data, such as the number of days in February in a leap year. You don't know, nor do you want to know.	Information hiding
Bob is part of a `WebDevTeam` object, together with Jill, a `Designer` object, and Jack, a `ProjectManager` object.	Aggregation and composition
`Designer`, `ProjectManager`, and `Programmer` are all based on and extend a `Person` object.	Inheritance
You can call the methods `Bob.talk()`, `Jill.talk()`, and `Jack.talk()` and they'll all work fine, albeit producing different results (Bob will probably talk more about performance, Jill about beauty, and Jack about deadlines). Each object inherited the method `talk` from `Person` and customized it.	Polymorphism and method overriding

Setting up your training environment

This book takes a "do-it-yourself" approach when it comes to writing code, because I firmly believe that the best way to really learn a programming language is by writing code. There are no cut-and-paste-ready code downloads that you simply put in your pages. On the contrary, you're expected to type in code, see how it works, and then tweak it and play around with it. When trying out the code examples, you're encouraged to enter the code into a JavaScript console. Let's see how you go about doing this.

As a developer, you most likely already have a number of web browsers installed on your system such as Firefox, Safari, Chrome, or Internet Explorer. All modern browsers have a JavaScript console feature, which you'll use throughout the book to help you learn and experiment with the language. More specifically, this book uses WebKit's console (available in Safari and Chrome), but the examples should work in any other console.

WebKit's Web Inspector

This example shows how you can use the console to type in some code that swaps the logo on the `google.com` home page with an image of your choice. As you can see, you can test your JavaScript code live on any page.

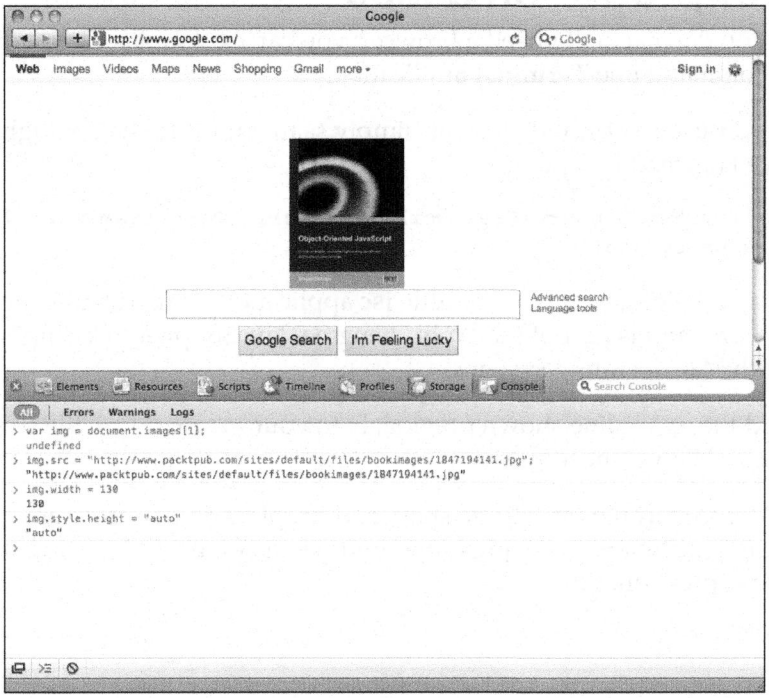

In order to bring up the console in Chrome or Safari, right-click anywhere on a page and select **Inspect Element**. The additional window that shows up is the Web Inspector feature. Select the **Console** tab and you're ready to go.

You type code directly into the console, and when you press *Enter*, your code is executed. The return value of the code is printed in the console. The code is executed in the context of the currently loaded page, so for example, if you type `location.href`, it will return the URL of the current page.

The console also has an autocomplete feature. It works similar to the normal command line prompt in your operating system. If, for example, you type `docu` and hit the *Tab* key or the right arrow key, `docu` will be autocompleted to `document`. Then, if you type `.` (the dot operator), you can iterate through all the available properties and methods you can call on the `document` object.

By using the up and down arrow keys, you can go through the list of already executed commands and bring them back in the console.

The console gives you only one line to type in, but you can execute several JavaScript statements by separating them with semicolons. If you need more lines, you can press *Shift* + *Enter* to go to a new line without executing the result just yet.

JavaScriptCore on a Mac

On a Mac, you don't actually need a browser; you can explore JavaScript directly from your command line **Terminal** application.

If you've never used **Terminal**, you can simply search for it in the Spotlight search. Once you've launched it, type:

```
alias jsc='/System/Library/Frameworks/JavaScriptCore.framework/Versions/
Current/Resources/jsc'
```

This command makes an alias to the little **jsc** application, which stands for "JavaScriptCore" and is part of the WebKit engine. JavaScriptCore is shipped together with Mac operating systems.

You can add the `alias` line shown previously to your `~/.profile` file so that `jsc` is always there when you need it.

Now, in order to start the interactive shell, you simply type `jsc` from any directory. Then you can type JavaScript expressions, and when you hit *Enter*, you'll see the result of the expression.

```
Terminal — jsc — 80×24
Last login: Tue May 31 01:07:35 on ttys002
stoyanstefanov:~ stoyanstefanov$ jsc
> 1+1
2
> var a = "hello";
undefined
> a
hello
> var b = "console";
undefined
> b
console
> a + " " + b
hello console
>
```

More consoles

All modern browsers have consoles built in. You have seen the Chrome/Safari console previously. In any Firefox version, you can install the Firebug extension, which comes with a console. Additionally, in newer Firefox releases, there's a console built in and accessible via the **Tools/Web Developer/Web Console** menu.

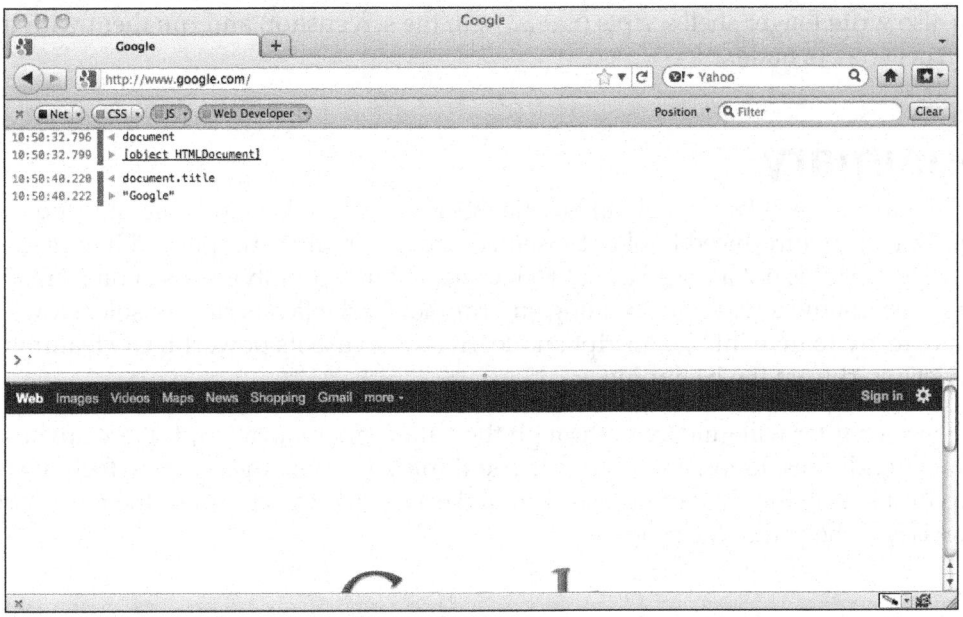

Internet Explorer, since Version 8, has an F12 Developer Tools feature, which has a console in its **Script** tab.

It's also a good idea to familiarize yourself with `Node.js`, and you can start by trying out its console. Install `Node.js` from `http://nodejs.org` and try the console in your command prompt (terminal).

```
stoyanstefanov — bash — 79×21
stoyanstefmbp15:~ stoyanstefanov$ node
> var a = 1; var b = 2;
undefined
> a + b;
3
>
(^C again to quit)
>
stoyanstefmbp15:~ stoyanstefanov$ cat test.js
var a = 101;
var b = 202;

console.log(a + b);
stoyanstefmbp15:~ stoyanstefanov$ node test.js
303
stoyanstefmbp15:~ stoyanstefanov$
```

As you can see, you can use the `Node.js` console to try out quick examples. But, you can also write longer shell scripts (`test.js` in the screenshot) and run them with the `scriptname.js` node.

Summary

In this chapter, you learned about how JavaScript came to be and where it is today. You were also introduced to object-oriented programming concepts and have seen how JavaScript is not a class-based OO language, but a prototype-based one. Finally, you learned how to use your training environment—the JavaScript console. Now you're ready to dive into JavaScript and learn how to use its powerful OO features. But let's start from the beginning.

The next chapter will guide you through the data types in JavaScript (there are just a few), conditions, loops, and arrays. If you think you know these topics, feel free to skip the next chapter, but not before you make sure you can complete the few short exercises at the end of the chapter.

2

Primitive Data Types, Arrays, Loops, and Conditions

Before diving into the object-oriented features of JavaScript, let's first take a look at some of the basics. This chapter walks you through the following:

- The primitive data types in JavaScript, such as strings and numbers
- Arrays
- Common operators, such as `+`, `-`, `delete`, and `typeof`
- Flow control statements, such as loops and if-else conditions

Variables

Variables are used to store data; they are placeholders for concrete values. When writing programs, it's convenient to use variables instead of the actual data, as it's much easier to write `pi` instead of `3.141592653589793`, especially when it happens several times inside your program. The data stored in a variable can be changed after it was initially assigned, hence the name "variable". You can also use variables to store data that is unknown to you while you write the code, such as the result of a later operation.

Using a variable requires two steps. You need to:

- Declare the variable
- Initialize it, that is, give it a value

To declare a variable, you use the `var` statement, like this:

```
var a;
var thisIsAVariable;
var _and_this_too;
var mix12three;
```

For the names of the variables, you can use any combination of letters, numbers, the underscore character, and the dollar sign. However, you can't start with a number, which means that this is invalid:

```
var 2three4five;
```

To initialize a variable means to give it a value for the first (initial) time. You have two ways to do so:

- Declare the variable first, then initialize it
- Declare and initialize it with a single statement

An example of the latter is:

```
var a = 1;
```

Now the variable named `a` contains the value `1`.

You can declare (and optionally initialize) several variables with a single `var` statement; just separate the declarations with a comma:

```
var v1, v2, v3 = 'hello', v4 = 4, v5;
```

For readability, this is often written using one variable per line:

```
var v1,
    v2,
    v3 = 'hello',
    v4 = 4,
    v5;
```

The $ character in variable names

You may see the dollar sign character ($) used in variable names, as in `$myvar` or less commonly `my$var`. This character is allowed to appear anywhere in a variable name, although previous versions of the ECMA standard discouraged its use in handwritten programs and suggested it should only be used in generated code (programs written by other programs). This suggestion is not well respected by the JavaScript community, and $ is in fact commonly used in practice as a function name.

Variables are case sensitive

Variable names are case sensitive. You can easily verify this statement using your JavaScript console. Try typing this, pressing *Enter* after each line:

```
var case_matters = 'lower';
var CASE_MATTERS = 'upper';
case_matters;
CASE_MATTER;
```

To save keystrokes, when you enter the third line, you can type `case` and press the *Tab* key (or right-arrow key). The console autocompletes the variable name to **case_matters**. Similarly, for the last line, type `CASE` and press *Tab*. The end result is shown in the following figure:

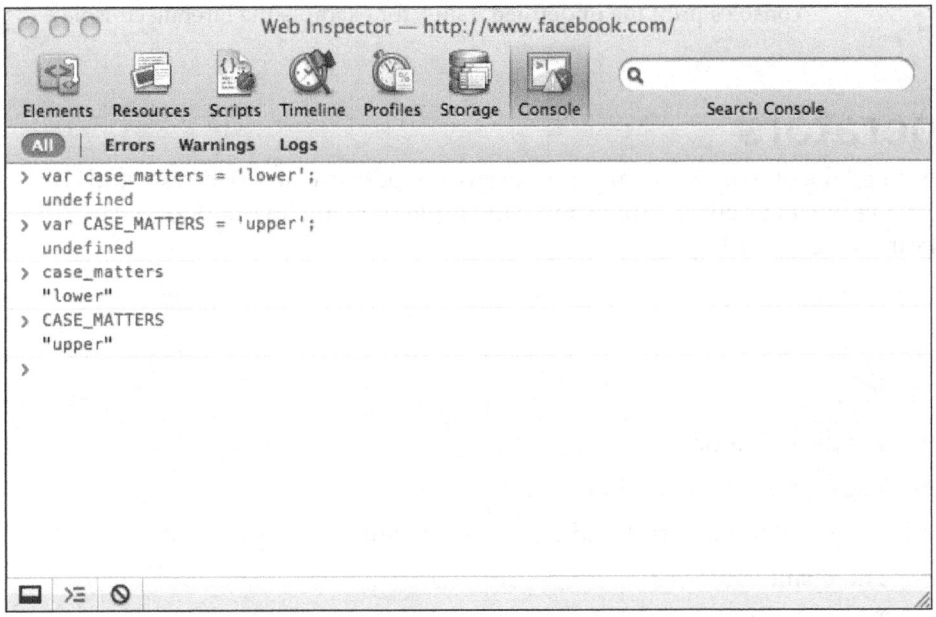

Throughout the rest of this book, only the code for the examples is given instead of a screenshot, like so:

```
> var case_matters = 'lower';
> var CASE_MATTERS = 'upper';
> case_matters;
"lower"

> CASE_MATTERS;
"upper"
```

The greater-than signs (>) show the code that you type; the rest is the result as printed in the console. Again, remember that when you see such code examples, you're strongly encouraged to type in the code yourself. Then, you can experiment by tweaking it a little here and there to get a better feeling of how exactly it works.

You can see in the screenshot that sometimes what you type in the console results in the word **undefined**. You can simply ignore this, but if you're curious, here's what happens: when evaluating (executing) what you type, the console prints the returned value. Some expressions (such as `var a = 1;`) don't return anything explicitly, in which case they implicitly return the special value **undefined** (more on it in a bit). When an expression returns some value (for example `case_matters` in the previous example or something such as `1 + 1`), the resulting value is printed out. Not all consoles print the **undefined** value, for example the Firebug console.

Operators

Operators take one or two values (or variables), perform an operation, and return a value. Let's check out a simple example of using an operator, just to clarify the terminology:

```
> 1 + 2;
3
```

In this code:

- `+` is the operator
- The operation is addition
- The input values are `1` and `2` (the input values are also called operands)
- The result value is `3`
- The whole thing is called an expression

Instead of using the values `1` and `2` directly in the expression, you can use variables. You can also use a variable to store the result of the operation, as the following example demonstrates:

```
> var a = 1;
> var b = 2;
> a + 1;
2
```

```
> b + 2;
4

> a + b;
3

> var c = a + b;
> c;
3
```

The following table lists the basic arithmetic operators:

Operator symbol	Operation	Example
+	Addition	`> 1 + 2;` **3**
-	Subtraction	`> 99.99 - 11;` **88.99**
*	Multiplication	`> 2 * 3;` **6**
/	Division	`> 6 / 4;` **1.5**

%	Modulo, the remainder of a division	`> 6 % 3;`
		0
		`> 5 % 3;`
		2
		It's sometimes useful to test if a number is even or odd. Using the modulo operator, it's easy to do just that. All odd numbers return 1 when divided by 2, while all even numbers return 0.
		`> 4 % 2;`
		0
		`> 5 % 2;`
		1

Operator symbol	Operation	Example

`++`	Increment a value by 1	Post-increment is when the input value is incremented after it's returned.
		`> var a = 123;`
		`> var b = a++;`
		`> b;`
		123
		`> a;`
		124
		The opposite is pre-increment. The input value is incremented by 1 first and then returned.
		`> var a = 123;`
		`> var b = ++a;`
		`> b;`
		124
		`> a;`
		124

`--`	Decrement a value by 1	Post-decrement:
		`> var a = 123;`
		`> var b = a--;`
		`> b;`
		123
		`> a;`
		122
		Pre-decrement:
		`> var a = 123;`
		`> var b = --a;`
		`> b;`
		122
		`> a;`
		122

`var a = 1;` is also an operation; it's the simple assignment operation, and `=` is the **simple assignment operator**.

There is also a family of operators that are a combination of an assignment and an arithmetic operator. These are called **compound operators**. They can make your code more compact. Let's see some of them with examples:

```
> var a = 5;
> a += 3;
8
```

In this example, `a += 3;` is just a shorter way of doing `a = a + 3;`:

```
> a -= 3;
5
```

Here, `a -= 3;` is the same as `a = a - 3;`.

Similarly:

```
> a *= 2;
10

> a /= 5;
2

> a %= 2;
0
```

In addition to the arithmetic and assignment operators discussed previously, there are other types of operators, as you'll see later in this and the following chapters.

Best practice

Always end your expressions with a semicolon. JavaScript has a semicolon insertion mechanism where it can add the semicolon if you forget it at the end of a line. However, this can also be a source of errors, so it's best to make sure you always explicitly state where you want to terminate your expressions. In other words, both expressions, `> 1 + 1` and `> 1 + 1;`, will work; but, throughout the book you'll always see the second type, terminated with a semicolon, just to emphasize this habit.

Primitive data types

Any value that you use is of a certain type. In JavaScript, there are just a few primitive data types:

1. Number: This includes floating point numbers as well as integers. For example, these values are all numbers: `1`, `100`, `3.14`.
2. String: These consist of any number of characters, for example `"a"`, `"one"`, and `"one 2 three"`.
3. Boolean: This can be either `true` or `false`.
4. Undefined: When you try to access a variable that doesn't exist, you get the special value `undefined`. The same happens when you declare a variable without assigning a value to it yet. JavaScript initializes the variable behind the scenes with the value `undefined`. The undefined data type can only have one value - the special value `undefined`.
5. Null: This is another special data type that can have only one value, namely the `null` value. It means no value, an empty value, or nothing. The difference with `undefined` is that if a variable has a value `null`, it's still defined, it just so happens that its value is nothing. You'll see some examples shortly.

Any value that doesn't belong to one of the five primitive types listed here is an object. Even `null` is considered an object, which is a little awkward—having an object (something) that is actually nothing. We'll learn more on objects in *Chapter 4, Objects*, but for the time being, just remember that in JavaScript the data types are either:

- Primitive (the five types listed previously)
- Non-primitive (objects)

Finding out the value type – the typeof operator

If you want to know the type of a variable or a value, you use the special `typeof` operator. This operator returns a string that represents the data type. The return values of using `typeof` are one of the following:

- `"number"`
- `"string"`
- `"boolean"`

- `"undefined"`
- `"object"`
- `"function"`

In the next few sections, you'll see `typeof` in action using examples of each of the five primitive data types.

Numbers

The simplest number is an integer. If you assign `1` to a variable and then use the `typeof` operator, it returns the string `"number"`:

```
> var n = 1;
> typeof n;
"number"

> n = 1234;
> typeof n;
"number"
```

In the preceding example, you can see that the second time you set a variable's value, you don't need the `var` statement.

Numbers can also be floating point (decimals):

```
> var n2 = 1.23;
> typeof n;
"number"
```

You can call `typeof` directly on the value without assigning it to a variable first:

```
> typeof 123;
"number"
```

Octal and hexadecimal numbers

When a number starts with a 0, it's considered an octal number. For example, the octal `0377` is the decimal `255`:

```
> var n3 = 0377;
> typeof n3;
"number"

> n3;
255
```

The last line in the preceding example prints the decimal representation of the octal value.

While you may not be intimately familiar with octal numbers, you've probably used hexadecimal values to define colors in CSS stylesheets.

In CSS, you have several options to define a color, two of them being:

- Using decimal values to specify the amount of R (red), G (green), and B (blue) ranging from 0 to 255. For example, `rgb(0, 0, 0)` is black and `rgb(255, 0, 0)` is red (maximum amount of red and no green or blue).
- Using hexadecimals and specifying two characters for each R, G, and B value. For example, `#000000` is black and `#ff0000` is red. This is because `ff` is the hexadecimal value for 255.

In JavaScript, you put `0x` before a hexadecimal value (also called hex for short):

```
> var n4 = 0x00;
> typeof n4;
"number"

> n4;
0

> var n5 = 0xff;
> typeof n5;
"number"

> n5;
255
```

Exponent literals

`1e1` (also written as `1e+1` or `1E1` or `1E+1`) represents the number one with one zero after it, or in other words, 10. Similarly, `2e+3` means the number 2 with 3 zeros after it, or 2000:

```
> 1e1;
10

> 1e+1;
10

> 2e+3;
2000

> typeof 2e+3;
"number"
```

`2e+3` means moving the decimal point three digits to the right of the number 2. There's also `2e-3`, meaning you move the decimal point three digits to the left of the number 2:

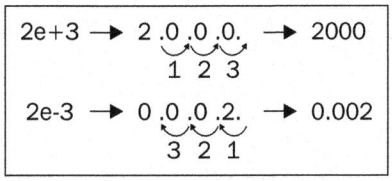


```
> 2e-3;
```
0.002

```
> 123.456E-3;
```
0.123456

```
> typeof 2e-3;
```
"number"

Infinity

There is a special value in JavaScript called `Infinity`. It represents a number too big for JavaScript to handle. `Infinity` is indeed a number, as typing `typeof Infinity` in the console will confirm. You can also quickly check that a number with 308 zeros is ok, but 309 zeros is too much. To be precise, the biggest number JavaScript can handle is `1.7976931348623157e+308`, while the smallest is `5e-324`.

```
> Infinity;
```
Infinity

```
> typeof Infinity;
```
"number"

```
> 1e309;
```
Infinity

```
> 1e308;
```
1e+308

Dividing by zero gives you infinity:

```
> var a = 6 / 0;
> a;
```
Infinity

Infinity is the biggest number (or rather a little bigger than the biggest), but how about the smallest? It's infinity with a minus sign in front of it; minus infinity:

```
> var i = -Infinity;
> i;
-Infinity

> typeof i;
"number"
```

Does this mean you can have something that's exactly twice as big as `Infinity`, from 0 up to infinity and then from 0 down to minus infinity? Well, not really. When you sum infinity and minus infinity, you don't get 0, but something that is called `NaN` (Not a Number):

```
> Infinity - Infinity;
NaN

> -Infinity + Infinity;
NaN
```

Any other arithmetic operation with `Infinity` as one of the operands gives you `Infinity`:

```
> Infinity - 20;
Infinity

> -Infinity * 3;
-Infinity

> Infinity / 2;
Infinity

> Infinity - 99999999999999999;
Infinity
```

NaN

What was this `NaN` in the previous example? It turns out that despite its name, "Not a Number", `NaN` is a special value that is also a number:

```
> typeof NaN;
"number"

> var a = NaN;
> a;
NaN
```

You get `NaN` when you try to perform an operation that assumes numbers, but the operation fails. For example, if you try to multiply `10` by the character `"f"`, the result is `NaN`, because `"f"` is obviously not a valid operand for a multiplication:

```
> var a = 10 * "f";
> a;
NaN
```

`NaN` is contagious, so if you have even one `NaN` in your arithmetic operation, the whole result goes down the drain:

```
> 1 + 2 + NaN;
NaN
```

Strings

A string is a sequence of characters used to represent text. In JavaScript, any value placed between single or double quotes is considered a string. This means that `1` is a number, but `"1"` is a string. When used with strings, `typeof` returns the string `"string"`:

```
> var s = "some characters";
> typeof s;
"string"

> var s = 'some characters and numbers 123 5.87';
> typeof s;
"string"
```

Here's an example of a number used in the string context:

```
> var s = '1';
> typeof s;
"string"
```

If you put nothing in quotes, it's still a string (an empty string):

```
> var s = ""; typeof s;
"string"
```

As you already know, when you use the plus sign with two numbers, this is the arithmetic addition operation. However, if you use the plus sign with strings, this is a string concatenation operation, and it returns the two strings glued together:

```
> var s1 = "web";
> var s2 = "site";
> var s = s1 + s2;
```

```
> s;
"website"

> typeof s;
"string"
```

The dual purpose of the `+` operator is a source of errors. Therefore, if you intend to concatenate strings, it's always best to make sure that all of the operands are strings. The same applies for addition; if you intend to add numbers, make sure the operands are numbers. You'll learn various ways to do so further in the chapter and the book.

String conversions

When you use a number-like string (for example `"1"`) as an operand in an arithmetic operation, the string is converted to a number behind the scenes. This works for all arithmetic operations except addition, because of its ambiguity:

```
> var s = '1';
> s = 3 * s;
> typeof s;
"number"

> s;
3

> var s = '1';
> s++;
> typeof s;
"number"

> s;
2
```

A lazy way to convert any number-like string to a number is to multiply it by 1 (another way is to use a function called `parseInt()`, as you'll see in the next chapter):

```
> var s = "100"; typeof s;
"string"

> s = s * 1;
100

> typeof s;
"number"
```

If the conversion fails, you'll get `NaN`:

```
> var movie = '101 dalmatians';
> movie * 1;
NaN
```

You convert a string to a number by multiplying by 1. The opposite—converting anything to a string—can be done by concatenating it with an empty string:

```
> var n = 1;
> typeof n;
"number"

> n = "" + n;
"1"

> typeof n;
"string"
```

Special strings

There are also strings with special meanings, as listed in the following table:

String	Meaning	Example
`\\`	`\` is the escape character.	`> var s = 'I don't know';`
`\'` `\"`	When you want to have quotes inside your string, you escape them so that JavaScript doesn't think they mean the end of the string. If you want to have an actual backslash in the string, escape it with another backslash.	This is an error, because JavaScript thinks the string is `I don` and the rest is invalid code. The following are valid: • `> var s = 'I don\'t know';` • `> var s = "I don\'t know";` • `> var s = "I don't know";` • `> var s = '"Hello", he said.';` • `> var s = "\"Hello\", he said.";` Escaping the escape: `> var s = "1\\2"; s;` **"1\2"**

String	Meaning	Example

`\n`	End of line.	`> var s = '\n1\n2\n3\n';`
		`> s;`
		"
		1
		2
		3
		"

`\r`	Carriage return.	Consider the following statements: • > var s = '1\r2'; • > var s = '1\n\r2'; • > var s = '1\r\n2'; The result of all of these is: `> s;` **"1** **2"**

`\t`	Tab.	`> var s = "1\t2";`
		`> s;`
		"1 2"

`\u`	`\u` followed by a character code allows you to use Unicode.	Here's my name in Bulgarian written with Cyrillic characters: `> "\u0421\u0442\u043E\u044F\u043D";` **"Стоян"**

There are also additional characters that are rarely used: `\b` (backspace), `\v` (vertical tab), and `\f` (form feed).

Booleans

There are only two values that belong to the Boolean data type: the values `true` and `false`, used without quotes:

```
> var b = true;
> typeof b;
"boolean"

> var b = false;
> typeof b;
"boolean"
```

If you quote `true` or `false`, they become strings:

```
> var b = "true";
> typeof b;
"string"
```

Logical operators

There are three operators, called logical operators, that work with Boolean values. These are:

- `!` - logical NOT (negation)
- `&&` - logical AND
- `||` - logical OR

You know that when something is not true, it must be false. Here's how this is expressed using JavaScript and the logical `!` operator:

```
> var b = !true;
> b;
false
```

If you use the logical NOT twice, you get the original value:

```
> var b = !!true;
> b;
true
```

If you use a logical operator on a non-Boolean value, the value is converted to Boolean behind the scenes:

```
> var b = "one";
> !b;
false
```

In the preceding case, the string value `"one"` is converted to a Boolean, `true`, and then negated. The result of negating `true` is `false`. In the next example, there's a double negation, so the result is `true`:

```
> var b = "one";
> !!b;
true
```

You can convert any value to its Boolean equivalent using a double negation. Understanding how any value converts to a Boolean is important. Most values convert to `true` with the exception of the following, which convert to `false`:

- The empty string `""`
- `null`
- `undefined`
- The number `0`
- The number `NaN`
- The Boolean `false`

These six values are referred to as falsy, while all others are truthy (including, for example, the strings `"0"`, `" "`, and `"false"`).

Let's see some examples of the other two operators—the logical AND (`&&`) and the logical OR (`||`). When you use `&&`, the result is `true` only if all of the operands are `true`. When you use `||`, the result is `true` if at least one of the operands is `true`:

```
> var b1 = true, b2 = false;
> b1 || b2;
true

> b1 && b2;
false
```

Here's a list of the possible operations and their results:

Operation	Result
`true && true`	`true`
`true && false`	`false`
`false && true`	`false`
`false && false`	`false`
`true || true`	`true`
`true || false`	`true`
`false || true`	`true`
`false || false`	`false`

You can use several logical operations one after the other:

```
> true && true && false && true;
false
```

```
> false || true || false;
true
```

You can also mix `&&` and `||` in the same expression. In such cases, you should use parentheses to clarify how you intend the operation to work. Consider these:

```
> false && false || true && true;
true

> false && (false || true) && true;
false
```

Operator precedence

You might wonder why the previous expression (`false && false || true && true`) returned `true`. The answer lies in the operator precedence. As you know from mathematics:

```
> 1 + 2 * 3;
7
```

This is because multiplication has higher precedence over addition, so `2 * 3` is evaluated first, as if you typed:

```
> 1 + (2 * 3);
7
```

Similarly for logical operations, `!` has the highest precedence and is executed first, assuming there are no parentheses that demand otherwise. Then, in the order of precedence, comes `&&` and finally `||`. In other words, the following two code snippets are the same:

```
> false && false || true && true;
true
```

and

```
> (false && false) || (true && true);
true
```

Best practice

Use parentheses instead of relying on operator precedence. This makes your code easier to read and understand.

The ECMAScript standard defines the precedence of operators. While it may be a good memorization exercise, this book doesn't offer it. First of all, you'll forget it, and second, even if you manage to remember it, you shouldn't rely on it. The person reading and maintaining your code will likely be confused.

Lazy evaluation

If you have several logical operations one after the other, but the result becomes clear at some point before the end, the final operations will not be performed because they don't affect the end result. Consider this:

```
> true || false || true || false || true;
true
```

Since these are all OR operations and have the same precedence, the result will be `true` if at least one of the operands is `true`. After the first operand is evaluated, it becomes clear that the result will be `true`, no matter what values follow. So, the JavaScript engine decides to be lazy (OK, efficient) and avoids unnecessary work by evaluating code that doesn't affect the end result. You can verify this short-circuiting behavior by experimenting in the console:

```
> var b = 5;
> true || (b = 6);
true

> b;
5

> true && (b = 6);
6

> b;
6
```

This example also shows another interesting behavior: if JavaScript encounters a non-Boolean expression as an operand in a logical operation, the non-Boolean is returned as a result:

```
> true || "something";
true

> true && "something";
"something"

> true && "something" && true;
true
```

This behavior is not something you should rely on because it makes the code harder to understand. It's common to use this behavior to define variables when you're not sure whether they were previously defined. In the next example, if the variable `mynumber` is defined, its value is kept; otherwise, it's initialized with the value `10`:

```
> var mynumber = mynumber || 10;
> mynumber;
10
```

This is simple and looks elegant, but be aware that it's not completely foolproof. If `mynumber` is defined and initialized to 0 (or to any of the six falsy values), this code might not behave as you expect:

```
> var mynumber = 0;
> var mynumber = mynumber || 10;
> mynumber;
10
```

Comparison

There's another set of operators that all return a Boolean value as a result of the operation. These are the comparison operators. The following table lists them together with example uses:

Operator symbol	Description	Example

`==`	Equality comparison: Returns true when both operands are equal. The operands are converted to the same type before being compared. Also called loose comparison.	`> 1 == 1;`
		true
		`> 1 == 2;`
		false
		`> 1 == '1';`
		true

`===`	Equality and type comparison: Returns `true` if both operands are equal and of the same type. It's better and safer to compare this way because there's no behind-the-scenes type conversions. It is also called strict comparison.	`> 1 === '1';`
		false
		`> 1 === 1;`
		true

Operator symbol	Description	Example

`!=`	Non-equality comparison: Returns `true` if the operands are not equal to each other (after a type conversion).	`> 1 != 1;`
		false
		`> 1 != '1';`
		false
		`> 1 != '2';`
		true

`!==`	Non-equality comparison without type conversion: Returns `true` if the operands are not equal or if they are of different types.	`> 1 !== 1;`
		false
		`> 1 !== '1';`
		true

`>`	Returns `true` if the left operand is greater than the right one.	`> 1 > 1;`
		false
		`> 33 > 22;`
		true

`>=`	Returns `true` if the left operand is greater than or equal to the right one.	> 1 >= 1; **true**
`<`	Returns `true` if the left operand is less than the right one.	> 1 < 1; **false** `> 1 < 2;` **true**
`<=`	Returns `true` if the left operand is less than or equal to the right one.	> 1 <= 1; **true** `> 1 <= 2;` **true**

Note that `NaN` is not equal to anything, not even itself:

```
> NaN == NaN;
```
false

Undefined and null

If you try to use a non-existing variable, you'll get an error:

```
> foo;
ReferenceError: foo is not defined
```

Using the `typeof` operator on a non-existing variable is not an error. You get the string `"undefined"` back:

```
> typeof foo;
"undefined"
```

If you declare a variable without giving it a value, this is, of course, not an error. But, the `typeof` still returns `"undefined"`:

```
> var somevar;
> somevar;
> typeof somevar;
"undefined"
```

This is because when you declare a variable without initializing it, JavaScript automatically initializes it with the value `undefined`:

```
> var somevar;
> somevar === undefined;
true
```

The `null` value, on the other hand, is not assigned by JavaScript behind the scenes; it's assigned by your code:

```
> var somevar = null;
null

> somevar;
null

> typeof somevar;
"object"
```

Although the difference between `null` and `undefined` is small, it could be critical at times. For example, if you attempt an arithmetic operation, you get different results:

```
> var i = 1 + undefined;
> i;
NaN

> var i = 1 + null;
> i;
1
```

This is because of the different ways `null` and `undefined` are converted to the other primitive types. The following examples show the possible conversions:

- Conversion to a number:

  ```
  > 1 * undefined;
  ```
  NaN

  ```
  > 1 * null;
  ```
  0

- Conversion to a Boolean:

  ```
  > !!undefined;
  ```
  false

  ```
  > !!null;
  ```
  false

- Conversion to a string:

  ```
  > "value: " + null;
  ```
  "value: null"

  ```
  > "value: " + undefined;
  ```
  "value: undefined"

Primitive data types recap

Let's quickly summarize some of the main points discussed so far:

- There are five primitive data types in JavaScript:
  - Number
  - String
  - Boolean
  - Undefined
  - Null
- Everything that is not a primitive data type is an object
- The primitive number data type can store positive and negative integers or floats, hexadecimal numbers, octal numbers, exponents, and the special numbers `NaN`, `Infinity`, and `-Infinity`
- The string data type contains characters in quotes
- The only values of the Boolean data type are `true` and `false`
- The only value of the null data type is the value `null`

- The only value of the undefined data type is the value `undefined`
- All values become `true` when converted to a Boolean, with the exception of the six falsy values:
  - `""`
  - `null`
  - `undefined`
  - `0`
  - `NaN`
  - `false`

Arrays

Now that you know about the basic primitive data types in JavaScript, it's time to move to a more powerful data structure—the array.

So, what is an array? It's simply a list (a sequence) of values. Instead of using one variable to store one value, you can use one array variable to store any number of values as elements of the array.

To declare a variable that contains an empty array, you use square brackets with nothing between them:

```
> var a = [];
```

To define an array that has three elements, you do this:

```
> var a = [1, 2, 3];
```

When you simply type the name of the array in the console, you get the contents of your array:

```
> a;
[1, 2, 3]
```

Now the question is how to access the values stored in these array elements. The elements contained in an array are indexed with consecutive numbers starting from zero. The first element has index (or position) 0, the second has index 1, and so on. Here's the three-element array from the previous example:

Index	Value
0	1
1	2
2	3

To access an array element, you specify the index of that element inside square brackets. So, `a[0]` gives you the first element of the array `a`, `a[1]` gives you the second, and so on:

```
> a[0];
1

> a[1];
2
```

Adding/updating array elements

Using the index, you can also update the values of the elements of the array. The next example updates the third element (index 2) and prints the contents of the new array:

```
> a[2] = 'three';
"three"

> a;
[1, 2, "three"]
```

You can add more elements by addressing an index that didn't exist before:

```
> a[3] = 'four';
"four"

> a;
[1, 2, "three", "four"]
```

If you add a new element, but leave a gap in the array, those elements in between don't exist and return the `undefined` value if accessed. Check out this example:

```
> var a = [1, 2, 3];
> a[6] = 'new';
"new"

> a;
[1, 2, 3, undefined x 3, "new"]
```

Deleting elements

To delete an element, you use the `delete` operator. However, after the deletion, the length of the array does not change. In a sense, you get a hole in the array:

```
> var a = [1, 2, 3];
> delete a[1];
true

> a;
[1, undefined, 3]

> typeof a[1];
"undefined"
```

Arrays of arrays

Arrays can contain all types of values, including other arrays:

```
> var a = [1, "two", false, null, undefined];
> a;
[1, "two", false, null, undefined]

> a[5] = [1, 2, 3];
[1, 2, 3]

> a;
[1, "two", false, null, undefined, Array[3]]
```

The **Array[3]** in the result is clickable in the console and it expands the array values. Let's see an example where you have an array of two elements, both of them being other arrays:

```
> var a = [[1, 2, 3], [4, 5, 6]];
> a;
[Array[3], Array[3]]
```

The first element of the array is `a[0]`, and it's also an array:

```
> a[0];
[1, 2, 3]
```

To access an element in the nested array, you refer to the element index in another set of square brackets:

```
> a[0][0];
1

> a[1][2];
6
```

Note that you can use the array notation to access individual characters inside a string:

```
> var s = 'one';
> s[0];
"o"

> s[1];
"n"

> s[2];
"e"
```

Array access to strings has been supported by many browsers for a while (not older IEs), but has been officially recognized only as late as ECMAScript 5.

There are more ways to have fun with arrays (and you'll get to those in *Chapter 4, Objects*), but let's stop here for now, remembering that:

- An array is a data store
- An array contains indexed elements
- Indexes start from zero and increment by one for each element in the array
- To access an element of an array, you use its index in square brackets
- An array can contain any type of data, including other arrays

Conditions and loops

Conditions provide a simple but powerful way to control the flow of code execution. **Loops** allow you to perform repetitive operations with less code. Let's take a look at:

- `if` conditions
- `switch` statements
- `while`, `do-while`, `for`, and `for-in` loops

The examples in the following sections require you to switch to the multiline Firebug console. Or, if you use the WebKit console, use *Shift* + *Enter* instead of *Enter* to add a new line.

The if condition

Here's a simple example of an `if` condition:

```
var result = '', a = 3;
if (a > 2) {
  result = 'a is greater than 2';
}
```

The parts of the `if` condition are:

- The `if` statement
- A condition in parentheses—"is `a` greater than 2?"
- A block of code wrapped in `{}` that executes if the condition is satisfied

The condition (the part in parentheses) always returns a Boolean value, and may also contain the following:

- A logical operation: `!`, `&&`, or `||`
- A comparison, such as `===`, `!=`, `>`, and so on
- Any value or variable that can be converted to a Boolean
- A combination of the above

The else clause

There can also be an optional `else` part of the `if` condition. The `else` statement is followed by a block of code that runs if the condition evaluates to `false`:

```
if (a > 2) {
  result = 'a is greater than 2';
} else {
  result = 'a is NOT greater than 2';
}
```

In between the `if` and the `else`, there can also be an unlimited number of `else if` conditions. Here's an example:

```
if (a > 2 || a < -2) {
  result = 'a is not between -2 and 2';
} else if (a === 0 && b === 0) {
  result = 'both a and b are zeros';
} else if (a === b) {
  result = 'a and b are equal';
} else {
  result = 'I give up';
}
```

You can also nest conditions by putting new conditions within any of the blocks:

```
if (a === 1) {
  if (b === 2) {
    result = 'a is 1 and b is 2';
  } else {
    result = 'a is 1 but b is definitely not 2';
  }
} else {
  result = 'a is not 1, no idea about b';
}
```

Code blocks

In the preceding examples, you saw the use of code blocks. Let's take a moment to clarify what a block of code is, because you use blocks extensively when constructing conditions and loops.

A block of code consists of zero or more expressions enclosed in curly brackets:

```
{
  var a = 1;
  var b = 3;
}
```

You can nest blocks within each other indefinitely:

```
{
  var a = 1;
  var b = 3;
  var c, d;
  {
    c = a + b;
```

```
    {
      d = a - b;
    }
  }
}
```

Best practice tips

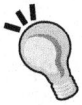

- Use end-of-line semicolons, as discussed previously in the chapter. Although the semicolon is optional when you have only one expression per line, it's good to develop the habit of using them. For best readability, the individual expressions inside a block should be placed one per line and separated by semicolons.
- Indent any code placed within curly brackets. Some programmers like one tab indentation, some use four spaces, and some use two spaces. It really doesn't matter, as long as you're consistent. In the preceding example, the outer block is indented with two spaces, the code in the first nested block is indented with four spaces, and the innermost block is indented with six spaces.
- Use curly brackets. When a block consists of only one expression, the curly brackets are optional, but for readability and maintainability, you should get into the habit of always using them, even when they're optional.

Checking if a variable exists

Let's apply the new knowledge about conditions for something practical. It's often necessary to check whether a variable exists. The laziest way to do this is to simply put the variable in the condition part of the `if`, for example, `if (somevar) {...}`. But, this is not necessarily the best method. Let's take a look at an example that tests whether a variable called `somevar` exists, and if so, sets the `result` variable to `yes`:

```
> var result = '';
> if (somevar) {
    result = 'yes';
  }
ReferenceError: somevar is not defined

> result;
""
```

This code obviously works because the end result was not "yes". But firstly, the code generated an error: `somevar` is not defined, and you don't want your code to behave like that. Secondly, just because `if (somevar)` returns `false` doesn't mean that `somevar` is not defined. It could be that `somevar` is defined and initialized but contains a falsy value like `false` or `0`.

A better way to check if a variable is defined is to use `typeof`:

```
> var result = "";
> if (typeof somevar !== "undefined") {
    result = "yes";
  }
> result;
""
```

`typeof` always returns a string, and you can compare this string with the string `"undefined"`. Note that the variable `somevar` may have been declared but not assigned a value yet, and you'll still get the same result. So, when testing with `typeof` like this, you're really testing whether the variable has any value other than the value `undefined`:

```
> var somevar;
> if (typeof somevar !== "undefined") {
    result = "yes";
  }
> result;
""

> somevar = undefined;
> if (typeof somevar !== "undefined") {
    result = "yes";
  }
> result;
""
```

If a variable is defined and initialized with any value other than `undefined`, its type returned by `typeof` is no longer `"undefined"`:

```
> somevar = 123;
> if (typeof somevar !== "undefined") {
    result = 'yes';
  }
> result;
"yes"
```

Alternative if syntax

When you have a simple condition, you can consider using an alternative `if` syntax. Take a look at this:

```
var a = 1;
var result = '';
if (a === 1) {
  result = "a is one";
} else {
  result = "a is not one";
}
```

You can also write this as:

```
> var a = 1;
> var result = (a === 1) ? "a is one" : "a is not one";
```

You should only use this syntax for simple conditions. Be careful not to abuse it, as it can easily make your code unreadable. Here's an example.

Let's say you want to make sure a number is within a certain range, say between 50 and 100:

```
> var a = 123;
> a = a > 100 ? 100 : a < 50 ? 50: a;
> a;
100
```

It may not be clear how this code works exactly because of the multiple `?`. Adding parentheses makes it a little clearer:

```
> var a = 123;
> a = (a > 100 ? 100 : a < 50) ? 50 : a;
> a;
50
```

```
> var a = 123;
> a = a > 100 ? 100 : (a < 50 ? 50 : a);
> a;
100
```

`?:` is called a ternary operator because it takes three operands.

Switch

If you find yourself using an `if` condition and having too many `else if` parts, you could consider changing the `if` to a `switch`:

```
var a = '1',
    result = '';
switch (a) {
case 1:
  result = 'Number 1';
  break;
case '1':
  result = 'String 1';
  break;
default:
  result = 'I don\'t know';
  break;
}
```

The result after executing this is `"String 1"`. Let's see what the parts of a switch are:

- The `switch` statement.
- An expression in parentheses. The expression most often contains a variable, but can be anything that returns a value.
- A number of `case` blocks enclosed in curly brackets.
- Each `case` statement is followed by an expression. The result of the expression is compared to the expression found after the `switch` statement. If the result of the comparison is `true`, the code that follows the colon after the case is executed.
- There is an optional `break` statement to signal the end of the `case` block. If this `break` statement is reached, the `switch` is all done. Otherwise, if the `break` is missing, the program execution enters the next `case` block.
- There's an optional default case marked with the `default` statement and followed by a block of code. The default case is executed if none of the previous cases evaluated to `true`.

In other words, the step-by-step procedure for executing a `switch` statement is as follows:

1. Evaluate the `switch` expression found in parentheses; remember it.
2. Move to the first `case` and compare its value with the one from step 1.
3. If the comparison in step 2 returns `true`, execute the code in the `case` block.
4. After the case block is executed, if there's a `break` statement at the end of it, exit the switch.
5. If there's no `break` or step 2 returned `false`, move on to the next `case` block.
6. Repeat steps 2 to 5.
7. If you are still here (no exit in step 4), execute the code following the `default` statement.

Best practice tips

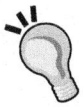

- Indent the code that follows the `case` lines. You can also indent `case` from the `switch`, but that doesn't give you much in terms of readability.
- Don't forget to `break`.
- Sometimes, you may want to omit the `break` intentionally, but that's rare. It's called a fall-through and should always be documented because it may look like an accidental omission. On the other hand, sometimes you may want to omit the whole code block following a `case` and have two cases sharing the same code. This is fine, but doesn't change the rule that if there's code that follows a `case` statement, this code should end with a `break`. In terms of indentation, aligning the `break` with the `case` or with the code inside the case is a personal preference; again, being consistent is what matters.
- Use the `default` case. This helps you make sure you always have a meaningful result after the `switch` statement, even if none of the cases matches the value being switched.

Loops

The `if-else` and `switch` statements allow your code to take different paths, as if you're at a crossroad and decide which way to go depending on a condition. Loops, on the other hand, allow your code to take a few roundabouts before merging back into the main road. How many repetitions? That depends on the result of evaluating a condition before (or after) each iteration.

Let's say you are (your program execution is) traveling from A to B. At some point, you reach a place where you evaluate a condition, C. The result of evaluating C tells you if you should go into a loop, L. You make one iteration and arrive at C again. Then, you evaluate the condition once again to see if another iteration is needed. Eventually, you move on your way to B.

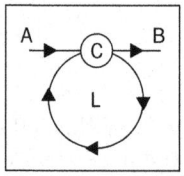

An infinite loop is when the condition is always `true` and your code gets stuck in the loop "forever". This is, of course, a logical error, and you should look out for such scenarios.

In JavaScript, there are four types of loops:

- `while` loops
- `do-while` loops
- `for` loops
- `for-in` loops

While loops

`while` loops are the simplest type of iteration. They look like this:

```
var i = 0;
while (i < 10) {
  i++;
}
```

The `while` statement is followed by a condition in parentheses and a code block in curly brackets. As long as the condition evaluates to `true`, the code block is executed over and over again.

Do-while loops

`do-while` loops are a slight variation of `while` loops. An example is shown as follows:

```
var i = 0;
do {
  i++;
} while (i < 10);
```

Here, the `do` statement is followed by a code block and a condition after the block. This means that the code block is always executed, at least once, before the condition is evaluated.

If you initialize `i` to `11` instead of `0` in the last two examples, the code block in the first example (the `while` loop) will not be executed, and `i` will still be `11` at the end, while in the second (the `do-while` loop), the code block will be executed once and `i` will become `12`.

For loops

`for` is the most widely used type of loop, and you should make sure you're comfortable with this one. It requires just a little bit more in terms of syntax.

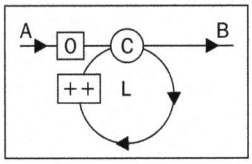

In addition to the condition C and the code block L, you have the following:

- Initialization—code that is executed before you even enter the loop (marked with `0` in the diagram)
- Increment—code that is executed after every iteration (marked with `++` in the diagram)

The most widely used `for` loop pattern is:

- In the initialization part, you define a variable (or set the initial value of an existing variable), most often called `i`
- In the condition part, you compare `i` to a boundary value, like `i < 100`
- In the increment part, you increase `i` by `1`, like `i++`

Here's an example:

```
var punishment = '';
for (var i = 0; i < 100; i++) {
  punishment += 'I will never do this again, ';
}
```

All three parts (initialization, condition, and increment) can contain multiple expressions separated by commas. Say you want to rewrite the example and define the variable `punishment` inside the initialization part of the loop:

```
for (var i = 0, punishment = ''; i < 100; i++) {
  punishment += 'I will never do this again, ';
}
```

Can you move the body of the loop inside the increment part? Yes, you can, especially as it's a one-liner. This gives you a loop that looks a little awkward, as it has no body. Note that this is just an intellectual exercise; it's not recommended that you write awkward-looking code:

```
for (
  var i = 0, punishment = '';
  i < 100;
  i++, punishment += 'I will never do this again, ') {

  // nothing here

}
```

These three parts are all optional. Here's another way of rewriting the same example:

```
var i = 0, punishment = '';
for (;;) {
  punishment += 'I will never do this again, ';
  if (++i == 100) {
    break;
  }
}
```

Although the last rewrite works exactly the same way as the original, it's longer and harder to read. It's also possible to achieve the same result by using a `while` loop. But, `for` loops make the code tighter and more robust because the mere syntax of the `for` loop makes you think about the three parts (initialization, condition, and increment), and thus helps you reconfirm your logic and avoid situations such as being stuck in an infinite loop.

The `for` loops can be nested within each other. Here's an example of a loop that is nested inside another loop and assembles a string containing 10 rows and 10 columns of asterisks. Think of `i` being the row and `j` being the column of an "image":

```
var res = '\n';
for (var i = 0; i < 10; i++) {
  for (var j = 0; j < 10; j++) {
    res += '* ';
  }
  res += '\n';
}
```

The result is a string like the following:

```
"
**********
**********
**********
**********
**********
**********
**********
**********
**********
**********
"
```

Here's another example that uses nested loops and a modulo operation to draw a snowflake-like result:

```
var res = '\n', i, j;
for (i = 1; i <= 7; i++) {
  for (j = 1; j <= 15; j++) {
    res += (i * j) % 8 ? ' ' : '*';
  }
  res += '\n';
}
```

The result is:

```
"
   *
 * * *
   *
*******
   *
 * * *
   *
"
```

For-in loops

The `for-in` loop is used to iterate over the elements of an array (or an object, as you'll see later). This is its only use; it cannot be used as a general-purpose repetition mechanism that replaces `for` or `while`. Let's see an example of using a `for-in` to loop through the elements of an array. But, bear in mind that this is for informational purposes only, as `for-in` is mostly suitable for objects, and the regular `for` loop should be used for arrays.

In this example, you iterate over all of the elements of an array and print out the index (the key) and the value of each element:

```
// example for information only
// for-in loops are used for objects
// regular for is better suited for arrays

var a = ['a', 'b', 'c', 'x', 'y', 'z'];

var result = '\n';

for (var i in a) {
  result += 'index: ' + i + ', value: ' + a[i] + '\n';
}
```

The result is:

```
"
index: 0, value: a
index: 1, value: b
index: 2, value: c
index: 3, value: x
index: 4, value: y
index: 5, value: z
"
```

Comments

One last thing for this chapter: comments. Inside your JavaScript program, you can put comments. These are ignored by the JavaScript engine and don't have any effect on how the program works. But, they can be invaluable when you revisit your code after a few months, or transfer the code to someone else for maintenance.

Two types of comments are allowed:

- Single line comments start with `//` and end at the end of the line.
- Multiline comments start with `/*` and end with `*/` on the same line or any subsequent line. Note that any code in between the comment start and the comment end is ignored.

Some examples are as follows:

```
// beginning of line

var a = 1; // anywhere on the line

/* multi-line comment on a single line */

/*
  comment that spans several lines
*/
```

There are even utilities, such as JSDoc and YUIDoc, that can parse your code and extract meaningful documentation based on your comments.

Summary

In this chapter, you learned a lot about the basic building blocks of a JavaScript program. Now you know the primitive data types:

- Number
- String
- Boolean
- Undefined
- Null

You also know quite a few operators:

- Arithmetic operators: `+`, `-`, `*`, `/`, and `%`
- Increment operators: `++` and `--`
- Assignment operators: `=`, `+=`, `-=`, `*=`, `/=`, and `%=`
- Special operators: `typeof` and `delete`
- Logical operators: `&&`, `||`, and `!`
- Comparison operators: `==`, `===`, `!=`, `!==`, `<`, `>`, `>=`, and `<=`
- The ternary operator `?:`

Then, you learned how to use arrays to store and access data, and finally you saw different ways to control the flow of your program—using conditions (`if-else` or `switch`) and loops (`while`, `do-while`, `for`, and `for-in`).

This is quite a bit of information; now take a moment to go through the exercises below, then give yourself a well-deserved pat on the back before diving into the next chapter. More fun is coming up!

Exercises

1. What is the result of executing each of these lines in the console? Why?

```
> var a; typeof a;
> var s = '1s'; s++;
> !!"false";
> !!undefined;
> typeof -Infinity;
> 10 % "0";
> undefined == null;
> false === "";
> typeof "2E+2";
> a = 3e+3; a++;
```

2. What is the value of `v` after the following?

```
> var v = v || 10;
```

   Experiment by first setting `v` to `100`, `0`, or `null`.

3. Write a small program that prints out the multiplication table. Hint: use a loop nested inside another loop.

3
Functions

Mastering functions is an important skill when you learn any programming language, and even more so when it comes to JavaScript. This is because JavaScript has many uses for functions, and much of the language's flexibility and expressiveness comes from them. Where most programming languages have a special syntax for some object-oriented features, JavaScript just uses functions. This chapter will cover:

- How to define and use a function
- Passing arguments to a function
- Predefined functions that are available to you "for free"
- The scope of variables in JavaScript
- The concept that functions are just data, albeit a special type of data

Understanding these topics will provide a solid base that will allow you to dive into the second part of the chapter, which shows some interesting applications of functions:

- Using anonymous functions
- Callbacks
- Immediate (self-invoking) functions
- Inner functions (functions defined inside other functions)
- Functions that return functions
- Functions that redefine themselves
- Closures

What is a function?

Functions allow you to group together some code, give this code a name, and reuse it later, addressing it by the name you gave it. Let's see an example:

```
function sum(a, b) {
  var c = a + b;
  return c;
}
```

The parts that make up a function are shown as follows:

- The `function` statement.
- The name of the function, in this case `sum`.
- The function parameters, in this case `a` and `b`. A function can take any number of parameters, separated by commas.
- A code block, also called the body of the function.
- The `return` statement. A function always returns a value. If it doesn't return a value explicitly, it implicitly returns the value `undefined`.

Note that a function can only return a single value. If you need to return more values, you can simply return an array that contains all of the values you need as elements of this array.

The preceding syntax is called a function declaration. It's just one of the ways to create a function in JavaScript, and more ways are coming up.

Calling a function

In order to make use of a function, you need to call it. You call a function simply by using its name optionally followed by any number of values in parentheses. "To invoke" a function is another way of saying "to call".

Let's call the function `sum()`, passing two arguments and assigning the value that the function returns to the variable `result`:

```
> var result = sum(1, 2);
> result;
3
```

Parameters

When defining a function, you can specify what parameters the function expects to receive when it's called. A function may not require any parameters, but if it does and you forget to pass them, JavaScript will assign the value `undefined` to the ones you skipped. In the next example, the function call returns `NaN` because it tries to sum `1` and `undefined`:

```
> sum(1);
NaN
```

Technically speaking, there is a difference between parameters and arguments, although the two are often used interchangeably. Parameters are defined together with the function, while arguments are passed to the function when it's called. Consider this:

```
> function sum(a, b) {
    return a + b;
  }
> sum(1, 2);
```

Here, `a` and `b` are parameters, while `1` and `2` are arguments.

JavaScript is not picky at all when it comes to accepting arguments. If you pass more than the function expects, the extra ones will be silently ignored:

```
> sum(1, 2, 3, 4, 5);
3
```

What's more, you can create functions that are flexible about the number of parameters they accept. This is possible thanks to the special value `arguments` that is created automatically inside each function. Here's a function that simply returns whatever arguments are passed to it:

```
> function args() {
    return arguments;
  }
> args();
[]

> args( 1, 2, 3, 4, true, 'ninja');
[1, 2, 3, 4, true, "ninja"]
```

By using `arguments`, you can improve the `sum()` function to accept any number of arguments and add them all up:

```
function sumOnSteroids() {
  var i,
      res = 0,
      number_of_params = arguments.length;
  for (i = 0; i < number_of_params; i++) {
    res += arguments[i];
  }
  return res;
}
```

If you test this function by calling it with a different number of arguments (or even none at all), you can verify that it works as expected:

```
> sumOnSteroids(1, 1, 1);
3

> sumOnSteroids(1, 2, 3, 4);
10

> sumOnSteroids(1, 2, 3, 4, 4, 3, 2, 1);
20

> sumOnSteroids(5);
5

> sumOnSteroids();
0
```

The expression `arguments.length` returns the number of arguments passed when the function was called. Don't worry if the syntax is unfamiliar, we'll examine it in detail in the next chapter. You'll also see that `arguments` is not an array (although it sure looks like one), but an array-like object.

Predefined functions

There are a number of functions that are built into the JavaScript engine and are available for you to use. Let's take a look at them. While doing so, you'll have a chance to experiment with functions, their arguments and return values, and become comfortable working with functions. Following is a list of the built-in functions:

- `parseInt()`
- `parseFloat()`
- `isNaN()`

- `isFinite()`
- `encodeURI()`
- `decodeURI()`
- `encodeURIComponent()`
- `decodeURIComponent()`
- `eval()`

The black box function

Often, when you invoke functions, your program doesn't need to know how these functions work internally. You can think of a function as a black box: you give it some values (as input arguments) and then you take the output result it returns. This is true for any function—one that's built into the JavaScript engine, one that you create, or one that a co-worker or someone else created.

parseInt()

`parseInt()` takes any type of input (most often a string) and tries to make an integer out of it. If it fails, it returns `NaN`:

```
> parseInt('123');
123

> parseInt('abc123');
NaN

> parseInt('1abc23');
1

> parseInt('123abc');
123
```

The function accepts an optional second parameter, which is the **radix**, telling the function what type of number to expect—decimal, hexadecimal, binary, and so on. For example, trying to extract a decimal number out of the string `FF` makes no sense, so the result is **NaN**, but if you try `FF` as a hexadecimal, then you get **255**:

```
> parseInt('FF', 10);
NaN

> parseInt('FF', 16);
255
```

Another example would be parsing a string with a base `10` (decimal) and base `8` (octal):

```
> parseInt('0377', 10);
377

> parseInt('0377', 8);
255
```

If you omit the second argument when calling `parseInt()`, the function will assume `10` (a decimal), with these exceptions:

- If you pass a string beginning with `0x`, then the radix is assumed to be `16` (a hexadecimal number is assumed).
- If the string you pass starts with `0`, the function assumes radix `8` (an octal number is assumed). Consider the following examples:

```
> parseInt('377');
377

> parseInt('0377');
255

> parseInt('0x377');
887
```

The safest thing to do is to always specify the radix. If you omit the radix, your code will probably still work in 99 percent of cases (because most often you parse decimals), but every once in a while it might cause you a bit of hair loss while debugging some edge cases. For example, imagine you have a form field that accepts calendar days or months and the user types `06` or `08`.

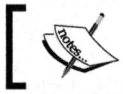

ECMAScript 5 removes the octal literal values and avoids the confusion with `parseInt()` and unspecified radix.

parseFloat()

`parseFloat()` is similar to `parseInt()`, but it also looks for decimals when trying to figure out a number from your input. This function takes only one parameter:

```
> parseFloat('123');
123

> parseFloat('1.23');
1.23
```

```
> parseFloat('1.23abc.00');
1.23

> parseFloat('a.bc1.23');
NaN
```

As with `parseInt()`, `parseFloat()` gives up at the first occurrence of an unexpected character, even though the rest of the string might have usable numbers in it:

```
> parseFloat('a123.34');
NaN

> parseFloat('12a3.34');
12
```

`parseFloat()` understands exponents in the input (unlike `parseInt()`):

```
> parseFloat('123e-2');
1.23

> parseFloat('1e10');
10000000000

> parseInt('1e10');
1
```

isNaN()

Using `isNaN()`, you can check if an input value is a valid number that can safely be used in arithmetic operations. This function is also a convenient way to check whether `parseInt()` or `parseFloat()` (or any arithmetic operation) succeeded:

```
> isNaN(NaN);
true

> isNaN(123);
false

> isNaN(1.23);
false

> isNaN(parseInt('abc123'));
true
```

The function will also try to convert the input to a number:

```
> isNaN('1.23');
false

> isNaN('a1.23');
true
```

The `isNaN()` function is useful because the special value `NaN` is not equal to anything including itself. In other words, `NaN === NaN` is `false`. So, `NaN` cannot be used to check if a value is a valid number.

isFinite()

`isFinite()` checks whether the input is a number that is neither `Infinity` nor `NaN`:

```
> isFinite(Infinity);
false

> isFinite(-Infinity);
false

> isFinite(12);
true

> isFinite(1e308);
true

> isFinite(1e309);
false
```

If you are wondering about the results returned by the last two calls, remember from the previous chapter that the biggest number in JavaScript is `1.7976931348623157e+308`, so `1e309` is effectively infinity.

Encode/decode URIs

In a **Uniform Resource Locator** (**URL**) or a **Uniform Resource Identifier** (**URI**), some characters have special meanings. If you want to "escape" those characters, you can use the functions `encodeURI()` or `encodeURIComponent()`. The first one will return a usable URL, while the second one assumes you're only passing a part of the URL, such as a query string for example, and will encode all applicable characters:

```
> var url = 'http://www.packtpub.com/script.php?q=this and that';
> encodeURI(url);
"http://www.packtpub.com/scr%20ipt.php?q=this%20and%20that"
```

```
> encodeURIComponent(url);
"http%3A%2F%2Fwww.packtpub.com%2Fscr%20ipt.php%3Fq%3Dthis%20and%20that"
```

The opposites of `encodeURI()` and `encodeURIComponent()` are `decodeURI()` and `decodeURIComponent()` respectively.

Sometimes, in legacy code, you might see the functions `escape()` and `unescape()` used to encode and decode URLs, but these functions have been deprecated; they encode differently and should not be used.

eval()

`eval()` takes a string input and executes it as a JavaScript code:

```
> eval('var ii = 2;');
> ii;
2
```

So, `eval('var ii = 2;')` is the same as `var ii = 2;`.

`eval()` can be useful sometimes, but should be avoided if there are other options. Most of the time there are alternatives, and in most cases the alternatives are more elegant and easier to write and maintain. "Eval is evil" is a mantra you can often hear from seasoned JavaScript programmers. The drawbacks of using `eval()` are:

- **Security** - JavaScript is powerful, which also means it can cause damage. If you don't trust the source of the input you pass to `eval()`, just don't use it.
- **Performance** - It's slower to evaluate "live" code than to have the code directly in the script.

A bonus – the alert() function

Let's take a look at another common function—`alert()`. It's not part of the core JavaScript (it's nowhere to be found in the ECMA specification), but it's provided by the host environment—the browser. It shows a string of text in a message box. It can also be used as a primitive debugging tool, although the debuggers in modern browsers are much better suited for this purpose.

Here's a screenshot showing the result of executing the code `alert("hello!")`:

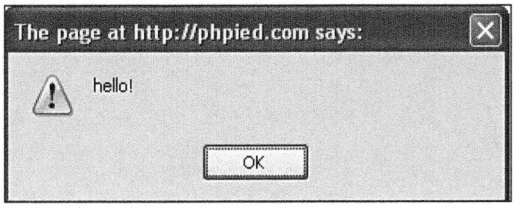

Before using this function, bear in mind that it blocks the browser thread, meaning that no other code will be executed until the user closes the alert. If you have a busy Ajax-type application, it's generally not a good idea to use `alert()`.

Scope of variables

It's important to note, especially if you have come to JavaScript from another language, that variables in JavaScript are not defined in a block scope, but in a function scope. This means that if a variable is defined inside a function, it's not visible outside of the function. However, if it's defined inside an `if` or a `for` code block, it's visible outside the block. The term "global variables" describes variables you define outside of any function (in the global program code), as opposed to "local variables", which are defined inside a function. The code inside a function has access to all global variables as well as to its own local ones.

In the next example:

- The `f()` function has access to the `global` variable
- Outside the `f()` function, the `local` variable doesn't exist

```
var global = 1;
function f() {
  var local = 2;
  global++;
  return global;
}
```

Let's test this:

```
> f();
2

> f();
3

> local;
ReferenceError: local is not defined
```

It's also important to note that if you don't use `var` to declare a variable, this variable is automatically assigned a global scope. Let's see an example:

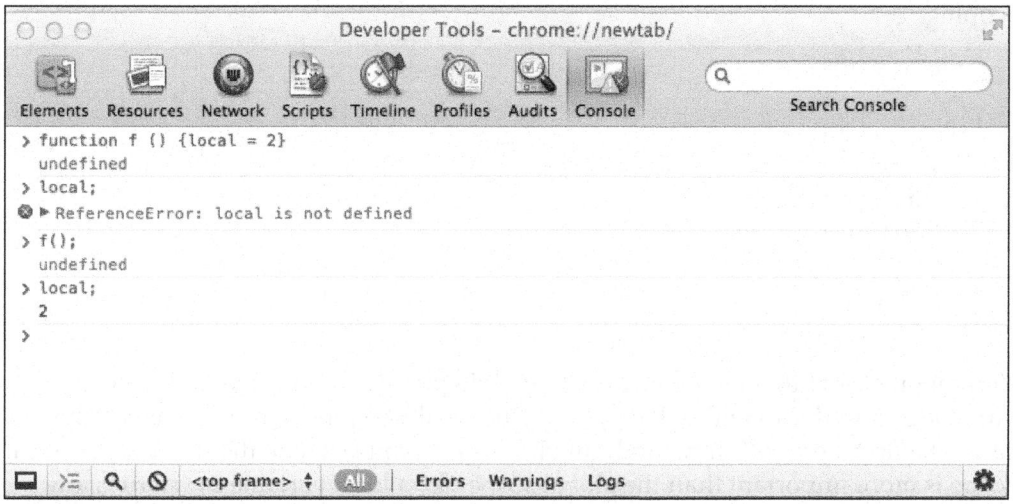

What happened? The function `f()` contains the variable `local`. Before calling the function, the variable doesn't exist. When you call the function for the first time, the variable `local` is created with a global scope. Then, if you access `local` outside the function, it will be available.

Best practice tips

- Minimize the number of global variables in order to avoid naming collisions. Imagine two people working on two different functions in the same script, and they both decide to use the same name for their global variable. This could easily lead to unexpected results and hard-to-find bugs.
- Always declare your variables with the `var` statement.
- Consider a "single var" pattern. Define all variables needed in your function at the very top of the function so you have a single place to look for variables and hopefully prevent accidental globals.

Variable hoisting

Here's an interesting example that shows an important aspect of local versus global scoping:

```
var a = 123;

function f() {
  alert(a);
  var a = 1;
  alert(a);
}

f();
```

You might expect that the first `alert()` will display **123** (the value of the global variable `a`) and the second will display **1** (the local variable `a`). But, this is not the case. The first alert will show **undefined**. This is because inside the function the local scope is more important than the global scope. So, a local variable overwrites any global variable with the same name. At the time of the first `alert()`, the variable `a` was not yet defined (hence the value `undefined`), but it still existed in the local space due to the special behavior called **hoisting**.

When your JavaScript program execution enters a new function, all the variables declared anywhere in the function are moved (or elevated, or hoisted) to the top of the function. This is an important concept to keep in mind. Further, only the declaration is hoisted, meaning only the presence of the variable is moved to the top. Any assignments stay where they are. In the preceding example, the declaration of the local variable `a` was hoisted to the top. Only the declaration was hoisted, but not the assignment to 1. It's as if the function was written like this:

```
var a = 123;

function f() {
  var a; // same as: var a = undefined;
  alert(a); // undefined
  a = 1;
  alert(a); // 1
}
```

You can also adopt the single var pattern mentioned previously in the best practice section. In this case, you'll be doing a sort of manual variable hoisting to prevent confusion with the JavaScript hoisting behavior.

Functions are data

Functions in JavaScript are actually data. This is an important concept that we'll need later on. This means that you can create a function and assign it to a variable:

```
var f = function () {
  return 1;
};
```

This way of defining a function is sometimes referred to as **function literal notation**.

The part `function () { return 1; }` is a **function expression**. A function expression can optionally have a name, in which case it becomes a **named function expression** (**NFE**). So, this is also allowed, although rarely seen in practice (and causes IE to mistakenly create two variables in the enclosing scope: `f` and `myFunc`):

```
var f = function myFunc() {
  return 1;
};
```

As you can see, there's no difference between a named function expression and a function declaration. But they are, in fact, different. The only way to distinguish between the two is to look at the context in which they are used. Function declarations may only appear in program code (in a body of another function or in the main program). You'll see many more examples of functions later on in the book that will clarify these concepts.

When you use the `typeof` operator on a variable that holds a function value, it returns the string `"function"`:

```
> function define() {
    return 1;
  }

> var express = function () {
    return 1;
  };

> typeof define;
"function"


> typeof express;
"function"
```

So, JavaScript functions are data, but a special kind of data with two important features:

- They contain code
- They are executable (they can be invoked)

As you have seen before, the way to execute a function is by adding parentheses after its name. As the next example demonstrates, this works regardless of how the function was defined. In the example, you can also see how a function is treated as a regular value: it can be copied to a different variable:

```
> var sum = function (a, b) {
    return a + b;
  };

> var add = sum;
> typeof add;
function

> add(1, 2);
3
```

Because functions are data assigned to variables, the same rules for naming functions apply as for naming variables—a function name cannot start with a number and it can contain any combination of letters, numbers, the underscore character, and the dollar sign.

Anonymous functions

As you now know, there exists a function expression syntax where you can have a function defined like this:

```
var f = function (a) {
  return a;
};
```

This is also often called an anonymous function (as it doesn't have a name), especially when such a function expression is used even without assigning it to a variable. In this case, there can be two elegant uses for such anonymous functions:

- You can pass an anonymous function as a parameter to another function. The receiving function can do something useful with the function that you pass.
- You can define an anonymous function and execute it right away.

Let's see these two applications of anonymous functions in more detail.

Callback functions

Because a function is just like any other data assigned to a variable, it can be defined, copied, and also passed as an argument to other functions.

Here's an example of a function that accepts two functions as parameters, executes them, and returns the sum of what each of them returns:

```
function invokeAdd(a, b) {
  return a() + b();
}
```

Now let's define two simple additional functions (using a function declaration pattern) that only return hardcoded values:

```
function one() {
  return 1;
}

function two() {
  return 2;
}
```

Now you can pass those functions to the original function, `invokeAdd()`, and get the result:

```
> invokeAdd(one, two);
3
```

Another example of passing a function as a parameter is to use anonymous functions (function expressions). Instead of defining `one()` and `two()`, you can simply do the following:

```
> invokeAdd(function () {return 1; }, function () {return 2; });
3
```

Or, you can make it more readable as shown in the following code:

```
> invokeAdd(
    function () { return 1; },
    function () { return 2; }
  );
3
```

Or, you can do the following:

```
> invokeAdd(
    function () {
      return 1;
    },
    function () {
      return 2;
    }
  );
3
```

When you pass a function, A, to another function, B, and then B executes A, it's often said that A is a **callback** function. If A doesn't have a name, then you can say that it's an anonymous callback function.

When are callback functions useful? Let's see some examples that demonstrate the benefits of callback functions, namely:

- They let you pass functions without the need to name them (which means there are fewer variables floating around)
- You can delegate the responsibility of calling a function to another function (which means there is less code to write)
- They can help with performance

Callback examples

Take a look at this common scenario: you have a function that returns a value, which you then pass to another function. In our example, the first function, `multiplyByTwo()`, accepts three parameters, loops through them, multiplies them by two, and returns an array containing the result. The second function, `addOne()`, takes a value, adds one to it, and returns it:

```
function multiplyByTwo(a, b, c) {
  var i, ar = [];
  for (i = 0; i < 3; i++) {
    ar[i] = arguments[i] * 2;
  }
  return ar;
}

function addOne(a) {
  return a + 1;
}
```

Let's test these functions:

```
> multiplyByTwo(1, 2, 3);
[2, 4, 6]

> addOne(100);
101
```

Now let's say you want to have an array, `myarr`, that contains three elements, and each of the elements is to be passed through both functions. First, let's start with a call to `multiplyByTwo()`:

```
> var myarr = [];
> myarr = multiplyByTwo(10, 20, 30);
[20, 40, 60]
```

Now loop through each element, passing it to `addOne()`:

```
> for (var i = 0; i < 3; i++) {
    myarr[i] = addOne(myarr[i]);
  }
> myarr;
[21, 41, 61]
```

As you can see, everything works fine, but there's room for improvement. For example: there were two loops. Loops can be expensive if they go through a lot of repetitions. You can achieve the same result with only one loop. Here's how to modify `multiplyByTwo()` so that it accepts a callback function and invokes that callback on every iteration:

```
function multiplyByTwo(a, b, c, callback) {
  var i, ar = [];
  for (i = 0; i < 3; i++) {
    ar[i] = callback(arguments[i] * 2);
  }
  return ar;
}
```

By using the modified function, all the work is done with just one function call, which passes the start values and the `callback` function:

```
> myarr = multiplyByTwo(1, 2, 3, addOne);
[3, 5, 7]
```

Instead of defining `addOne()`, you can use an anonymous function, therefore saving an extra global variable:

```
> multiplyByTwo(1, 2, 3, function (a) {
    return a + 1;
  });
[3, 5, 7]
```

Anonymous functions are easy to change should the need arise:

```
> multiplyByTwo(1, 2, 3, function (a) {
    return a + 2;
  });
[4, 6, 8]
```

Immediate functions

So far, we have discussed using anonymous functions as callbacks. Let's see another application of an anonymous function: calling a function immediately after it's defined. Here's an example:

```
(
  function () {
    alert('boo');
  }
)();
```

The syntax may look a little scary at first, but all you do is simply place a function expression inside parentheses followed by another set of parentheses. The second set says "execute now" and is also the place to put any arguments that your anonymous function might accept:

```
(
  function (name) {
    alert('Hello ' + name + '!');
  }
)('dude');
```

Alternatively, you can move the closing of the first set of parentheses to the end. Both of these work:

```
(function () {
  // ...
}());
```

```
// vs.

(function () {
  // ...
})();
```

One good application of immediate (self-invoking) anonymous functions is when you want to have some work done without creating extra global variables. A drawback, of course, is that you cannot execute the same function twice. This makes immediate functions best suited for one-off or initialization tasks.

An immediate function can also optionally return a value if you need one. It's not uncommon to see code that looks like the following:

```
var result = (function () {
  // something complex with
  // temporary local variables...
  // ...

  // return something;
}());
```

In this case, you don't need to wrap the function expression in parentheses, you only need the parentheses that invoke the function. So, the following also works:

```
var result = function () {
  // something complex with
  // temporary local variables
  // return something;
}();
```

This syntax works, but may look slightly confusing: without reading the end of the function, you don't know if `result` is a function or the return value of the immediate function.

Inner (private) functions

Bearing in mind that a function is just like any other value, there's nothing that stops you from defining a function inside another function:

```
function outer(param) {
  function inner(theinput) {
    return theinput * 2;
  }
  return 'The result is ' + inner(param);
}
```

Using a function expression, this can also be written as:

```
var outer = function (param) {
  var inner = function (theinput) {
    return theinput * 2;
  };
  return 'The result is ' + inner(param);
};
```

When you call the global function `outer()`, it will internally call the local function `inner()`. Since `inner()` is local, it's not accessible outside `outer()`, so you can say it's a private function:

```
> outer(2);
```
"The result is 4"

```
> outer(8);
```
"The result is 16"

```
> inner(2);
```
ReferenceError: inner is not defined

The benefits of using private functions are as follows:

- You keep the global namespace clean (less likely to cause naming collisions)
- Privacy—you expose only the functions you decide to the "outside world", keeping to yourself functionality that is not meant to be consumed by the rest of the application

Functions that return functions

As mentioned earlier, a function always returns a value, and if it doesn't do it explicitly with `return`, then it does so implicitly by returning `undefined`. A function can return only one value, and this value can just as easily be another function:

```
function a() {
  alert('A!');
  return function () {
    alert('B!');
  };
}
```

In this example, the function `a()` does its job (says **A!**) and returns another function that does something else (says **B!**). You can assign the return value to a variable and then use this variable as a normal function:

```
> var newFunc = a();
> newFunc();
```

Here, the first line will alert **A!** and the second will alert **B!**.

If you want to execute the returned function immediately without assigning it to a new variable, you can simply use another set of parentheses. The end result will be the same:

```
> a()();
```

Function, rewrite thyself!

Because a function can return a function, you can use the new function to replace the old one. Continuing with the previous example, you can take the value returned by the call to `a()` to overwrite the actual `a()` function:

```
> a = a();
```

The above alerts **A!**, but the next time you call `a()` it alerts **B!**. This is useful when a function has some initial one-off work to do. The function overwrites itself after the first call in order to avoid doing unnecessary repetitive work every time it's called.

In the preceding example, the function was redefined from the outside—the returned value was assigned back to the function. But, the function can actually rewrite itself from the inside:

```
function a() {
  alert('A!');
  a = function () {
    alert('B!');
  };
}
```

If you call this function for the first time, it will:

- Alert **A!** (consider this as being the one-off preparatory work)
- Redefine the global variable `a`, assigning a new function to it

Every subsequent time that the function is called, it will alert **B!**

Here's another example that combines several of the techniques discussed in the last few sections of this chapter:

```
var a = (function () {

  function someSetup() {
```

```
    var setup = 'done';
  }

  function actualWork() {
    alert('Worky-worky');
  }

  someSetup();
  return actualWork;

}());
```

In this example:

- You have private functions: `someSetup()` and `actualWork()`.
- You have an immediate function: an anonymous function that calls itself using the parentheses following its definition.
- The function executes for the first time, calls `someSetup()`, and then returns a reference to the variable `actualWork`, which is a function. Notice that there are no parentheses in the `return` statement, because you're returning a function reference, not the result of invoking this function.
- Because the whole thing starts with `var a =`, the value returned by the self-invoked function is assigned to `a`.

If you want to test your understanding of the topics just discussed, answer the following questions. What will the preceding code alert when:

- It is initially loaded?
- You call `a()` afterwards?

These techniques could be really useful when working in the browser environment. Different browsers can have different ways of achieving the same result. If you know that the browser features won't change between function calls, you can have a function determine the best way to do the work in the current browser, then redefine itself so that the "browser capability detection" is done only once. You'll see concrete examples of this scenario later in this book.

Closures

The rest of the chapter is about closures (what better way to close a chapter?). Closures can be a little hard to grasp initially, so don't feel discouraged if you don't "get it" during the first read. You should go through the rest of the chapter and experiment with the examples on you own, but if you feel you don't fully understand the concept, you can come back to it later when the topics discussed previously in this chapter have had a chance to sink in.

Before moving on to closures, let's first review and expand on the concept of scope in JavaScript.

Scope chain

As you know, in JavaScript, there is no curly braces scope, but there is function scope. A variable defined in a function is not visible outside the function, but a variable defined in a code block (for example an `if` or a `for` loop) is visible outside the block:

```
> var a = 1;
> function f() {
    var b = 1;
    return a;
  }
> f();
1

> b;
ReferenceError: b is not defined
```

The variable `a` is in the global space, while `b` is in the scope of the function `f()`. So:

- Inside `f()`, both `a` and `b` are visible
- Outside `f()`, `a` is visible, but `b` is not

If you define a function `inner()` nested inside `outer()`, `inner()` will have access to variables in its own scope, plus the scope of its "parents". This is known as a scope chain, and the chain can be as long (deep) as you need it to be:

```
var global = 1;
function outer() {
  var outer_local = 2;
  function inner() {
    var inner_local = 3;
    return inner_local + outer_local + global;
```

```
    }
    return inner();
  }
```

Let's test that `inner()` has access to all variables:

```
> outer();
6
```

Breaking the chain with a closure

Let's introduce closures with an illustration. Let's look at this code and see what's happening there:

```
var a = "global variable";
var F = function () {
  var b = "local variable";
  var N = function () {
    var c = "inner local";
  };
};
```

First, there is the global scope `G`. Think of it as the universe, as if it contains everything:

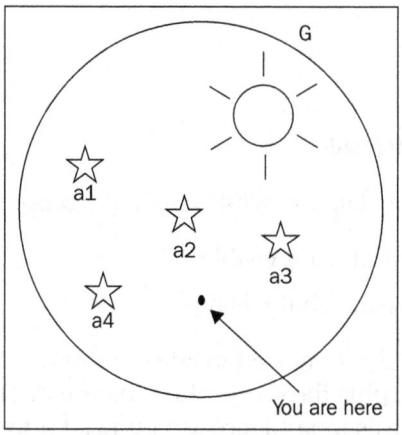

It can contain global variables such as `a1` and `a2` and global functions such as `F`:

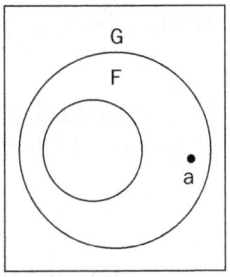

Functions have their own private space and can use it to store other variables such as `b` and inner functions such as `N` (for *iNNer*). At some point, you end up with a picture like this:

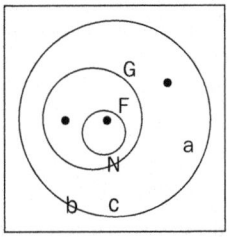

If you're at point `a`, you're inside the global space. If you're at point `b`, which is inside the space of the function `F`, then you have access to the global space and to the `F` space. If you're at point `c`, which is inside the function `N`, then you can access the global space, the `F` space, and the `N` space. You cannot reach from `a` to `b`, because `b` is invisible outside `F`. But, you can get from `c` to `b` if you want, or from `N` to `b`. The interesting part—the closure effect—happens when somehow `N` breaks out of `F` and ends up in the global space:

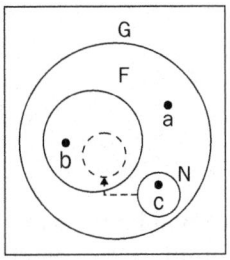

What happens then? `N` is in the same global space as `a`. And, as functions remember the environment in which they were defined, `N` will still have access to the `F` space, and hence can access `b`. This is interesting, because `N` is where `a` is and yet `N` does have access to `b`, but `a` doesn't.

And how does `N` break the chain? By making itself global (omitting `var`) or by having `F` deliver (or `return`) it to the global space. Let's see how this is done in practice.

Closure #1

Take a look at this function, which is the same as before, only `F` returns `N` and also `N` returns `b`, to which it has access via the scope chain:

```
var a = "global variable";
var F = function () {
  var b = "local variable";
  var N = function () {
    var c = "inner local";
    return b;
  };
  return N;
};
```

The function `F` contains the variable `b`, which is local, and therefore inaccessible from the global space:

```
> b;
ReferenceError: b is not defined
```

The function `N` has access to its private space, to the `F()` function's space, and to the global space. So, it can see `b`. Since `F()` is callable from the global space (it's a global function), you can call it and assign the returned value to another global variable. The result: a new global function that has access to the `F()` function's private space:

```
> var inner = F();
> inner();
"local variable"
```

Closure #2

The final result of the next example will be the same as the previous example, but the way to achieve it is a little different. `F()` doesn't return a function, but instead it creates a new global function, `inner()`, inside its body.

Let's start by declaring a placeholder for the global function-to-be. This is optional, but it's always good to declare your variables. Then, you can define the function `F()` as follows:

```
var inner; // placeholder
var F = function () {
  var b = "local variable";
  var N = function () {
    return b;
  };
  inner = N;
};
```

Now what happens if you invoke `F()`?:

```
> F();
```

A new function, `N()`,is defined inside `F()` and assigned to the global `inner`. During definition time, `N()` was inside `F()`, so it had access to the `F()` function's scope. `inner()` will keep its access to the `F()` function's scope, even though it's part of the global space:

```
> inner();
"local variable".
```

A definition and closure #3

Every function can be considered a closure. This is because every function maintains a secret link to the environment (the scope) in which it was created. But, most of the time this scope is destroyed unless something interesting happens (as shown above) that causes this scope to be maintained.

Based on what you've seen so far, you can say that a closure is created when a function keeps a link to its parent scope even after the parent has returned. And, every function is a closure because, at the very least, every function maintains access to the global scope, which is never destroyed.

Let's see one more example of a closure, this time using the function parameters. Function parameters behave like local variables to this function, but they are implicitly created (you don't need to use `var` for them). You can create a function that returns another function, which in turn returns its parent's parameter:

```
function F(param) {
  var N = function () {
    return param;
  };
```

```
    param++;
    return N;
  }
```

You use the function like this:

```
> var inner = F(123);
> inner();
124
```

Notice how `param++` was incremented after the function was defined and yet, when called, `inner()` returned the updated value. This demonstrates that the function maintains a reference to the scope where it was defined, not to the variables and their values found in the scope during the function definition.

Closures in a loop

Let's take a look at a canonical rookie mistake when it comes to closures. It can easily lead to hard-to-spot bugs, because on the surface, everything looks normal.

Let's loop three times, each time creating a new function that returns the loop sequence number. The new functions will be added to an array and the array is returned at the end. Here's the function:

```
function F() {
  var arr = [], i;
  for (i = 0; i < 3; i++) {
    arr[i] = function () {
      return i;
    };
  }
  return arr;
}
```

Let's run the function, assigning the result to the array `arr`:

```
> var arr = F();
```

Now you have an array of three functions. Let's invoke them by adding parentheses after each array element. The expected behavior is to see the loop sequence printed out: `0`, `1`, and `2`. Let's try:

```
> arr[0]();
3

> arr[1]();
3
```

```
> arr[2]();
3
```

Hmm, not quite as expected. What happened here? All three functions point to the same local variable `i`. Why? The functions don't remember values, they only keep a link (reference) to the environment where they were created. In this case, the variable `i` happens to live in the environment where the three functions were defined. So, all functions, when they need to access the value, reach back to the environment and find the most current value of `i`. After the loop, the `i` variable's value is `3`. So, all three functions point to the same value.

Why three and not two is another good question to think about for better understanding the `for` loop.

So, how do you implement the correct behavior? The answer is to use another closure:

```
function F() {
  var arr = [], i;
  for (i = 0; i < 3; i++) {
    arr[i] = (function (x) {
      return function () {
        return x;
      };
    }(i));
  }
  return arr;
}
```

This gives you the expected result:

```
> var arr = F();
> arr[0]();
0

> arr[1]();
1

> arr[2]();
2
```

Here, instead of just creating a function that returns `i`, you pass the `i` variable's current value to another immediate function. In this function, `i` becomes the local value `x`, and `x` has a different value every time.

Alternatively, you can use a "normal" (as opposed to an immediate) inner function to achieve the same result. The key is to use the middle function to "localize" the value of `i` at every iteration:

```
function F() {

  function binder(x) {
    return function () {
      return x;
    };
  }

  var arr = [], i;
  for (i = 0; i < 3; i++) {
    arr[i] = binder(i);
  }
  return arr;
}
```

Getter/setter

Let's see two more examples of using closures. The first one involves the creation of getter and setter functions. Imagine you have a variable that should contain a specific type of values or a specific range of values. You don't want to expose this variable because you don't want just any part of the code to be able to alter its value. You protect this variable inside a function and provide two additional functions: one to get the value and one to set it. The one that sets it could contain some logic to validate a value before assigning it to the protected variable. Let's make the validation part simple (for the sake of keeping the example short) and only accept number values.

You place both the getter and the setter functions inside the same function that contains the `secret` variable so that they share the same scope:

```
var getValue, setValue;

(function () {

  var secret = 0;

  getValue = function () {
```

```
    return secret;
  };

  setValue = function (v) {
    if (typeof v === "number") {
      secret = v;
    }
  };

}());
```

In this case, the function that contains everything is an immediate function. It defines `setValue()` and `getValue()` as global functions, while the `secret` variable remains local and inaccessible directly:

```
> getValue();
0

> setValue(123);
> getValue();
123

> setValue(false);
> getValue();
123
```

Iterator

The last closure example (also the last example in the chapter) shows the use of a closure to accomplish an iterator functionality.

You already know how to loop through a simple array, but there might be cases where you have a more complicated data structure with different rules as to what the sequence of values has. You can wrap the complicated "who's next" logic into an easy-to-use `next()` function. Then, you simply call `next()` every time you need the consecutive value.

For this example, let's just use a simple array and not a complex data structure. Here's an initialization function that takes an input array and also defines a secret pointer, `i`, that will always point to the next element in the array:

```
function setup(x) {
  var i = 0;
  return function () {
    return x[i++];
  };
}
```

Calling the `setup()` function with a data array will create the `next()` function for you:

```
> var next = setup(['a', 'b', 'c']);
```

From there it's easy and fun: calling the same function over and over again gives you the next element:

```
> next();
"a"

> next();
"b"

> next();
"c"
```

Summary

You have now completed the introduction to the fundamental concepts related to functions in JavaScript. You've been laying the groundwork that will allow you to quickly grasp the concepts of object-oriented JavaScript and the patterns used in modern JavaScript programming. So far, we've been avoiding the OO features, but as you have reached this point in the book, it's only going to get more interesting from here on in. Let's take a moment and review the topics discussed in this chapter:

- The basics of how to define and invoke (call) a function using either a function declaration syntax or a function expression
- Function parameters and their flexibility
- Built-in functions—`parseInt()`, `parseFloat()`, `isNaN()`, `isFinite()`, and `eval()`—and the four functions to encode/decode a URL
- The scope of variables in JavaScript—no curly braces scope, variables have only function scope and the scope chain
- Functions as data—a function is like any other piece of data that you assign to a variable and a lot of interesting applications follow from this, such as:
    - Private functions and private variables
    - Anonymous functions
    - Callbacks
    - Immediate functions
    - Functions overwriting themselves
- Closures

Exercises

1. Write a function that converts a hexadecimal color, for example blue (`#0000FF`), into its RGB representation `rgb(0, 0, 255)`. Name your function `getRGB()` and test it with the following code. Hint: treat the string as an array of characters:

```
> var a = getRGB("#00FF00");
> a;
"rgb(0, 255, 0)"
```

2. What do each of these lines print in the console?

```
> parseInt(1e1);
> parseInt('1e1');
> parseFloat('1e1');
> isFinite(0/10);
> isFinite(20/0);
> isNaN(parseInt(NaN));
```

3. What does this following code alert?

```
var a = 1;

function f() {
  function n() {
    alert(a);
  }
  var a = 2;
  n();
}

f();
```

4. All these examples alert **"Boo!"**. Can you explain why?
   - Example 1:

     ```
     var f = alert;
     eval('f("Boo!")');
     ```

   - Example 2:

     ```
     var e;
     var f = alert;
     eval('e=f')('Boo!');
     ```

   - Example 3:

     ```
     (function(){
       return alert;}
     )()('Boo!');
     ```

4
Objects

Now that you've mastered JavaScript's primitive data types, arrays, and functions, it's time to make true to the promise of the book title and talk about objects.

In this chapter, you will learn:

- How to create and use objects
- What are the constructor functions
- What types of built-in JavaScript objects exist and what they can do for you

From arrays to objects

As you already know from *Chapter 2, Primitive Data Types, Arrays, Loops, and Conditions,* an array is just a list of values. Each value has an index (a numeric key) that starts from zero and increments by one for each value.

```
> var myarr = ['red', 'blue', 'yellow', 'purple'];
> myarr;
```
["red", "blue", "yellow", "purple".

```
> myarr[0];
```
"red"

```
> myarr[3];
```
"purple"

If you put the indexes in one column and the values in another, you'll end up with a table of key/value pairs shown as follows:

Key	Value
0	red
1	blue
2	yellow
3	purple

An object is similar to an array, but with the difference that you define the keys yourself. You're not limited to using only numeric indexes and you can use friendlier keys, such as `first_name`, `age`, and so on.

Let's take a look at a simple object and examine its parts:

```
var hero = {
  breed: 'Turtle',
  occupation: 'Ninja'
};
```

You can see that:

- The name of the variable that refers to the object is `hero`
- Instead of `[` and `]`, which you use to define an array, you use `{` and `}` for objects
- You separate the elements (called properties) contained in the object with commas
- The key/value pairs are divided by colons, as in `key: value`

The keys (names of the properties) can optionally be placed in quotation marks. For example, these are all the same:

```
var hero = {occupation: 1};
var hero = {"occupation": 1};
var hero = {'occupation': 1};
```

It's recommended that you don't quote the names of the properties (it's less typing), but there are cases when you must use quotes:

- If the property name is one of the reserved words in JavaScript (see *Appendix A, Reserved Words*)

- If it contains spaces or special characters (anything other than letters, numbers, and the _ and $ characters)
- If it starts with a number

In other words, if the name you have chosen for a property is not a valid name for a variable in JavaScript, then you need to wrap it in quotes.

Have a look at this bizarre-looking object:

```
var o = {
  $omething: 1,
  'yes or no': 'yes',
  '!@#$%^&*': true
};
```

This is a valid object. The quotes are required for the second and the third properties, otherwise you'll get an error.

Later in this chapter, you'll see other ways to define objects and arrays in addition to `[]` and `{}`. But first, let's introduce this bit of terminology: defining an array with `[]` is called **array literal** notation, and defining an object using the curly braces `{}` is called **object literal** notation.

Elements, properties, methods, and members

When talking about arrays, you say that they contain elements. When talking about objects, you say that they contain properties. There isn't any significant difference in JavaScript; it's just the terminology that people are used to, likely from other programming languages.

A property of an object can point to a function, because functions are just data. Properties that point to functions are also called methods. In the following example, `talk` is a method:

```
var dog = {
  name: 'Benji',
  talk: function () {
    alert('Woof, woof!');
  }
};
```

As you have seen in the previous chapter, it's also possible to store functions as array elements and invoke them, but you'll not see much code like this in practice:

```
> var a = [];
> a[0] = function (what) { alert(what); };
> a[0]('Boo!');
```

You can also see people using the word members to refer to properties of an object, most often when it doesn't matter if the property is a function or not.

Hashes and associative arrays

In some programming languages, there is a distinction between:

- A regular array, also called an **indexed** or **enumerated** array (the keys are numbers)
- An associative array, also called a **hash** or a dictionary (the keys are strings)

JavaScript uses arrays to represent indexed arrays and objects to represent associative arrays. If you want a hash in JavaScript, you use an object.

Accessing an object's properties

There are two ways to access a property of an object:

- Using the square bracket notation, for example `hero['occupation']`
- Using the dot notation, for example `hero.occupation`

The dot notation is easier to read and write, but it cannot always be used. The same rules apply as for quoting property names: if the name of the property is not a valid variable name, you cannot use the dot notation.

Let's take the `hero` object again:

```
var hero = {
  breed: 'Turtle',
  occupation: 'Ninja'
};
```

Accessing a property with the dot notation:

```
> hero.breed;
"Turtle"
```

Accessing a property with the bracket notation:

```
> hero['occupation'];
"Ninja"
```

Accessing a non-existing property returns `undefined`:

```
> 'Hair color is ' + hero.hair_color;
"Hair color is undefined"
```

Objects can contain any data, including other objects:

```
var book = {
  name: 'Catch-22',
  published: 1961,
  author: {
    firstname: 'Joseph',
    lastname: 'Heller'
  }
};
```

To get to the `firstname` property of the object contained in the `author` property of the `book` object, you use:

```
> book.author.firstname;
"Joseph"
```

Using the square brackets notation:

```
> book['author']['lastname'];
"Heller"
```

It works even if you mix both:

```
> book.author['lastname'];
"Heller"

> book['author'].lastname;
"Heller"
```

Another case where you need square brackets is when the name of the property you need to access is not known beforehand. During runtime, it's dynamically stored in a variable:

```
> var key = 'firstname';
> book.author[key];
"Joseph"
```

Calling an object's methods

You know a method is just a property that happens to be a function, so you access methods the same way as you would access properties: using the dot notation or using square brackets. Calling (invoking) a method is the same as calling any other function: you just add parentheses after the method name, which effectively says "Execute!".

```
> var hero = {
    breed: 'Turtle',
    occupation: 'Ninja',
    say: function () {
      return 'I am ' + hero.occupation;
    }
  };
> hero.say();
"I am Ninja"
```

If there are any parameters that you want to pass to a method, you proceed as with normal functions:

```
> hero.say('a', 'b', 'c');
```

Because you can use the array-like square brackets to access a property, this means you can also use brackets to access and invoke methods:

```
> hero['say']();
```

This is not a common practice unless the method name is not known at the time of writing code, but is instead defined at runtime:

```
var method = 'say';
hero[method]();
```

Best practice tip: no quotes (unless you have to)

Use the dot notation to access methods and properties and don't quote properties in your object literals.

Altering properties/methods

JavaScript allows you to alter the properties and methods of existing objects at any time. This includes adding new properties or deleting them. You can start with a "blank" object and add properties later. Let's see how you can go about doing this.

An object without properties is shown as follows:

```
> var hero = {};
```

A "blank" object

In this section, you started with a "blank" object, `var hero = {};`. Blank is in quotes because this object is not really empty and useless. Although at this stage it has no properties of its own, it has already inherited some. You'll learn more about own versus inherited properties later. So, an object in ES3 is never really "blank" or "empty". In ES5 though, there is a way to create a completely blank object that doesn't inherit anything, but let's not get ahead too much.

Accessing a non-existing property is shown as follows:

```
> typeof hero.breed;
"undefined"
```

Adding two properties and a method:

```
> hero.breed = 'turtle';
> hero.name = 'Leonardo';
> hero.sayName = function () {
    return hero.name;
  };
```

Calling the method:

```
> hero.sayName();
"Leonardo"
```

Deleting a property:

```
> delete hero.name;
true
```

Calling the method again will no longer find the deleted `name` property:

```
> hero.sayName();
"undefined"
```

Malleable objects

You can always change any object at any time, such as adding and removing properties and changing their values. But, there are exceptions to this rule. A few properties of some built-in objects are not changeable (for example, `Math.PI`, as you'll see later). Also, ES5 allows you to prevent changes to objects; you'll learn more about it in *Appendix C, Built-in Objects.*

Using the this value

In the previous example, the `sayName()` method used `hero.name` to access the `name` property of the `hero` object. When you're inside a method though, there is another way to access the object the method belongs to: by using the special value `this`.

```
> var hero = {
    name: 'Rafaelo',
    sayName: function () {
      return this.name;
    }
  };
> hero.sayName();
"Rafaelo"
```

So, when you say `this`, you're actually saying "this object" or "the current object".

Constructor functions

There is another way to create objects: by using constructor functions. Let's see an example:

```
function Hero() {
  this.occupation = 'Ninja';
}
```

In order to create an object using this function, you use the `new` operator, like this:

```
> var hero = new Hero();
> hero.occupation;
"Ninja"
```

A benefit of using constructor functions is that they accept parameters, which can be used when creating new objects. Let's modify the constructor to accept one parameter and assign it to the `name` property:

```
function Hero(name) {
  this.name = name;
  this.occupation = 'Ninja';
  this.whoAreYou = function () {
    return "I'm " +
           this.name +
           " and I'm a " +
           this.occupation;
  };
}
```

Now you can create different objects using the same constructor:

```
> var h1 = new Hero('Michelangelo');
> var h2 = new Hero('Donatello');
> h1.whoAreYou();
"I'm Michelangelo and I'm a Ninja"

> h2.whoAreYou();
"I'm Donatello and I'm a Ninja"
```

Best practice

By convention, you should capitalize the first letter of your constructor functions so that you have a visual clue that this is not intended to be called as a regular function.

If you call a function that is designed to be a constructor but you omit the `new` operator, this is not an error, but it doesn't give you the expected result.

```
> var h = Hero('Leonardo');
> typeof h;
"undefined"
```

What happened here? There is no `new` operator, so a new object was *not* created. The function was called like any other function, so `h` contains the value that the function returns. The function does not return anything (there's no `return`), so it actually returns **undefined**, which gets assigned to `h`.

In this case, what does `this` refer to? It refers to the global object.

The global object

You have already learned a bit about global variables (and how you should avoid them). You also know that JavaScript programs run inside a host environment (the browser for example). Now that you know about objects, it's time for the whole truth: the host environment provides a global object and all global variables are accessible as properties of the global object.

If your host environment is the web browser, the global object is called `window`. Another way to access the global object (and this is also true in most other environments) is to use `this` outside a constructor function, for example in the global program code outside any function.

As an illustration, you can declare a global variable outside any function, such as:

```
> var a = 1;
```

Then, you can access this global variable in various ways:

- As a variable `a`
- As a property of the global object, for example `window['a']` or `window.a`
- As a property of the global object referred to as `this`:

```
> var a = 1;
> window.a;
1

> this.a;
1
```

Let's go back to the case where you define a constructor function and call it without the `new` operator. In such cases, `this` refers to the global object and all the properties set to `this` become properties of `window`.

Declaring a constructor function and calling it without `new` returns **"undefined"**:

```
> function Hero(name) {
    this.name = name;
  }
> var h = Hero('Leonardo');
> typeof h;
"undefined"

> typeof h.name;
TypeError: Cannot read property 'name' of undefined
```

Because you had `this` inside `Hero`, a global variable (a property of the global object) called `name` was created:

```
> name;
"Leonardo"

> window.name;
"Leonardo"
```

If you call the same constructor function using `new`, then a new object is returned and `this` refers to it:

```
> var h2 = new Hero('Michelangelo');
> typeof h2;
"object"

> h2.name;
"Michelangelo"
```

The built-in global functions you have seen in *Chapter 3, Functions*, can also be invoked as methods of the `window` object. So, the following two calls have the same result:

```
> parseInt('101 dalmatians');
101

> window.parseInt('101 dalmatians');
101
```

And, when outside a function called as a constructor (with `new`), also:

```
> this.parseInt('101 dalmatians');
101
```

The constructor property

When an object is created, a special property is assigned to it behind the scenes—the `constructor` property. It contains a reference to the constructor function used to create this object.

Continuing from the previous example:

```
> h2.constructor;
function Hero(name) {
  this.name = name;
}
```

Because the `constructor` property contains a reference to a function, you might as well call this function to produce a new object. The following code is like saying, "I don't care how object `h2` was created, but I want another one just like it":

```
> var h3 = new h2.constructor('Rafaello');
> h3.name;
"Rafaello"
```

If an object was created using the object literal notation, its constructor is the built-in `Object()` constructor function (there is more about this later in this chapter):

```
> var o = {};
> o.constructor;
function Object() { [native code] }

> typeof o.constructor;
"function"
```

The instanceof operator

With the `instanceof` operator, you can test if an object was created with a specific constructor function:

```
> function Hero() {}
> var h = new Hero();
> var o = {};
> h instanceof Hero;
true

> h instanceof Object;
true

> o instanceof Object;
true
```

Note that you don't put parentheses after the function name (you don't use `h instanceof Hero()`). This is because you're not invoking this function, but just referring to it by name, as with any other variable.

Functions that return objects

In addition to using constructor functions and the `new` operator to create objects, you can also use a normal function to create objects without `new`. You can have a function that does a bit of preparatory work and has an object as a return value.

For example, here's a simple `factory()` function that produces objects:

```
function factory(name) {
  return {
    name: name
  };
}
```

Using the `factory()` function:

```
> var o = factory('one');
> o.name;
"one"

> o.constructor;
function Object() { [native code] }
```

In fact, you can also use constructor functions and return objects different from `this`. This means you can modify the default behavior of the constructor function. Let's see how.

Here's the normal constructor scenario:

```
> function C() {
    this.a = 1;
  }
> var c = new C();
> c.a;
1
```

But now look at this scenario:

```
> function C2() {
    this.a = 1;
    return {b: 2};
  }
> var c2 = new C2();
> typeof c2.a;
"undefined"

> c2.b;
2
```

What happened here? Instead of returning the object `this`, which contains the property `a`, the constructor returned another object that contains the property `b`. This is possible only if the return value is an object. Otherwise, if you try to return anything that is not an object, the constructor will proceed with its usual behavior and return `this`.

If you think about how objects are created inside constructor functions, you can imagine that a variable called `this` is defined at the top of the function and then returned at the end. It's as if something like this happens:

```
function C() {
  // var this = {}; // pseudo code, you can't do this
  this.a = 1;
  // return this;
}
```

Passing objects

When you assign an object to a different variable or pass it to a function, you only pass a reference to that object. Consequently, if you make a change to the reference, you're actually modifying the original object.

Here's an example of how you can assign an object to another variable and then make a change to the copy. As a result, the original object is also changed:

```
> var original = {howmany: 1};
> var mycopy = original;
> mycopy.howmany;
1

> mycopy.howmany = 100;
100

> original.howmany;
100
```

The same thing applies when passing objects to functions:

```
> var original = {howmany: 100};
> var nullify = function (o) { o.howmany = 0; };
> nullify(original);
> original.howmany;
0
```

Comparing objects

When you compare objects, you'll get `true` only if you compare two references to the same object. Comparing two distinct objects that happen to have the exact same methods and properties returns `false`.

Let's create two objects that look the same:

```
> var fido  = {breed: 'dog'};
> var benji = {breed: 'dog'};
```

Comparing them returns `false`:

```
> benji === fido;
false

> benji == fido;
false
```

You can create a new variable, `mydog`, and assign one of the objects to it. This way, `mydog` actually points to the same object:

```
> var mydog = benji;
```

In this case, `benji` is `mydog` because they are the same object (changing the `mydog` variable's properties will change the `benji` variable's properties). The comparison returns **true**:

```
> mydog === benji;
true
```

And, because `fido` is a different object, it does not compare to `mydog`:

```
> mydog === fido;
false
```

Objects in the WebKit console

Before diving into the built-in objects in JavaScript, let's quickly say a few words about working with objects in the WebKit console.

After playing around with the examples in this chapter, you might have already noticed how objects are displayed in the console. If you create an object and type its name, you'll get an arrow pointing to the word **Object**.

The object is clickable and expands to show you a list of all of the properties of the object. If a property is also an object, there is an arrow next to it too, so you can expand this as well. This is handy as it gives you an insight into exactly what this object contains.

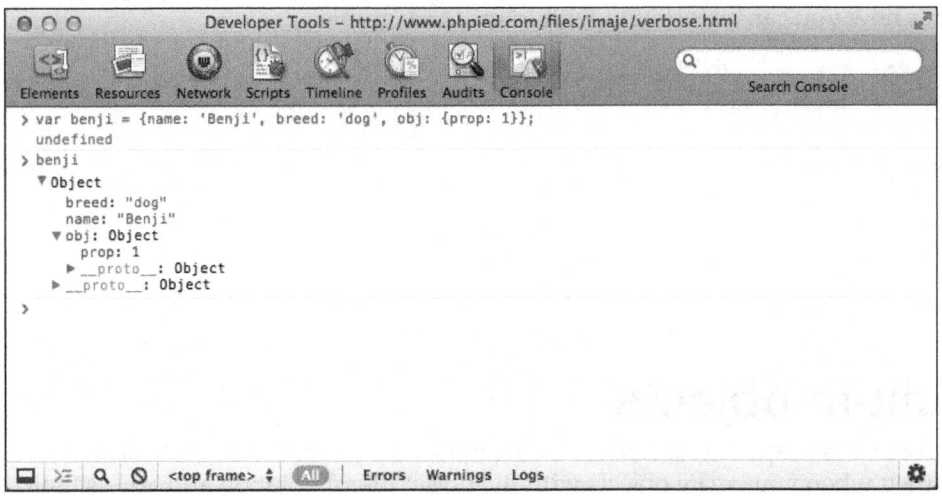

You can ignore `__proto__` for now; there's more about it in the next chapter.

console.log

The console also offers you an object called `console` and a few methods, such as `console.log()` and `console.error()`, which you can use to display any value you want in the console.

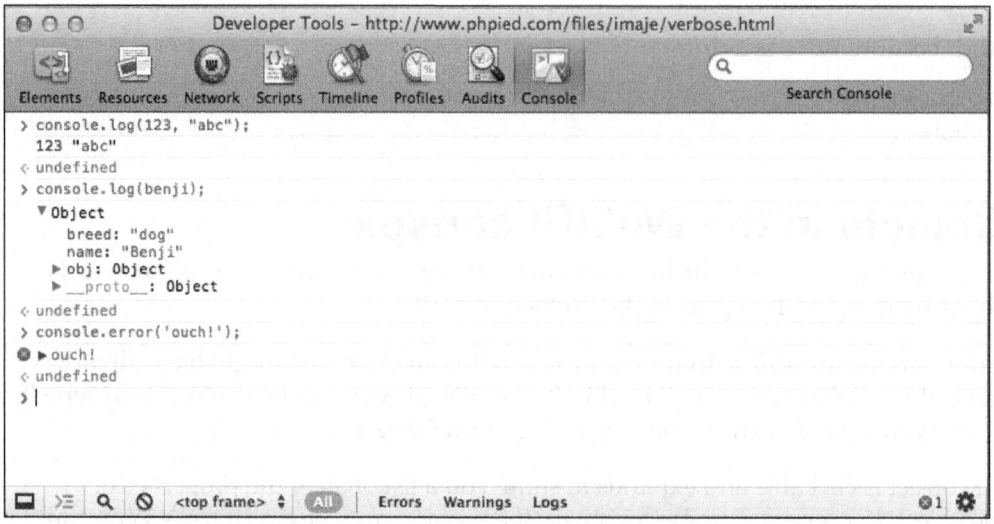

`console.log()` is convenient when you want to quickly test something, as well as in your real scripts when you want to dump some intermediate debugging information. Here's how you can experiment with loops for example:

```
> for (var i = 0; i < 5; i++) {
    console.log(i);
  }
0
1
2
3
4
```

Built-in objects

Earlier in this chapter, you came across the `Object()` constructor function. It's returned when you create objects with the object literal notation and access their `constructor` property. `Object()` is one of the built-in constructors; there are a few others, and in the rest of this chapter you'll see all of them.

The built-in objects can be divided into three groups:

- **Data wrapper objects**: These are `Object`, `Array`, `Function`, `Boolean`, `Number`, and `String`. These objects correspond to the different data types in JavaScript. There is a data wrapper object for every different value returned by `typeof` (discussed in *Chapter 2, Primitive Data Types, Arrays, Loops, and Conditions*), with the exception of "undefined" and "null".
- **Utility objects**: These are `Math`, `Date`, and `RegExp`, and can come in handy.
- **Error objects**: These include the generic `Error` object as well as other more specific objects that can help your program recover its working state when something unexpected happens.

Only a handful of methods of the built-in objects will be discussed in this chapter. For a full reference, see *Appendix C, Built-in Objects*.

If you're confused about what a built-in object is and what a built-in constructor is, well, they are the same thing. In a moment, you'll see how functions, and therefore constructor functions, are also objects.

Object

`Object` is the parent of all JavaScript objects, which means that every object you create inherits from it. To create a new "empty" object, you can use the literal notation or the `Object()` constructor function. The following two lines are equivalent:

```
> var o = {};
> var o = new Object();
```

As mentioned before, an "empty" (or "blank") object is not completely useless because it already contains several *inherited* methods and properties. In this book, "empty" means an object like `{}` that has no properties of its own other than the ones it automatically gets. Let's see a few of the properties that even "blank" objects already have:

- The `o.constructor` property returns a reference to the constructor function
- `o.toString()` is a method that returns a string representation of the object
- `o.valueOf()` returns a single-value representation of the object; often this is the object itself

Let's see these methods in action. First, create an object:

```
> var o = new Object();
```

Calling `toString()` returns a string representation of the object:

```
> o.toString();
"[object Object]"
```

`toString()` will be called internally by JavaScript when an object is used in a string context. For example, `alert()` works only with strings, so if you call the `alert()` function passing an object, the `toString()` method will be called behind the scenes. These two lines produce the same result:

```
> alert(o);
> alert(o.toString());
```

Another type of string context is the string concatenation. If you try to concatenate an object with a string, the object's `toString()` method is called first:

```
> "An object: " + o;
"An object: [object Object]"
```

`valueOf()` is another method that all objects provide. For the simple objects (whose constructor is `Object()`), the `valueOf()` method returns the object itself:

```
> o.valueOf() === o;
true
```

To summarize:

- You can create objects either with `var o = {};` (object literal notation, the preferred method) or with `var o = new Object();`
- Any object, no matter how complex, inherits from the `Object` object, and therefore offers methods such as `toString()` and properties such as `constructor`

Array

`Array()` is a built-in function that you can use as a constructor to create arrays:

```
> var a = new Array();
```

This is equivalent to the array literal notation:

```
> var a = [];
```

No matter how the array is created, you can add elements to it as usual:

```
> a[0] = 1;
> a[1] = 2;
> a;
[1, 2]
```

When using the `Array()` constructor, you can also pass values that will be assigned to the new array's elements:

```
> var a = new Array(1, 2, 3, 'four');
> a;
[1, 2, 3, "four"]
```

An exception to this is when you pass a single number to the constructor. In this case, the number is considered to be the length of the array:

```
> var a2 = new Array(5);
> a2;
[undefined x 5]
```

Because arrays are created with a constructor, does this mean that arrays are in fact objects? Yes, and you can verify this by using the `typeof` operator:

```
> typeof [1, 2, 3];
"object"
```

Because arrays are objects, this means that they inherit the properties and methods of the parent `Object`:

```
> var a = [1, 2, 3, 'four'];
> a.toString();
"1,2,3,four"

> a.valueOf();
[1, 2, 3, "four"]

> a.constructor;
function Array() { [native code] }
```

Arrays are objects, but of a special type because:

- The names of their properties are automatically assigned using numbers starting from 0
- They have a `length` property that contains the number of elements in the array
- They have more built-in methods in addition to those inherited from the parent `Object`

Let's examine the differences between an array and an object, starting by creating the empty array `a` and the empty object `o`:

```
> var a = [], o = {};
```

Array objects have a `length` property automatically defined for them, while normal objects do not:

```
> a.length;
0

> typeof o.length;
"undefined"
```

It's OK to add both numeric and non-numeric properties to both arrays and objects:

```
> a[0] = 1;
> o[0] = 1;
> a.prop = 2;
> o.prop = 2;
```

The `length` property is always up-to-date with the number of numeric properties, while it ignores the non-numeric ones:

```
> a.length;
1
```

The `length` property can also be set by you. Setting it to a greater value than the current number of items in the array makes room for additional elements. If you try to access these non-existing elements, you'll get the value `undefined`:

```
> a.length = 5;
5

> a;
[1, undefined x 4]
```

Setting the `length` property to a lower value removes the trailing elements:

```
> a.length = 2;
2

> a;
[1, undefined x 1]
```

A few array methods

In addition to the methods inherited from the parent `Object`, array objects also have specialized methods for working with arrays, such as `sort()`, `join()`, and `slice()`, among others (see *Appendix C, Built-in Objects*, for the full list).

Let's take an array and experiment with some of these methods:

```
> var a = [3, 5, 1, 7, 'test'];
```

The `push()` method appends a new element to the end of the array. The `pop()` method removes the last element. `a.push('new')` works like `a[a.length] = 'new'` and `a.pop()` is like `a.length--`.

`push()` returns the length of the changed array, whereas `pop()` returns the removed element:

```
> a.push('new');
6

> a;
[3, 5, 1, 7, "test", "new"]

> a.pop();
"new"

> a;
[3, 5, 1, 7, "test"]
```

The `sort()` method sorts the array and returns it. In the next example, after the sort, both `a` and `b` point to the same array:

```
> var b = a.sort();
> b;
[1, 3, 5, 7, "test"]

> a === b;
true
```

The `join()` method returns a string containing the values of all the elements in the array glued together using the string parameter passed to `join()`:

```
> a.join(' is not ');
"1 is not 3 is not 5 is not 7 is not test"
```

The `slice()` method returns a piece of the array without modifying the source array. The first parameter to `slice()` is the start index (zero-based) and the second is the end index (both indices are zero-based):

```
> b = a.slice(1, 3);
[3, 5]

> b = a.slice(0, 1);
[1]

> b = a.slice(0, 2);
[1, 3]
```

After all the slicing, the source array is still the same:

```
> a;
[1, 3, 5, 7, "test"]
```

The `splice()` method modifies the source array. It removes a slice, returns it, and optionally fills the gap with new elements. The first two parameters define the start index and length (number of elements) of the slice to be removed; the other parameters pass the new values:

```
> b = a.splice(1, 2, 100, 101, 102);
[3, 5]

> a;
[1, 100, 101, 102, 7, "test"]
```

Filling the gap with new elements is optional and you can skip it:

```
> a.splice(1, 3);
[100, 101, 102]

> a;
[1, 7, "test"]
```

Function

You already know that functions are a special data type. But, it turns out that there's more to it than that: functions are actually objects. There is a built-in constructor function called `Function()` that allows for an alternative (but not necessarily recommended) way to create a function.

The following example shows three ways to define a function:

```
> function sum(a, b) { // function declaration
    return a + b;
  }
```

```
> sum(1, 2);
3

> var sum = function (a, b) { // function expression
    return a + b;
  };
> sum(1, 2)
3

> var sum = new Function('a', 'b', 'return a + b;');
> sum(1, 2)
3
```

When using the `Function()` constructor, you pass the parameter names first (as strings) and then the source code for the body of the function (again as a string). The JavaScript engine needs to evaluate the source code you pass and create the new function for you. This source code evaluation suffers from the same drawbacks as the `eval()` function, so defining functions using the `Function()` constructor should be avoided when possible.

If you use the `Function()` constructor to create functions that have lots of parameters, bear in mind that the parameters can be passed as a single comma-delimited list; so, for example, these are the same:

```
> var first = new Function(
    'a, b, c, d',
    'return arguments;'
  );
> first(1, 2, 3, 4);
  [1, 2, 3, 4]

> var second = new Function(
    'a, b, c',
    'd',
    'return arguments;'
  );
> second(1, 2, 3, 4);
  [1, 2, 3, 4]

> var third = new Function(
    'a',
    'b',
    'c',
    'd',
    'return arguments;'
  );
> third(1, 2, 3, 4);
  [1, 2, 3, 4]
```

Best practice

Do not use the `Function()` constructor. As with `eval()` and `setTimeout()` (discussed later in the book), always try to stay away from passing JavaScript code as a string.

Properties of function objects

Like any other object, functions have a `constructor` property that contains a reference to the `Function()` constructor function. This is true no matter which syntax you used to create the function.

```
> function myfunc(a) {
    return a;
  }
> myfunc.constructor;
function Function() { [native code] }
```

Functions also have a `length` property, which contains the number of formal parameters the function expects.

```
> function myfunc(a, b, c) {
    return true;
  }
> myfunc.length;
  3
```

Prototype

One of the most widely used properties of function objects is the `prototype` property. You'll see this property discussed in detail in the next chapter, but for now, let's just say:

- The `prototype` property of a function object points to another object
- Its benefits shine only when you use this function as a constructor
- All objects created with this function keep a reference to the `prototype` property and can use its properties as their own

Let's see a quick example to demonstrate the `prototype` property. Take a simple object that has a property `name` and a method `say()`.

```
var ninja = {
  name: 'Ninja',
  say: function () {
    return 'I am a ' + this.name;
  }
};
```

When you create a function (even one without a body), you can verify that it automatically has a `prototype` property that points to a new object.

```
> function F() {}
> typeof F.prototype;
"object"
```

It gets interesting when you modify the `prototype` property. You can add properties to it or you can replace the default object with any other object. Let's assign `ninja` to the prototype.

```
> F.prototype = ninja;
```

Now, and here's where the magic happens, using the function `F()` as a constructor function, you can create a new object, `baby_ninja`, which will have access to the properties of `F.prototype` (which points to `ninja`) as if it were its own.

```
> var baby_ninja = new F();
> baby_ninja.name;
"Ninja"

> baby_ninja.say();
"I am a Ninja"
```

There will be much more on this topic later. In fact, the whole next chapter is about the `prototype` property.

Methods of function objects

Function objects, being a descendant of the top parent `Object`, get the default methods such as `toString()`. When invoked on a function, the `toString()` method returns the source code of the function.

```
> function myfunc(a, b, c) {
    return a + b + c;
  }
> myfunc.toString();
"function myfunc(a, b, c) {
 return a + b + c;
}"
```

If you try to peek into the source code of the built-in functions, you'll get the string `[native code]` instead of the body of the function.

```
> parseInt.toString();
"function parseInt() { [native code] }"
```

As you can see, you can use `toString()` to differentiate between native methods and developer-defined ones.

The behavior of the function's `toString()` is environment-dependent, and it does differ among browsers in terms of spacing and new lines.

Call and apply

Function objects have `call()` and `apply()` methods. You can use them to invoke a function and pass any arguments to it.

These methods also allow your objects to "borrow" methods from other objects and invoke them as their own. This is an easy and powerful way to reuse code.

Let's say you have a `some_obj` object, which contains the method `say()`.

```
var some_obj = {
  name: 'Ninja',
  say: function (who) {
    return 'Haya ' + who + ', I am a ' + this.name;
  }
};
```

You can call the `say()` method, which internally uses `this.name` to gain access to its own `name` property.

```
> some_obj.say('Dude');
"Haya Dude, I am a Ninja"
```

Now let's create a simple object, `my_obj`, which only has a `name` property.

```
> var my_obj = {name: 'Scripting guru'};
```

`my_obj` likes the `some_obj` object's `say()` method so much that it wants to invoke it as its own. This is possible using the `call()` method of the `say()` function object.

```
> some_obj.say.call(my_obj, 'Dude');
"Haya Dude, I am a Scripting guru"
```

It worked! But what happened here? You invoked the `call()` method of the `say()` function object passing two parameters: the object `my_obj` and the string `'Dude'`. The result is that when `say()` is invoked, the references to the `this` value that it contains point to `my_obj`. This way, `this.name` doesn't return **Ninja**, but **Scripting guru** instead.

If you have more parameters to pass when invoking the `call()` method, you just keep adding them.

```
some_obj.someMethod.call(my_obj, 'a', 'b', 'c');
```

If you don't pass an object as a first parameter to `call()` or you pass `null`, the global object is assumed.

The method `apply()` works the same way as `call()`, but with the difference that all parameters you want to pass to the method of the other object are passed as an array. The following two lines are equivalent:

```
some_obj.someMethod.apply(my_obj, ['a', 'b', 'c']);
some_obj.someMethod.call(my_obj, 'a', 'b', 'c');
```

Continuing the previous example, you can use:

```
> some_obj.say.apply(my_obj, ['Dude']);
```
"Haya Dude, I am a Scripting guru"

The arguments object revisited

In the previous chapter, you have seen how, from inside a function, you have access to something called `arguments`, which contains the values of all the parameters passed to the function:

```
> function f() {
    return arguments;
  }
> f(1, 2, 3);
```
[1, 2, 3]

`arguments` looks like an array, but it is actually an array-like object. It resembles an array because it contains indexed elements and a `length` property. However, the similarity ends there, as `arguments` doesn't provide any of the array methods, such as `sort()` or `slice()`.

However, you can convert `arguments` to an array and benefit from all the array goodies. Here's what you can do, practicing your newly-learned `call()` method:

```
> function f() {
    var args = [].slice.call(arguments);
    return args.reverse();
  }

> f(1, 2, 3, 4);
```
[4, 3, 2, 1]

As you can see, you can borrow `slice()` using `[].slice` or the more verbose `Array.prototype.slice`.

Inferring object types

You can see that you have this array-like `arguments` object looking so much like an array object. How can you reliably tell the difference between the two? Additionally, `typeof` returns `object` when used with arrays. Therefore, how can you tell the difference between an object and an array?

The silver bullet is the `Object` object's `toString()` method. It gives you the internal class name used to create a given object.

```
> Object.prototype.toString.call({});
"[object Object]"

> Object.prototype.toString.call([]);
"[object Array]"
```

You have to call the original `toString()` method as defined in the prototype of the `Object` constructor. Otherwise, if you call the `Array` function's `toString()`, it will give you a different result, as it's been overridden for the specific purposes of the array objects:

```
> [1, 2, 3].toString();
"1,2,3"
```

This is the same as:

```
> Array.prototype.toString.call([1, 2, 3]);
"1,2,3"
```

Let's have some more fun with `toString()`. Make a handy reference to save typing:

```
> var toStr = Object.prototype.toString;
```

Differentiate between an array and the array-like object `arguments`:

```
> (function () {
    return toStr.call(arguments);
  }());
"[object Arguments]"
```

You can even inspect DOM elements:

```
> toStr.call(document.body);
"[object HTMLBodyElement]"
```

Boolean

Your journey through the built-in objects in JavaScript continues, and the next three are fairly straightforward; they merely wrap the primitive data types Boolean, number, and string.

You already know a lot about Booleans from *Chapter 2, Primitive Data Types, Arrays, Loops, and Conditions*. Now, let's meet the `Boolean()` constructor:

```
> var b = new Boolean();
```

It's important to note that this creates a new object, `b`, and not a primitive Boolean value. To get the primitive value, you can call the `valueOf()` method (inherited from `Object` and customized):

```
> var b = new Boolean();
> typeof b;
"object"

> typeof b.valueOf();
"boolean"

> b.valueOf();
false
```

Overall, objects created with the `Boolean()` constructor are not too useful, as they don't provide any methods or properties other than the inherited ones.

The `Boolean()` function, when called as a normal function without `new`, converts non-Booleans to Booleans (which is like using a double negation `!!value`):

```
> Boolean("test");
true

> Boolean("");
false

> Boolean({});
true
```

Apart from the six falsy values, everything else is true in JavaScript, including all objects. This also means that all Boolean objects created with `new Boolean()` are also true, as they are objects:

```
> Boolean(new Boolean(false));
true
```

This can be confusing, and since Boolean objects don't offer any special methods, it's best to just stick with regular primitive Boolean values.

Number

Similarly to `Boolean()`, the `Number()` function can be used as:

- A constructor function (with `new`) to create objects.
- A normal function in order to try to convert any value to a number. This is similar to the use of `parseInt()` or `parseFloat()`.

```
> var n = Number('12.12');
> n;
12.12

> typeof n;
"number"

> var n = new Number('12.12');
> typeof n;
"object"
```

Because functions are objects, they can also have properties. The `Number()` function has constant built-in properties that you cannot modify:

```
> Number.MAX_VALUE;
1.7976931348623157e+308

> Number.MIN_VALUE;
5e-324

> Number.POSITIVE_INFINITY;
Infinity

> Number.NEGATIVE_INFINITY;
-Infinity

> Number.NaN;
NaN
```

The number objects provide three methods: `toFixed()`, `toPrecision()`, and `toExponential()` (see *Appendix C, Built-in Objects*, for more details):

```
> var n = new Number(123.456);
> n.toFixed(1);
"123.5"
```

Note that you can use these methods without explicitly creating a number object first. In such cases, the number object is created (and destroyed) for you behind the scenes:

```
> (12345).toExponential();
"1.2345e+4"
```

Like all objects, number objects also provide the `toString()` method. When used with number objects, this method accepts an optional radix parameter (10 being the default):

```
> var n = new Number(255);
> n.toString();
"255"

> n.toString(10);
"255"

> n.toString(16);
"ff"

> (3).toString(2);
"11"

> (3).toString(10);
"3"
```

String

You can use the `String()` constructor function to create string objects. String objects provide convenient methods for text manipulation.

Here's an example that shows the difference between a string object and a primitive string data type:

```
> var primitive = 'Hello';
> typeof primitive;
"string"

> var obj = new String('world');
> typeof obj;
"object"
```

A string object is similar to an array of characters. String objects have an indexed property for each character (introduced in ES5, but long supported in many browsers except old IEs) and they also have a `length` property.

```
> obj[0];
"w"

> obj[4];
"d"

> obj.length;
5
```

To extract the primitive value from the string object, you can use the `valueOf()` or `toString()` methods inherited from `Object`. You'll probably never need to do this, as `toString()` is called behind the scenes if you use an object in a primitive string context.

```
> obj.valueOf();
"world"

> obj.toString();
"world"

> obj + "";
"world"
```

Primitive strings are not objects, so they don't have any methods or properties. But, JavaScript also offers you the syntax to treat primitive strings as objects (just like you saw already with primitive numbers).

In the following example, string objects are being created (and then destroyed) behind the scenes every time you treat a primitive string as if it were an object:

```
> "potato".length;
6

> "tomato"[0];
"t"

> "potatoes"["potatoes".length - 1];
"s"
```

One final example to illustrate the difference between a string primitive and a string object: let's convert them to Boolean. The empty string is a falsy value, but any string object is truthy (because all objects are truthy):

```
> Boolean("");
false

> Boolean(new String(""));
true
```

Similarly to `Number()` and `Boolean()`, if you use the `String()` function without `new`, it converts the parameter to a primitive:

```
> String(1);
"1"
```

If you pass an object to `String()`, this object's `toString()` method will be called first:

```
> String({p: 1});
  "[object Object]"

> String([1, 2, 3]);
  "1,2,3"

> String([1, 2, 3]) === [1, 2, 3].toString();
  true
```

A few methods of string objects

Let's experiment with a few of the methods you can call on string objects (see *Appendix C, Built-in Objects,* for the full list).

Start off by creating a string object:

```
> var s = new String("Couch potato");
```

`toUpperCase()` and `toLowerCase()` transforms the capitalization of the string:

```
> s.toUpperCase();
"COUCH POTATO"

> s.toLowerCase();
"couch potato"
```

`charAt()` tells you the character found at the position you specify, which is the same as using square brackets (treating a string as an array of characters):

```
> s.charAt(0);
"C"

> s[0];
"C"
```

If you pass a non-existing position to `charAt()`, you get an empty string:

```
> s.charAt(101);
""
```

`indexOf()` allows you to search within a string. If there is a match, the method returns the position at which the first match is found. The position count starts at 0, so the second character in "Couch" is "o" at position 1:

```
> s.indexOf('o');
1
```

You can optionally specify where (at what position) to start the search. The following finds the second "o", because `indexOf()` is instructed to start the search at position 2:

```
> s.indexOf('o', 2);
7
```

`lastIndexOf()` starts the search from the end of the string (but the position of the match is still counted from the beginning):

```
> s.lastIndexOf('o');
11
```

You can also search for strings, not only characters, and the search is case sensitive:

```
> s.indexOf('Couch');
0
```

If there is no match, the function returns position -1:

```
> s.indexOf('couch');
-1
```

For a case-insensitive search, you can transform the string to lowercase first and then search:

```
> s.toLowerCase().indexOf('couch');
0
```

When you get 0, this means that the matching part of the string starts at position 0. This can cause confusion when you check with `if`, because `if` converts the position 0 to a Boolean `false`. So, while this is syntactically correct, it is logically wrong:

```
if (s.indexOf('Couch')) {...}
```

The proper way to check if a string contains another string is to compare the result of `indexOf()` to the number `-1`:

```
if (s.indexOf('Couch') !== -1) {...}
```

`slice()` and `substring()` return a piece of the string when you specify start and end positions:

```
> s.slice(1, 5);
"ouch"

> s.substring(1, 5);
"ouch"
```

Note that the second parameter you pass is the end position, not the length of the piece. The difference between these two methods is how they treat negative arguments. `substring()` treats them as zeros, while `slice()` adds them to the length of the string. So, if you pass parameters `(1, -1)` to both methods, it's the same as `substring(1, 0)` and `slice(1, s.length - 1)`:

```
> s.slice(1, -1);
"ouch potat"

> s.substring(1, -1);
"C"
```

There's also the non-standard method `substr()`, but you should try to avoid it in favor of `substring()`.

The `split()` method creates an array from the string using another string that you pass as a separator:

```
> s.split(" ");
["Couch", "potato"]
```

`split()` is the opposite of `join()`, which creates a string from an array:

```
> s.split(' ').join(' ');
"Couch potato"
```

`concat()` glues strings together, the way the `+` operator does for primitive strings:

```
> s.concat("es");
"Couch potatoes"
```

Note that while some of the preceding methods discussed return new primitive strings, none of them modify the source string. After all the method calls listed previously, the initial string is still the same:

```
> s.valueOf();
"Couch potato"
```

You have seen how to use `indexOf()` and `lastIndexOf()` to search within strings, but there are more powerful methods (`search()`, `match()`, and `replace()`) that take regular expressions as parameters. You'll see these later in the `RegExp()` constructor function.

At this point, you're done with all of the data wrapper objects, so let's move on to the utility objects `Math`, `Date`, and `RegExp`.

Math

`Math` is a little different from the other built-in global objects you have seen previously. It's not a function, and therefore cannot be used with `new` to create objects. `Math` is a built-in global object that provides a number of methods and properties for mathematical operations.

The `Math` object's properties are constants, so you can't change their values. Their names are all in uppercase to emphasize the difference between them and a normal property (similar to the constant properties of the `Number()` constructor). Let's see a few of these constant properties:

- The constant π:

  ```
  > Math.PI;
  3.141592653589793
  ```

- Square root of 2:

  ```
  > Math.SQRT2;
  1.4142135623730951
  ```

- Euler's constant:

  ```
  > Math.E;
  2.718281828459045
  ```

- Natural logarithm of 2:

  ```
  > Math.LN2;
  0.6931471805599453
  ```

- Natural logarithm of 10:

```
> Math.LN10;
2.302585092994046
```

Now you know how to impress your friends the next time they (for whatever reason) start wondering, "What was the value of *e*? I can't remember." Just type `Math.E` in the console and you have the answer.

Let's take a look at some of the methods the `Math` object provides (the full list is in *Appendix C, Built-in Objects*).

Generating random numbers:

```
> Math.random();
0.3649461670235814
```

The `random()` function returns a number between 0 and 1, so if you want a number between, let's say, 0 and 100, you can do the following:

```
> 100 * Math.random();
```

For numbers between any two values, use the formula `((max - min) * Math.random()) + min`. For example, a random number between 2 and 10 would be:

```
> 8 * Math.random() + 2;
9.175650496668485
```

If you only need an integer, you can use one of the following rounding methods:

- `floor()` to round down
- `ceil()` to round up
- `round()` to round to the nearest

For example, to get either 0 or 1:

```
> Math.round(Math.random());
```

If you need the lowest or the highest among a set of numbers, you have the `min()` and `max()` methods. So, if you have a form on a page that asks for a valid month, you can make sure that you always work with sane data (a value between 1 and 12):

```
> Math.min(Math.max(1, input), 12);
```

The `Math` object also provides the ability to perform mathematical operations for which you don't have a designated operator. This means that you can raise to a power using `pow()`, find the square root using `sqrt()`, and perform all the trigonometric operations—`sin()`, `cos()`, `atan()`, and so on.

For example, to calculate 2 to the power of 8:

```
> Math.pow(2, 8);
256
```

And to calculate the square root of 9:

```
> Math.sqrt(9);
3
```

Date

`Date()` is a constructor function that creates date objects. You can create a new object by passing:

- Nothing (defaults to today's date)
- A date-like string
- Separate values for day, month, time, and so on
- A timestamp

Following is an object instantiated with today's date/time:

```
> new Date();
Wed Feb 27 2013 23:49:28 GMT-0800 (PST)
```

The console displays the result of the `toString()` method called on the date object, so you get this long string **Wed Feb 27 2013 23:49:28 GMT-0800 (PST)** as a representation of the date object.

Here are a few examples of using strings to initialize a date object. Note how many different formats you can use to specify the date:

```
> new Date('2015 11 12');
Thu Nov 12 2015 00:00:00 GMT-0800 (PST)

> new Date('1 1 2016');
Fri Jan 01 2016 00:00:00 GMT-0800 (PST)

> new Date('1 mar 2016 5:30');
Tue Mar 01 2016 05:30:00 GMT-0800 (PST)
```

The `Date` constructor can figure out a date from different strings, but this is not really a reliable way of defining a precise date, for example when passing user input to the constructor. The better way is to pass numeric values to the `Date()` constructor representing:

- Year

- Month: 0 (January) to 11 (December)
- Day: 1 to 31
- Hour: 0 to 23
- Minutes: 0 to 59
- Seconds: 0 to 59
- Milliseconds: 0 to 999

Let's see some examples.

Passing all the parameters:

```
> new Date(2015, 0, 1, 17, 05, 03, 120);
Tue Jan 01 2015 17:05:03 GMT-0800 (PST)
```

Passing date and hour:

```
> new Date(2015, 0, 1, 17);
Tue Jan 01 2015 17:00:00 GMT-0800 (PST)
```

Watch out for the fact that the month starts from 0, so 1 is February:

```
> new Date(2016, 1, 28);
Sun Feb 28 2016 00:00:00 GMT-0800 (PST)
```

If you pass a greater than allowed value, your date "overflows" forward. Because there's no February 30 in 2016, this means it has to be March 1st (2016 is a leap year):

```
> new Date(2016, 1, 29);
Mon Feb 29 2016 00:00:00 GMT-0800 (PST)

> new Date(2016, 1, 30);
Tue Mar 01 2016 00:00:00 GMT-0800 (PST)
```

Similarly, December 32nd becomes January 1st of the next year:

```
> new Date(2012, 11, 31);
Mon Dec 31 2012 00:00:00 GMT-0800 (PST)

> new Date(2012, 11, 32);
Tue Jan 01 2013 00:00:00 GMT-0800 (PST)
```

Finally, a date object can be initialized with a timestamp (the number of milliseconds since the UNIX epoch, where 0 milliseconds is January 1, 1970):

```
> new Date(1357027200000);
Tue Jan 01 2013 00:00:00 GMT-0800 (PST)
```

If you call `Date()` without `new`, you get a string representing the current date, whether or not you pass any parameters. The following example gives the current time (current when this example was run):

```
> Date();
Wed Feb 27 2013 23:51:46 GMT-0800 (PST)

> Date(1, 2, 3, "it doesn't matter");
Wed Feb 27 2013 23:51:52 GMT-0800 (PST)

> typeof Date();
"string"

> typeof new Date();
"object"
```

Methods to work with date objects

Once you've created a date object, there are lots of methods you can call on that object. Most of the methods can be divided into `set*()` and `get*()` methods, for example, `getMonth()`, `setMonth()`, `getHours()`, `setHours()`, and so on. Let's see some examples.

Creating a date object:

```
> var d = new Date(2015, 1, 1);
> d.toString();
Sun Feb 01 2015 00:00:00 GMT-0800 (PST)
```

Setting the month to March (months start from 0):

```
> d.setMonth(2);
1425196800000

> d.toString();
Sun Mar 01 2015 00:00:00 GMT-0800 (PST)
```

Getting the month:

```
> d.getMonth();
2
```

In addition to all the methods of date objects, there are also two methods (plus one more added in ES5) that are properties of the `Date()` function/object. These do not need a date object; they work just like the `Math` object's methods. In class-based languages, such methods would be called static because they don't require an instance.

`Date.parse()` takes a string and returns a timestamp:

```
> Date.parse('Jan 11, 2018');
1515657600000
```

`Date.UTC()` takes all the parameters for year, month, day, and so on, and produces a timestamp in Universal Time:

```
> Date.UTC(2018, 0, 11);
1515628800000
```

Because the `new Date()` constructor can accept timestamps, you can pass the result of `Date.UTC()` to it. Using the following example, you can see how `UTC()` works with Universal Time, while `new Date()` works with local time:

```
> new Date(Date.UTC(2018, 0, 11));
Wed Jan 10 2018 16:00:00 GMT-0800 (PST)

> new Date(2018, 0, 11);
Thu Jan 11 2018 00:00:00 GMT-0800 (PST)
```

The ES5 addition to the `Date` constructor is the method `now()`, which returns the current timestamp. It provides a more convenient way to get the timestamp instead of using the `getTime()` method on a date object as you would in ES3:

```
> Date.now();
1362038353044

> Date.now() === new Date().getTime();
true
```

You can think of the internal representation of the date being an integer timestamp and all other methods being "sugar" on top of it. So, it makes sense that the `valueOf()` is a timestamp:

```
> new Date().valueOf();
1362418306432
```

Also dates cast to integers with the + operator:

```
> +new Date();
1362418318311
```

Calculating birthdays

Let's see one final example of working with `Date` objects. I was curious about which day my birthday falls on in 2016:

```
> var d = new Date(2016, 5, 20);
> d.getDay();
1
```

Starting the count from 0 (Sunday), 1 means Monday. Is that so?

```
> d.toDateString();
"Mon Jun 20 2016"
```

OK, good to know, but Monday is not necessarily the best day for a party. So, how about a loop that shows how many times June 20th is a Friday from year 2016 to year 3016, or better yet, let's see the distribution of all the days of the week. After all, with all the progress in DNA hacking, we're all going to be alive and kicking in 3016.

First, let's initialize an array with seven elements, one for each day of the week. These will be used as counters. Then, as a loop goes up to 3016, let's increment the counters:

```
var stats = [0, 0, 0, 0, 0, 0, 0];
```

The loop:

```
for (var i = 2016; i < 3016; i++) {
   stats[new Date(i, 5, 20).getDay()]++;
}
```

And the result:

```
> stats;
[140, 146, 140, 145, 142, 142, 145]
```

142 Fridays and 145 Saturdays. Woo-hoo!

RegExp

Regular expressions provide a powerful way to search and manipulate text. Different languages have different implementations (think "dialects") of the regular expressions syntax. JavaScript uses the Perl 5 syntax.

Instead of saying "regular expression", people often shorten it to "regex" or "regexp".

A regular expression consists of:

- A pattern you use to match text
- Zero or more modifiers (also called flags) that provide more instructions on how the pattern should be used

The pattern can be as simple as literal text to be matched verbatim, but that's rare, and in such cases you're better off using `indexOf()`. Most of the time, the pattern is more complex and could be difficult to understand. Mastering regular expression's patterns is a large topic, which won't be discussed in full detail here; instead, you'll see what JavaScript provides in terms of syntax, objects, and methods in order to support the use of regular expressions. You can also refer to *Appendix D, Regular Expressions*, to help you when you're writing patterns.

JavaScript provides the `RegExp()` constructor, which allows you to create regular expression objects:

```
> var re = new RegExp("j.*t");
```

There is also the more convenient *regexp literal notation*:

```
> var re = /j.*t/;
```

In the preceding example, `j.*t` is the regular expression pattern. It means "match any string that starts with `j`, ends with `t`, and has zero or more characters in between". The asterisk (`*`) means "zero or more of the preceding"; the dot (`.`) means "any character". The pattern needs to be quoted when passed to a `RegExp()` constructor.

Properties of RegExp objects

Regular expression objects have the following properties:

- `global`: If this property is `false`, which is the default, the search stops when the first match is found. Set this to `true` if you want all matches.
- `ignoreCase`: When the match is case insensitive, the defaults to `false` (meaning the default is a case sensitive match).
- `multiline`: Search matches that may span over more than one line default to `false`.
- `lastIndex`: The position at which to start the search; this defaults to 0.
- `source`: Contains the regexp pattern.

None of these properties, except for `lastIndex`, can be changed once the object has been created.

The first three items in the preceding list represent the regex modifiers. If you create a regex object using the constructor, you can pass any combination of the following characters as a second parameter:

- `g` for `global`
- `i` for `ignoreCase`
- `m` for `multiline`

These letters can be in any order. If a letter is passed, the corresponding modifier property is set to `true`. In the following example, all modifiers are set to `true`:

```
> var re = new RegExp('j.*t', 'gmi');
```

Let's verify:

```
> re.global;
true
```

Once set, the modifier cannot be changed:

```
> re.global = false;
> re.global;
true
```

To set any modifiers using the *regex literal*, you add them after the closing slash:

```
> var re = /j.*t/ig;
> re.global;
true
```

Methods of RegExp objects

Regex objects provide two methods you can use to find matches: `test()` and `exec()`. They both accept a string parameter. `test()` returns a Boolean (`true` when there's a match, `false` otherwise), while `exec()` returns an array of matched strings. Obviously, `exec()` is doing more work, so use `test()` unless you really need to do something with the matches. People often use regular expressions to validate data, in this case, `test()` should be enough.

In the following example, there is no match because of the capital `J`:

```
> /j.*t/.test("Javascript");
false
```

A case insensitive test gives a positive result:

```
> /j.*t/i.test("Javascript");
true
```

The same test using `exec()` returns an array, and you can access the first element as shown below:

```
> /j.*t/i.exec("Javascript")[0];
"Javascript"
```

String methods that accept regular expressions as arguments

Previously in this chapter, you learned about string objects and how you can use the `indexOf()` and `lastIndexOf()` methods to search within text. Using these methods, you can only specify literal string patterns to search. A more powerful solution would be to use regular expressions to find text. String objects offer you this ability.

String objects provide the following methods that accept regular expression objects as parameters:

- `match()` returns an array of matches
- `search()` returns the position of the first match
- `replace()` allows you to substitute matched text with another string
- `split()` also accepts a regexp when splitting a string into array elements

search() and match()

Let's see some examples of using the `search()` and `match()` methods. First, you create a string object:

```
> var s = new String('HelloJavaScriptWorld');
```

Using `match()`, you get an array containing only the first match:

```
> s.match(/a/);
["a"]
```

Using the `g` modifier, you perform a global search, so the result array contains two elements:

```
> s.match(/a/g);
["a", "a"]
```

A case insensitive match is as follows:

```
> s.match(/j.*a/i);
["Java"]
```

The `search()` method gives you the position of the matching string:

```
> s.search(/j.*a/i);
5
```

replace()

`replace()` allows you to replace the matched text with some other string. The following example removes all capital letters (it replaces them with blank strings):

```
> s.replace(/[A-Z]/g, '');
"elloavacriptorld"
```

If you omit the `g` modifier, you're only going to replace the first match:

```
> s.replace(/[A-Z]/, '');
"elloJavaScriptWorld"
```

When a match is found, if you want to include the matched text in the replacement string, you can access it using `$&`. Here's how to add an underscore before the match while keeping the match:

```
> s.replace(/[A-Z]/g, "_$&");
"_Hello_Java_Script_World"
```

When the regular expression contains groups (denoted by parentheses), the matches of each group are available as `$1` for the first group, `$2` the second, and so on.

```
> s.replace(/([A-Z])/g, "_$1");
"_Hello_Java_Script_World"
```

Imagine you have a registration form on your web page that asks for an e-mail address, username, and password. The user enters their e-mail, and then your JavaScript kicks in and suggests the username, taking it from the e-mail address:

```
> var email = "stoyan@phpied.com";
> var username = email.replace(/(.*)@.*/, "$1");
> username;
"stoyan"
```

Replace callbacks

When specifying the replacement, you can also pass a function that returns a string. This gives you the ability to implement any special logic you may need before specifying the replacements:

```
> function replaceCallback(match) {
    return "_" + match.toLowerCase();
```

```
}

> s.replace(/[A-Z]/g, replaceCallback);
"_hello_java_script_world"
```

The callback function receives a number of parameters (the previous example ignores all but the first one):

- The first parameter is the match
- The last is the string being searched
- The one before last is the position of the match
- The rest of the parameters contain any strings matched by any groups in your regex pattern

Let's test this. First, let's create a variable to store the entire `arguments` array passed to the callback function:

```
> var glob;
```

Next, define a regular expression that has three groups and matches e-mail addresses in the format `something@something.something`:

```
> var re = /(.*)@(.*)\.(.*)/;
```

Finally, let's define a callback function that stores the arguments in `glob` and then returns the replacement:

```
var callback = function () {
  glob = arguments;
  return arguments[1] + ' at ' +
         arguments[2] + ' dot ' +
         arguments[3];
};
```

Now perform a test:

```
> "stoyan@phpied.com".replace(re, callback);
"stoyan at phpied dot com"
```

Here's what the callback function received as arguments:

```
> glob;
["stoyan@phpied.com", "stoyan", "phpied", "com", 0,
"stoyan@phpied.com"]
```

split()

You already know about the `split()` method, which creates an array from an input string and a delimiter string. Let's take a string of comma-separated values and split it:

```
> var csv = 'one, two,three ,four';
> csv.split(',');
["one", " two", "three ", "four"]
```

Because the input string happens to have random inconsistent spaces before and after the commas, the array result has spaces too. With a regular expression, you can fix this using `\s*`, which means "zero or more spaces":

```
> csv.split(/\s*,\s*/);
["one", "two", "three", "four"]
```

Passing a string when a RegExp is expected

One last thing to note is that the four methods that you have just seen (`split()`, `match()`, `search()`, and `replace()`) can also take strings as opposed to regular expressions. In this case, the string argument is used to produce a new regex as if it was passed to `new RegExp()`.

An example of passing a string to `replace` is shown as follows:

```
> "test".replace('t', 'r');
"rest"
```

The above is the same as:

```
> "test".replace(new RegExp('t'), 'r');
"rest"
```

When you pass a string, you cannot set modifiers the way you do with a normal constructor or regex literal. There's a common source of errors when using a string instead of a regular expression object for string replacements, and it's due to the fact that the `g` modifier is `false` by default. The outcome is that only the first string is replaced, which is inconsistent with most other languages and a little confusing. For example:

```
> "pool".replace('o', '*');
"p*ol"
```

Most likely, you want to replace all occurrences:

```
> "pool".replace(/o/g, '*');
"p**l"
```

Error objects

Errors happen, and it's good to have the mechanisms in place so that your code can realize that there has been an error condition and can recover from it in a graceful manner. JavaScript provides the statements `try`, `catch`, and `finally` to help you deal with errors. If an error occurs, an error object is thrown. Error objects are created by using one of these built-in constructors: `EvalError`, `RangeError`, `ReferenceError`, `SyntaxError`, `TypeError`, and `URIError`. All of these constructors inherit from `Error`.

Let's just cause an error and see what happens. What's a simple way to cause an error? Just call a function that doesn't exist. Type this into the console:

```
> iDontExist();
```

You'll get something like this:

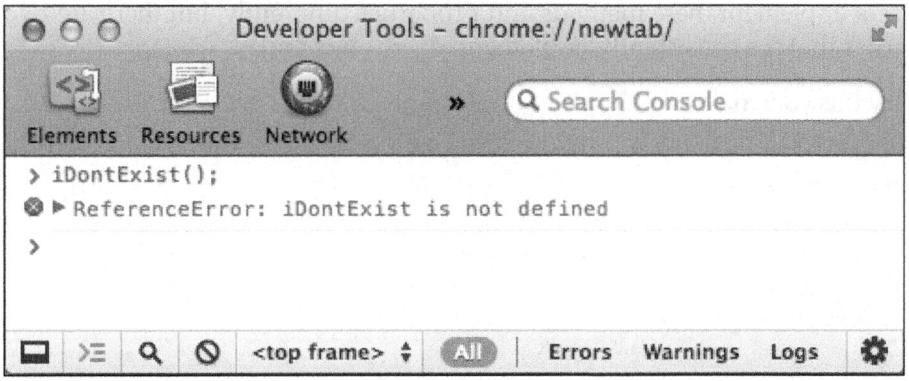

The display of errors can vary greatly between browsers and other host environments. In fact, most recent browsers tend to hide the errors from the users. However, you cannot assume that all of your users have disabled the display of errors, and it is your responsibility to ensure an error-free experience for them. The previous error propagated to the user because the code didn't try to trap (catch) this error. The code didn't expect the error and was not prepared to handle it. Fortunately, it's trivial to trap the error. All you need is the `try` statement followed by a `catch` statement.

This code hides the error from the user:

```
try {
  iDontExist();
} catch (e) {
  // do nothing
}
```

Here you have:

- The `try` statement followed by a block of code
- The `catch` statement followed by a variable name in parentheses and another block of code

There can be an optional `finally` statement (not used in this example) followed by a block of code, which is executed regardless of whether there was an error or not.

In the previous example, the code block that follows the `catch` statement didn't do anything, but this is the place where you put the code that can help recover from the error, or at least give feedback to the user that your application is aware that there was a special condition.

The variable `e` in the parentheses after the `catch` statement contains an error object. Like any other object, it contains properties and methods. Unfortunately, different browsers implement these methods and properties differently, but there are two properties that are consistently implemented—`e.name` and `e.message`.

Let's try this code now:

```
try {
  iDontExist();
} catch (e) {
  alert(e.name + ': ' + e.message);
} finally {
  alert('Finally!');
}
```

This will present an `alert()` showing `e.name` and `e.message` and then another `alert()` saying **Finally!**.

In Firefox and Chrome, the first alert will say **ReferenceError: iDontExist is not defined**. In Internet Explorer, it will be **TypeError: Object expected**. This tells us two things:

- `e.name` contains the name of the constructor that was used to create the error object
- Because the error objects are not consistent across host environments (browsers), it would be somewhat tricky to have your code act differently depending on the type of error (the value of `e.name`)

You can also create error objects yourself using `new Error()` or any of the other error constructors, and then let the JavaScript engine know that there's an erroneous condition using the `throw` statement.

For example, imagine a scenario where you call the `maybeExists()` function and after that make calculations. You want to trap all errors in a consistent way, no matter whether the error is that `maybeExists()` doesn't exist or that your calculations found a problem. Consider this code:

```
try {
  var total = maybeExists();
  if (total === 0) {
    throw new Error('Division by zero!');
  } else {
    alert(50 / total);
  }
} catch (e) {
  alert(e.name + ': ' + e.message);
} finally {
  alert('Finally!');
}
```

This code will `alert()` different messages depending on whether or not `maybeExists()` is defined and the values it returns:

- If `maybeExists()` doesn't exist, you get **ReferenceError: maybeExists() is not defined** in Firefox and **TypeError: Object expected** in IE
- If `maybeExists()` returns 0, you'll get **Error: Division by zero!**
- If `maybeExists()` returns 2, you'll get an alert that says **25**

In all cases, there will be a second alert that says **Finally!**.

Instead of throwing a generic error, `throw new Error('Division by zero!')`, you can be more specific if you choose to, for example, throw `throw new RangeError('Division by zero!')`. Alternatively, you don't need a constructor, you can simply throw a normal object:

```
throw {
  name: "MyError",
  message: "OMG! Something terrible has happened"
}
```

This gives you cross-browser control over the error name.

Summary

In *Chapter 2, Primitive Data Types, Arrays, Loops, and Conditions*, you saw that there are five primitive data types (number, string, Boolean, null, and undefined) and we also said that everything that is not a primitive piece of data is an object. Now you also know that:

- Objects are like arrays, but you specify the keys.
- Objects contain properties.
- Properties can be functions (functions are data; remember `var f = function () {};`). Properties that are functions are also called methods.
- Arrays are actually objects with predefined numeric properties and an auto-incrementing `length` property.
- Array objects have a number of convenient methods (such as `sort()` or `slice()`).
- Functions are also objects and they have properties (such as `length` and `prototype`) and methods (such as `call()` and `apply()`).

Regarding the five primitive data types, apart from `undefined` and `null`, the other three have the corresponding constructor functions: `Number()`, `String()`, and `Boolean()`. Using these, you can create objects, called wrapper objects, which contain methods for working with primitive data elements.

`Number()`, `String()`, and `Boolean()` can be invoked:

- With the `new` operator – to create new objects
- Without the `new` operator – to convert any value to the corresponding primitive data type

Other built-in constructor functions you're now familiar with include: `Object()`, `Array()`, `Function()`, `Date()`, `RegExp()`, and `Error()`. You're also familiar with `Math`: a global object that is not a constructor.

Now you can see how objects have a central role in JavaScript programming, as pretty much everything is an object or can be wrapped by an object.

Finally, let's wrap up the literal notations you're now familiar with:

Name	Literal	Constructor	Example
Object	{}	`new Object()`	`{prop: 1}`
Array	[]	`new Array()`	`[1,2,3,'test']`
Regular expression	/pattern/ modifiers	`new RegExp('pattern', 'modifiers')`	`/java.*/img`

Exercises

1. Look at this code:

```
function F() {
  function C() {
    return this;
  }
  return C();
}
var o = new F();
```

   Does the value of `this` refer to the global object or the object `o`?

2. What's the result of executing this piece of code?

```
function C(){
  this.a = 1;
  return false;
}
console.log(typeof new C());
```

3. What's the result of executing the following piece of code?

```
> c = [1, 2, [1, 2]];
> c.sort();
> c.join('--');
> console.log(c);
```

4. Imagine the `String()` constructor didn't exist. Create a constructor function, `MyString()`, that acts like `String()` as closely as possible. You're not allowed to use any built-in string methods or properties, and remember that `String()` doesn't exist. You can use this code to test your constructor:

```
> var s = new MyString('hello');
> s.length;
  5

> s[0];
  "h"

> s.toString();
  "hello"

> s.valueOf();
  "hello"

> s.charAt(1);
  "e"
```

```
> s.charAt('2');
  "l"

> s.charAt('e');
  "h"

> s.concat(' world!');
  "hello world!"

> s.slice(1, 3);
  "el"

> s.slice(0, -1);
  "hell"

> s.split('e');
  ["h", "llo"]

> s.split('l');
  ["he", "", "o"]
```

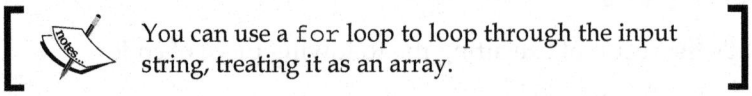

You can use a `for` loop to loop through the input string, treating it as an array.

5. Update your `MyString()` constructor to include a `reverse()` method.

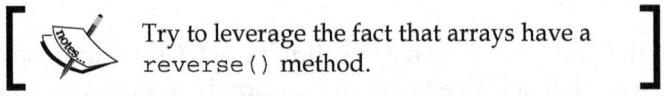

Try to leverage the fact that arrays have a `reverse()` method.

6. Imagine `Array()` doesn't exist and the array literal notation doesn't exist either. Create a constructor called `MyArray()` that behaves as close to `Array()` as possible. Test it with the following code:

```
> var a = new MyArray(1, 2, 3, "test");
> a.toString();
  "1,2,3,test"

> a.length;
  4

> a[a.length - 1];
  "test"

> a.push('boo');
  5

> a.toString();
  "1,2,3,test,boo"
```

```
> a.pop();
  "boo"

> a.toString();
  "1,2,3,test"

> a.join(',');
  "1,2,3,test"

> a.join(' isn\'t ');
  "1 isn't 2 isn't 3 isn't test"
```

If you found this exercise amusing, don't stop with the `join()` method; go on with as many methods as possible.

7. Imagine `Math` didn't exist. Create a `MyMath` object that also provides additional methods:
   - `MyMath.rand(min, max, inclusive)` – generates a random number between `min` and `max`, inclusive if `inclusive` is `true` (default)
   - `MyMath.min(array)` – returns the smallest number in a given array
   - `MyMath.max(array)` – returns the largest number in a given array

5
Prototype

In this chapter, you'll learn about the prototype property of the function objects. Understanding how the prototype works is an important part of learning the JavaScript language. After all, JavaScript is often classified as having a prototype-based object model. There's nothing particularly difficult about the prototype, but it's a new concept, and as such may sometimes take a bit of time to sink in. Like closures (see *Chapter 3, Functions*), the prototype is one of those things in JavaScript, which once you "get", they seem so obvious and make perfect sense. As with the rest of the book, you're strongly encouraged to type in and play around with the examples—this makes it much easier to learn and remember the concepts.

The following topics are discussed in this chapter:

- Every function has a `prototype` property and it contains an object
- Adding properties to the prototype object
- Using the properties added to the prototype
- The difference between own properties and properties of the prototype
- `__proto__`, the secret link every object keeps to its prototype
- Methods such as `isPrototypeOf()`, `hasOwnProperty()`, and `propertyIsEnumerable()`
- Enhancing built-in objects, such as arrays or strings (and why that can be a bad idea)

The prototype property

The functions in JavaScript are objects, and they contain methods and properties. Some of the methods that you're already familiar with are `apply()` and `call()`, and some of the other properties are `length` and `constructor`. Another property of the function objects is `prototype`.

If you define a simple function, `foo()`, you can access its properties as you would do with any other object.

```
> function foo(a, b) {
    return a * b;
  }
> foo.length;
2

> foo.constructor;
function Function() { [native code] }
```

The `prototype` property is a property that is available to you as soon as you define the function. Its initial value is an "empty" object.

```
> typeof foo.prototype;
"object"
```

It's as if you added this property yourself as follows:

```
> foo.prototype = {};
```

You can augment this empty object with properties and methods. They won't have any effect on the `foo()` function itself; they'll only be used if you call `foo()` as a constructor.

Adding methods and properties using the prototype

In the previous chapter, you learned how to define constructor functions that you can use to create (construct) new objects. The main idea is that inside a function invoked with `new`, you have access to the value `this`, which refers to the object to be returned by the constructor. Augmenting (adding methods and properties to) `this` is how you add functionality to the object being constructed.

Let's take a look at the constructor function `Gadget()`, which uses `this` to add two properties and one method to the objects it creates.

```
function Gadget(name, color) {
  this.name = name;
  this.color = color;
  this.whatAreYou = function () {
    return 'I am a ' + this.color + ' ' + this.name;
  };
}
```

Adding methods and properties to the `prototype` property of the constructor function is another way to add functionality to the objects this constructor produces. Let's add two more properties, `price` and `rating`, as well as a `getInfo()` method. Since `prototype` already points to an object, you can just keep adding properties and methods to it as follows:

```
Gadget.prototype.price = 100;
Gadget.prototype.rating = 3;
Gadget.prototype.getInfo = function () {
  return 'Rating: ' + this.rating +
         ', price: ' + this.price;
};
```

Alternatively, instead of adding properties to the `prototype` object one by one, you can overwrite the prototype completely, replacing it with an object of your choice.

```
Gadget.prototype = {
  price: 100,
  rating: ...  /* and so on... */
};
```

Using the prototype's methods and properties

All the methods and properties you have added to the prototype are available as soon as you create a new object using the constructor. If you create a `newtoy` object using the `Gadget()` constructor, you can access all the methods and properties already defined.

```
> var newtoy = new Gadget('webcam', 'black');
> newtoy.name;
"webcam"
```

```
> newtoy.color;
"black"

> newtoy.whatAreYou();
"I am a black webcam"

> newtoy.price;
100

> newtoy.rating;
3

> newtoy.getInfo();
"Rating: 3, price: 100"
```

It's important to note that the prototype is "live". Objects are passed by reference in JavaScript, and therefore, the prototype is not copied with every new object instance. What does this mean in practice? It means that you can modify the prototype at any time and all the objects (even those created before the modification) will "see" the changes.

Let's continue the example by adding a new method to the prototype:

```
Gadget.prototype.get = function (what) {
  return this[what];
};
```

Even though `newtoy` was created *before* the `get()` method was defined, `newtoy` still has access to the new method:

```
> newtoy.get('price');
100

> newtoy.get('color');
"black"
```

Own properties versus prototype properties

In the preceding example, `getInfo()` was used internally to access the properties of the object. It could've also used `Gadget.prototype` to achieve the same output.

```
Gadget.prototype.getInfo = function () {
  return 'Rating: ' + Gadget.prototype.rating +
         ', price: ' + Gadget.prototype.price;
};
```

What's the difference? To answer this question, let's examine how the prototype works in more detail.

Let's take the `newtoy` object again.

```
var newtoy = new Gadget('webcam', 'black');
```

When you try to access a property of `newtoy`, say, `newtoy.name`, the JavaScript engine looks through all of the properties of the object searching for one called `name`, and if it finds it, it returns its value.

```
> newtoy.name;
"webcam"
```

What if you try to access the `rating` property? The JavaScript engine examines all of the properties of `newtoy` and doesn't find the one called `rating`. Then, the script engine identifies the prototype of the constructor function used to create this object (the same as if you do `newtoy.constructor.prototype`). If the property is found in the prototype object, the following property is used:

```
> newtoy.rating;
3
```

You can do the same and access the prototype directly. Every object has a constructor property, which is a reference to the function that created the object, so in this case:

```
> newtoy.constructor === Gadget;
true

> newtoy.constructor.prototype.rating;
3
```

Now, let's take this lookup one step further. Every object has a constructor. The prototype is an object, so it must have a constructor too, which, in turn, has a prototype. You can go up the *prototype chain* and you will eventually end up with the built-in `Object()` object, which is the highest-level parent. In practice, this means that if you try `newtoy.toString()` and `newtoy` doesn't have its own `toString()` method and its prototype doesn't either, in the end you'll get the object's `toString()` method:

```
> newtoy.toString();
"[object Object]"
```

Overwriting a prototype's property with an own property

As the above discussion demonstrates, if one of your objects doesn't have a certain property of its own, it can use one (if it exists) somewhere up the prototype chain. What if the object does have its own property and the prototype also has one with the same name? Then, the own property takes precedence over the prototype's.

Consider a scenario where a property name exists as both an own property and a property of the prototype object.

```
> function Gadget(name) {
    this.name = name;
  }
> Gadget.prototype.name = 'mirror';
```

Creating a new object and accessing its `name` property gives you the object's own `name` property.

```
> var toy = new Gadget('camera');
> toy.name;
"camera"
```

You can tell where the property was defined by using `hasOwnProperty()`.

```
> toy.hasOwnProperty('name');
true
```

If you delete the toy object's own `name` property, the prototype's property with the same name "shines through".

```
> delete toy.name;
true

> toy.name;
"mirror"

> toy.hasOwnProperty('name');
false
```

Of course, you can always recreate the object's own property.

```
> toy.name = 'camera';
> toy.name;
"camera"
```

You can play around with the method `hasOwnProperty()` to find out the origins of a particular property you're curious about. The method `toString()` was mentioned earlier. Where is it coming from?

```
> toy.toString();
"[object Object]"

> toy.hasOwnProperty('toString');
false
```

```
> toy.constructor.hasOwnProperty('toString');
false

> toy.constructor.prototype.hasOwnProperty('toString');
false

> Object.hasOwnProperty('toString');
false

> Object.prototype.hasOwnProperty('toString');
true
```

Ahaa!

Enumerating properties

If you want to list all the properties of an object, you can use a `for-in` loop. In *Chapter 2, Primitive Data Types, Arrays, Loops, and Conditions*, you saw that you can also loop through all the elements of an array with `for-in`, but as mentioned there, `for` is better suited for arrays and `for-in` is for objects. Let's take an example of constructing a query string for a URL from an object:

```
var params = {
  productid: 666,
  section: 'products'
};

var url = 'http://example.org/page.php?',
    i,
    query = [];

for (i in params) {
  query.push(i + '=' + params[i]);
}

url += query.join('&');
```

This produces the `url` string as follows:

```
"http://example.org/page.php?productid=666&section=products"
```

There are a few details to be aware of:

- Not all properties show up in a `for-in` loop. For example, the length (for arrays) and constructor properties don't show up. The properties that do show up are called **enumerable**. You can check which ones are enumerable with the help of the `propertyIsEnumerable()` method that every object provides. In ES5, you can specify which properties are enumerable, while in ES3 you don't have that control.
- Prototypes that come through the prototype chain also show up, provided they are enumerable. You can check if a property is an object's own property or a prototype's property using the `hasOwnProperty()` method.
- `propertyIsEnumerable()` returns `false` for all of the prototype's properties, even those that are enumerable and show up in the `for-in` loop.

Let's see these methods in action. Take this simplified version of `Gadget()`:

```
function Gadget(name, color) {
  this.name = name;
  this.color = color;
  this.getName = function () {
    return this.name;
  };
}
Gadget.prototype.price = 100;
Gadget.prototype.rating = 3;
```

Create a new object as follows:

```
var newtoy = new Gadget('webcam', 'black');
```

Now, if you loop using a `for-in` loop, you see all of the object's properties, including those that come from the prototype:

```
for (var prop in newtoy) {
  console.log(prop + ' = ' + newtoy[prop]);
}
```

The result also contains the object's methods (since methods are just properties that happen to be functions):

```
name = webcam
color = black
getName = function () {
 return this.name;
}
price = 100
rating = 3
```

If you want to distinguish between the object's own properties and the prototype's properties, use `hasOwnProperty()`. Try the following first:

```
> newtoy.hasOwnProperty('name');
true

> newtoy.hasOwnProperty('price');
false
```

Let's loop again, but this time showing only the object's own properties.

```
for (var prop in newtoy) {
  if (newtoy.hasOwnProperty(prop)) {
    console.log(prop + '=' + newtoy[prop]);
  }
}
```

The result is as follows:

```
name=webcam
color=black
getName = function () {
 return this.name;
}
```

Now let's try `propertyIsEnumerable()`. This method returns `true` for the object's own properties that are not built-in.

```
> newtoy.propertyIsEnumerable('name');
true
```

Most built-in properties and methods are not enumerable.

```
> newtoy.propertyIsEnumerable('constructor');
false
```

Any properties coming down the prototype chain are not enumerable.

```
> newtoy.propertyIsEnumerable('price');
false
```

Note, however, that such properties are enumerable if you reach the object contained in the prototype and invoke its `propertyIsEnumerable()` method.

```
> newtoy.constructor.prototype.propertyIsEnumerable('price');
true
```

isPrototypeOf()

Objects also have the `isPrototypeOf()` method. This method tells you whether that specific object is used as a prototype of another object.

Let's take a simple object named `monkey`.

```
var monkey = {
  hair: true,
  feeds: 'bananas',
  breathes: 'air'
};
```

Now let's create a `Human()` constructor function and set its prototype property to point to `monkey`.

```
function Human(name) {
  this.name = name;
}
Human.prototype = monkey;
```

Now if you create a new `Human` object called `george` and ask "is `monkey` the prototype of `george`?", you'll get `true`.

```
> var george = new Human('George');
> monkey.isPrototypeOf(george);
true
```

Note that you have to know, or suspect, who the prototype is and then ask "is it true that your `prototype` is `monkey`?" in order to confirm your suspicion. But what if you don't suspect anything and you have no idea? Can you just ask the object to tell you its prototype? The answer is you can't in all browsers, but you can in most of them. Most recent browsers have implemented the addition to ES5 called `Object.getPrototypeOf()`.

```
> Object.getPrototypeOf(george).feeds;
"bananas"

> Object.getPrototypeOf(george) === monkey;
true
```

For some of the pre-ES5 environments that don't have `getPrototypeOf()`, you can use the special property `__proto__`.

The secret __proto__ link

As you already know, the `prototype` property is consulted when you try to access a property that does not exist in the current object.

Consider another object called `monkey` and use it as a prototype when creating objects with the `Human()` constructor.

```
> var monkey = {
    feeds: 'bananas',
    breathes: 'air'
  };
> function Human() {}
> Human.prototype = monkey;
```

Now, let's create a `developer` object and give it some properties.

```
> var developer = new Human();
> developer.feeds = 'pizza';
> developer.hacks = 'JavaScript';
```

Now let's access these properties. For example, `hacks` is a property of the `developer` object.

```
> developer.hacks;
"JavaScript"
```

`feeds` could also be found in the object.

```
> developer.feeds;
"pizza"
```

`breathes` doesn't exist as a property of the `developer` object, so the prototype is looked up, as if there is a secret link, or a secret passageway, that leads to the prototype object.

```
> developer.breathes;
"air"
```

The secret link is exposed in most modern JavaScript environments as the `__proto__` property (the word "proto" with two underscores before and two after).

```
> developer.__proto__ === monkey;
true
```

You can use this secret property for learning purposes, but it's not a good idea to use it in your real scripts because it does not exist in all browsers (notably Internet Explorer), so your scripts won't be portable.

Be aware that `__proto__` is not the same as `prototype`, since `__proto__` is a property of the instances (objects), whereas `prototype` is a property of the constructor functions used to create those objects.

```
> typeof developer.__proto__;
"object"

> typeof developer.prototype;
"undefined"

> typeof developer.constructor.prototype;
"object"
```

Once again, you should use `__proto__` only for learning or debugging purposes. Or, if you're lucky enough and your code only needs to work in ES5-compliant environments, you can use `Object.getPrototypeOf()`.

Augmenting built-in objects

The objects created by the built-in constructor functions such as `Array`, `String`, and even `Object` and `Function` can be augmented (or enhanced) through the use of prototypes. This means that you can, for example, add new methods to the `Array` prototype, and in this way you can make them available to all arrays. Let's see how to do this.

In PHP, there is a function called `in_array()`, which tells you if a value exists in an array. In JavaScript, there is no `inArray()` method (although in ES5 there's `indexOf()`, which you can use for the same purpose). So, let's implement it and add it to `Array.prototype`.

```
Array.prototype.inArray = function (needle) {
  for (var i = 0, len = this.length; i < len; i++) {
    if (this[i] === needle) {
      return true;
    }
  }
  return false;
};
```

Now all arrays have access to the new method. Let's test this.

```
> var colors = ['red', 'green', 'blue'];
> colors.inArray('red');
true

> colors.inArray('yellow');
false
```

That was nice and easy! Let's do it again. Imagine your application often needs to spell words backwards and you feel there should be a built-in `reverse()` method for string objects. After all, arrays have `reverse()`. You can easily add a `reverse()` method to the `String` prototype by borrowing `Array.prototype.reverse()` (there was a similar exercise at the end of *Chapter 4, Objects*).

```
String.prototype.reverse = function () {
  return Array.prototype.reverse.
                apply(this.split('')).join('');
};
```

This code uses `split()` to create an array from a string, then calls the `reverse()` method on this array, which produces a reversed array. The resulting array is then turned back into a string using `join()`. Let's test the new method.

```
> "bumblebee".reverse();
"eebelbmub"
```

That is a nice name for a big and scary (and potentially hairy) mythical creature, isn't it?

Augmenting built-in objects – discussion

Augmenting built-in objects through the prototype is a powerful technique, and you can use it to shape JavaScript in any way you like. Because of its power, though, you should always thoroughly consider your options before using this approach.

The reason is that once you know JavaScript, you're expecting it to work the same way, no matter which third-party library or widget you're using. Modifying core objects could confuse the users and maintainers of your code and create unexpected errors.

JavaScript evolves and browser's vendors continuously support more features. What you consider a missing method today and decide to add to a core prototype could be a built-in method tomorrow. In this case, your method is no longer needed. Additionally, what if you have already written a lot of code that uses the method and your method is slightly different from the new built-in implementation?

The most common and acceptable use case for augmenting built-in prototypes is to add support for new features (ones that are already standardized by the ECMAScript committee and implemented in new browsers) to old browsers. One example would be adding an ES5 method to old versions of IE. These extensions are known as **shims** or **polyfills**.

When augmenting prototypes, you first check if the method exists before implementing it yourself. This way, you use the native implementation in the browser if one exists. For example, let's add the `trim()` method for strings, which is a method that exists in ES5 but is missing in older browsers.

```
if (typeof String.prototype.trim !== 'function') {
  String.prototype.trim = function () {
    return this.replace(/^\s+|\s+$/g,'');
  };
}

> " hello ".trim();
"hello"
```

Best practice

If you decide to augment a built-in object or its prototype with a new property, do check for the existence of the new property first.

Prototype gotchas

There are two important behaviors to consider when dealing with prototypes:

- The prototype chain is live except when you completely replace the prototype object
- `prototype.constructor` is not reliable

Let's create a simple constructor function and two objects.

```
> function Dog() {
    this.tail = true;
  }
> var benji = new Dog();
> var rusty = new Dog();
```

Even after you've created the objects `benji` and `rusty`, you can still add properties to the prototype of `Dog()` and the existing objects will have access to the new properties. Let's throw in the method `say()`.

```
> Dog.prototype.say = function () {
    return 'Woof!';
  };
```

Both objects have access to the new method.

```
> benji.say();
"Woof!"

 rusty.say();
"Woof!"
```

Up to this point, if you consult your objects asking which constructor function was used to create them, they'll report it correctly.

```
> benji.constructor === Dog;
true

> rusty.constructor === Dog;
true
```

Now, let's completely overwrite the prototype object with a brand new object.

```
> Dog.prototype = {
    paws: 4,
    hair: true
  };
```

It turns out that the old objects do not get access to the new prototype's properties; they still keep the secret link pointing to the old prototype object.

```
> typeof benji.paws;
"undefined"

> benji.say();
"Woof!"

> typeof benji.__proto__.say;
"function"

> typeof benji.__proto__.paws;
"undefined"
```

Any new objects you create from now on will use the updated prototype.

```
> var lucy = new Dog();
> lucy.say();
TypeError: lucy.say is not a function

> lucy.paws;
4
```

The secret `__proto__` link points to the new prototype object.

```
> typeof lucy.__proto__.say;
"undefined"

> typeof lucy.__proto__.paws;
"number"
```

Now the `constructor` property of the new object no longer reports correctly. You would expect it to point to `Dog()`, but instead it points to `Object()`.

```
> lucy.constructor;
function Object() { [native code] }

> benji.constructor;
function Dog() {
 this.tail = true;
}
```

You can easily prevent this confusion by resetting the `constructor` property after you overwrite the prototype completely.

```
> function Dog() {}
> Dog.prototype = {};
> new Dog().constructor === Dog;
false

> Dog.prototype.constructor = Dog;
> new Dog().constructor === Dog;
true
```

Best practice

When you overwrite the prototype, remember to reset the `constructor` property.

Summary

Let's summarize the most important topics you have learned in this chapter:

- All functions have a property called `prototype`. Initially it contains an "empty" object (an object without any own properties).
- You can add properties and methods to the prototype object. You can even replace it completely with an object of your choice.
- When you create an object using a function as a constructor (with `new`), the object gets a secret link pointing to the prototype of the constructor, and can access the prototype's properties.
- An object's own properties take precedence over a prototype's properties with the same name.
- Use the method `hasOwnProperty()` to differentiate between an object's own properties and prototype properties.
- There is a prototype chain. When you execute `foo.bar`, and if your object `foo` doesn't have a property called `bar`, the JavaScript interpreter looks for a `bar` property in the prototype. If none is found, it keeps searching in the prototype's prototype, then the prototype of the prototype's prototype, and it will keep going all the way up to `Object.prototype`.
- You can augment the prototypes of built-in constructor functions and all objects will see your additions. Assign a function to `Array.prototype.flip` and all arrays will immediately get a `flip()` method, as in `[1,2,3].flip()`. But do check if the method/property you want to add already exists, so you can future-proof your scripts.

Exercises

1. Create an object called `shape` that has the type `property` and a `getType()` method.
2. Define a `Triangle()` constructor function whose prototype is `shape`. Objects created with `Triangle()` should have three own properties—`a`, `b`, and `c`, representing the lengths of the sides of a triangle.
3. Add a new method to the prototype called `getPerimeter()`.

4. Test your implementation with the following code:

```
> var t = new Triangle(1, 2, 3);
> t.constructor === Triangle;
    true

> shape.isPrototypeOf(t);
    true

> t.getPerimeter();
    6

> t.getType();
    "triangle"
```

5. Loop over `t` showing only own properties and methods (none of the prototype's).
6. Make the following code work:

```
> [1, 2, 3, 4, 5, 6, 7, 8, 9].shuffle();
    [2, 4, 1, 8, 9, 6, 5, 3, 7]
```

6
Inheritance

If you go back to *Chapter 1, Object-oriented JavaScript* and review the *Object-oriented programming* section, you'll see that you already know how to apply most of them to JavaScript. You know what objects, methods, and properties are. You know that there are no classes in JavaScript, although you can achieve the same using constructor functions. Encapsulation? Yes, the objects encapsulate both the data and the means (methods) to do something with the data. Aggregation? Sure, an object can contain other objects. In fact, this is almost always the case since methods are functions, and functions are also objects.

Now, let's focus on the inheritance part. This is one of the most interesting features, as it allows you to reuse existing code, thus promoting laziness, which is likely to be what brought human species to computer programming in the first place.

JavaScript is a dynamic language and there is usually more than one way to achieve any given task. Inheritance is not an exception. In this chapter, you'll see some common patterns for implementing inheritance. Having a good understanding of these patterns will help you pick the right one, or the right mix, depending on your task, project or your style.

Prototype chaining

Let's start with the default way of implementing inheritance—inheritance chaining through the prototype.

As you already know, every function has a `prototype` property, which points to an object. When a function is invoked using the `new` operator, an object is created and returned. This new object has a secret link to the prototype object. The secret link (called `__proto__` in some environments) allows methods and properties of the prototype object to be used as if they belonged to the newly-created object.

The prototype object is just a regular object and, therefore, it also has the secret link to its prototype. And so a chain is created, called a **prototype chain**:

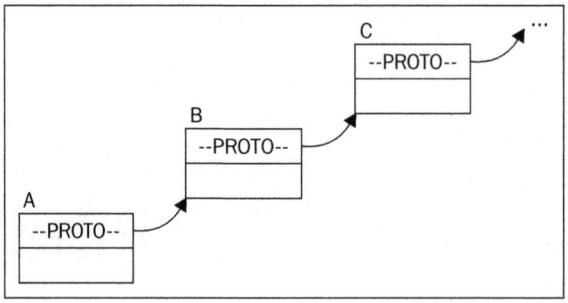

In this illustration, an object A contains a number of properties. One of the properties is the hidden `__proto__` property, which points to another object, B. B's `__proto__` property points to C. This chain ends with the `Object.prototype` object—the grandparent, and every object inherits from it.

This is all good to know, but how does it help you? The practical side is that when object A lacks a property but B has it, A can still access this property as its own. The same applies if B also doesn't have the required property, but C does. This is how inheritance takes place: an object can access any property found somewhere down the inheritance chain.

Throughout the rest of this chapter, you'll see different examples that use the following hierarchy: a generic Shape parent is inherited by a 2D shape, which in turn is inherited by any number of specific two-dimensional shapes such as a Triangle, Rectangle, and so on.

Prototype chaining example

Prototype chaining is the default way to implement inheritance. In order to implement the hierarchy, let's define three constructor functions.

```
function Shape(){
this.name = 'Shape';
this.toString = function () {
return this.name;
};
}

function TwoDShape(){
this.name = '2D shape';
```

```
}

function Triangle(side, height){
this.name = 'Triangle';
this.side = side;
this.height = height;
this.getArea = function () {
return this.side * this.height / 2;
};
}
```

The code that performs the inheritance magic is as follows:

```
TwoDShape.prototype = new Shape();
Triangle.prototype = new TwoDShape();
```

What's happening here? You take the object contained in the `prototype` property of `TwoDShape` and instead of augmenting it with individual properties, you completely overwrite it with another object, created by invoking the `Shape()` constructor with `new`. The same for `Triangle`: its prototype is replaced with an object created by `new TwoDShape()`. It's important to remember that JavaScript works with objects, not classes. You need to create an instance using the `new Shape()` constructor and after that you can inherit its properties; you don't inherit from `Shape()` directly. Additionally, after inheriting, you can modify the `Shape()` constructor, overwrite it, or even delete it, and this will have no effect on `TwoDShape`, because all you needed is one instance to inherit from.

As you know from the previous chapter, overwriting the prototype (as opposed to just adding properties to it), has side effects on the `constructor` property. Therefore, it's a good idea to reset the `constructor` after inheriting:

```
TwoDShape.prototype.constructor = TwoDShape;
Triangle.prototype.constructor = Triangle;
```

Now, let's test what has happened so far. Creating a `Triangle` object and calling its own `getArea()` method works as expected:

```
>var my = new Triangle(5, 10);
>my.getArea();
25
```

Although the `my` object doesn't have its own `toString()` method, it inherited one and you can call it. Note, how the inherited method `toString()` binds the `this` object to `my`.

```
>my.toString();
"Triangle"
```

It's fascinating to consider what the JavaScript engine does when you call `my.toString()`:

- It loops through all of the properties of `my` and doesn't find a method called `toString()`.
- It looks at the object that `my.__proto__` points to; this object is the instance `new TwoDShape()` created during the inheritance process.
- Now, the JavaScript engine loops through the instance of `TwoDShape` and doesn't find a `toString()` method. It then checks the `__proto__` of that object. This time `__proto__` points to the instance created by `new Shape()`.
- The instance of `new Shape()` is examined and `toString()` is finally found.
- This method is invoked in the context of `my`, meaning that `this` points to `my`.

If you ask `my`, "who's your constructor?" it reports it correctly because of the reset of the `constructor` property after the inheritance:

```
>my.constructor === Triangle;
true
```

Using the `instanceof` operator you can validate that `my` is an instance of all three constructors.

```
> my instanceof Shape;
true

> my instanceofTwoDShape;
true

> my instanceof Triangle;
true

> my instanceof Array;
false
```

The same happens when you call `isPropertyOf()` on the constructors passing `my`:

```
>Shape.prototype.isPrototypeOf(my);
true

>TwoDShape.prototype.isPrototypeOf(my);
true

>Triangle.prototype.isPrototypeOf(my);
true

>String.prototype.isPrototypeOf(my);
false
```

You can also create objects using the other two constructors. Objects created with `new TwoDShape()` also get the method `toString()`, inherited from `Shape()`.

```
>var td = new TwoDShape();
>td.constructor === TwoDShape;
true

>td.toString();
"2D shape"

>var s = new Shape();
>s.constructor === Shape;
true
```

Moving shared properties to the prototype

When you create objects using a constructor function, own properties are added using `this`. This could be inefficient in cases where properties don't change across instances. In the previous example, `Shape()` was defined like so:

```
function Shape(){
this.name = 'Shape';
}
```

This means that every time you create a new object using `new Shape()` a new `name` property is created and stored somewhere in the memory. The other option is to have the `name` property added to the prototype and shared among all the instances:

```
function Shape() {}
Shape.prototype.name = 'Shape';
```

Now, every time you create an object using `new Shape()`, this object doesn't get its own property `name`, but uses the one added to the prototype. This is more efficient, but you should only use it for properties that don't change from one instance to another. Methods are ideal for this type of sharing.

Let's improve on the preceding example by adding all methods and suitable properties to the `prototype`. In the case of `Shape()` and `TwoDShape()` everything is meant to be shared:

```
// constructor
function Shape() {}

// augment prototype
Shape.prototype.name = 'Shape';
```

```
Shape.prototype.toString = function () {
return this.name;
};

// another constructor
function TwoDShape() {}

// take care of inheritance
TwoDShape.prototype = new Shape();
TwoDShape.prototype.constructor = TwoDShape;

// augment prototype
TwoDShape.prototype.name = '2D shape';
```

As you can see, you have to take care of inheritance first before augmenting the prototype. Otherwise anything you add to `TwoDShape.prototype` gets wiped out when you inherit.

The `Triangle` constructor is a little different, because every object it creates is a new triangle, which is likely to have different dimensions. So it's good to keep `side` and `height` as own properties and share the rest. The method `getArea()`, for example, is the same regardless of the actual dimensions of each triangle. Again, you do the inheritance bit first and then augment the prototype.

```
function Triangle(side, height) {
this.side = side;
this.height = height;
}
// take care of inheritance
Triangle.prototype = new TwoDShape();
Triangle.prototype.constructor = Triangle;

// augment prototype
Triangle.prototype.name = 'Triangle';
Triangle.prototype.getArea = function () {
return this.side * this.height / 2;
};
```

All the preceding test code work exactly the same, for example:

```
>var my = new Triangle(5, 10);
>my.getArea();
25

>my.toString();
"Triangle"
```

There is only a slight behind-the-scenes difference when calling `my.toString()`. The difference is that there is one more lookup to be done before the method is found in the `Shape.prototype`, as opposed to in the `new Shape()` instance like it was in the previous example.

You can also play with `hasOwnProperty()` to see the difference between the own property versus a property coming down the prototype chain.

```
>my.hasOwnProperty('side');
true

>my.hasOwnProperty('name');
false
```

The calls to `isPrototypeOf()` and the `instanceof` operator from the previous example work exactly the same:

```
>TwoDShape.prototype.isPrototypeOf(my);
true

> my instanceof Shape;
true
```

Inheriting the prototype only

As explained previously, for reasons of efficiency you should add the reusable properties and methods to the prototype. If you do so, then it's a good idea to inherit only the prototype, because all the reusable code is there. This means that inheriting the `Shape.prototype` object is better than inheriting the object created with `new Shape()`. After all, `new Shape()` only gives you own shape properties that are not meant to be reused (otherwise they would be in the prototype). You gain a little more efficiency by:

- Not creating a new object for the sake of inheritance alone
- Having less lookups during runtime (when it comes to searching for `toString()` for example)

Here's the updated code; the changes are highlighted:

```
function Shape() {}
// augment prototype
Shape.prototype.name = 'Shape';
Shape.prototype.toString = function () {
```

```
return this.name;
};

function TwoDShape() {}
// take care of inheritance
TwoDShape.prototype = Shape.prototype;
TwoDShape.prototype.constructor = TwoDShape;
// augment prototype
TwoDShape.prototype.name = '2D shape';

function Triangle(side, height) {
this.side = side;
this.height = height;
}

// take care of inheritance
Triangle.prototype = TwoDShape.prototype;
Triangle.prototype.constructor = Triangle;
// augment prototype
Triangle.prototype.name = 'Triangle';
Triangle.prototype.getArea = function () {
return this.side * this.height / 2;
};
```

The test code gives you the same result:

```
>var my = new Triangle(5, 10);
>my.getArea();
25

>my.toString();
"Triangle"
```

What's the difference in the lookups when calling `my.toString()`? First, as usual, the JavaScript engine looks for a method `toString()` of the `my` object itself. The engine doesn't find such a method, so it inspects the prototype. The prototype turns out to be pointing to the same object that the prototype of `TwoDShape` points to and also the same object that `Shape.prototype` points to. Remember, that objects are not copied by value, but only by reference. So the lookup is only a two-step process as opposed to four (in the previous example) or three (in the first example).

Simply copying the prototype is more efficient but it has a side effect: because all the prototypes of the children and parents point to the same object, when a child modifies the prototype, the parents get the changes, and so do the siblings.

Look at this line:

```
Triangle.prototype.name = 'Triangle';
```

It changes the `name` property, so it effectively changes `Shape.prototype.name` too. If you create an instance using `new Shape()`, its `name` property says **"Triangle"**:

```
>var s = new Shape();
>s.name;
"Triangle"
```

This method is more efficient but may not suit all your use cases.

A temporary constructor – new F()

A solution to the previously outlined problem, where all prototypes point to the same object and the parents get children's properties, is to use an intermediary to break the chain. The intermediary is in the form of a temporary constructor function. Creating an empty function `F()` and setting its `prototype` to the prototype of the parent constructor, allows you to call `new F()` and create objects that have no properties of their own, but inherit everything from the parent's `prototype`.

Let's take a look at the modified code:

```
function Shape() {}
// augment prototype
Shape.prototype.name = 'Shape';
Shape.prototype.toString = function () {
return this.name;
};

function TwoDShape() {}
// take care of inheritance
var F = function () {};
F.prototype = Shape.prototype;
TwoDShape.prototype = new F();
TwoDShape.prototype.constructor = TwoDShape;
// augment prototype
TwoDShape.prototype.name = '2D shape';

function Triangle(side, height) {
this.side = side;
this.height = height;
}

// take care of inheritance
```

```
var F = function () {};
F.prototype = TwoDShape.prototype;
Triangle.prototype = new F();
Triangle.prototype.constructor = Triangle;
// augment prototype
Triangle.prototype.name = 'Triangle';
Triangle.prototype.getArea = function () {
return this.side * this.height / 2;
};
```

Creating `my` triangle and testing the methods:

```
>var my = new Triangle(5, 10);
>my.getArea();
25

>my.toString();
"Triangle"
```

Using this approach, the prototype chain stays in place:

```
>my.__proto__ === Triangle.prototype;
true

>my.__proto__.constructor === Triangle;
true

>my.__proto__.__proto__ === TwoDShape.prototype;
true

>my.__proto__.__proto__.__proto__.constructor === Shape;
true
```

And also the parents' properties are not overwritten by the children:

```
>var s = new Shape();
>s.name;
"Shape"

>"I am a " + new TwoDShape(); // calling toString()
"I am a 2D shape"
```

At the same time, this approach supports the idea that only properties and methods added to the prototype should be inherited, and own properties should not. The rationale behind this is that own properties are likely to be too specific to be reusable.

Uber – access to the parent from a child object

Classical OO languages usually have a special syntax that gives you access to the parent class, also referred to as superclass. This could be convenient when a child wants to have a method that does everything the parent's method does plus something in addition. In such cases, the child calls the parent's method with the same name and works with the result.

In JavaScript, there is no such special syntax, but it's trivial to achieve the same functionality. Let's rewrite the last example and, while taking care of inheritance, also create an `uber` property that points to the parent's prototype object.

```
function Shape() {}
// augment prototype
Shape.prototype.name = 'Shape';
Shape.prototype.toString = function () {
varconst = this.constructor;
returnconst.uber
    ? this.const.uber.toString() + ', ' + this.name
    : this.name;
};

function TwoDShape() {}
// take care of inheritance
var F = function () {};
F.prototype = Shape.prototype;
TwoDShape.prototype = new F();
TwoDShape.prototype.constructor = TwoDShape;
TwoDShape.uber = Shape.prototype;
// augment prototype
TwoDShape.prototype.name = '2D shape';

function Triangle(side, height) {
this.side = side;
this.height = height;
}

// take care of inheritance
var F = function () {};
F.prototype = TwoDShape.prototype;
Triangle.prototype = new F();
Triangle.prototype.constructor = Triangle;
Triangle.uber = TwoDShape.prototype;
```

```
// augment prototype
Triangle.prototype.name = 'Triangle';
Triangle.prototype.getArea = function () {
return this.side * this.height / 2;
};
```

The new things here are:

- A new`uber` property points to the parent's prototype
- The updated `toString()` method

Previously, `toString()` only returned `this.name`. Now, in addition to that, there is a check to see whether `this.constructor.uber` exists and, if it does, call its `toString()` first. `this.constructor` is the function itself, and `this.constructor.uber` points to the parent's `prototype`. The result is that when you call `toString()` for a `Triangle` instance, all `toString()` methods up the prototype chain are called:

```
>var my = new Triangle(5, 10);
>my.toString();
"Shape, 2D shape, Triangle"
```

The name of the property `uber` could've been "superclass" but this would suggest that JavaScript has classes. Ideally it could've been "super" (as in Java), but "super" is a reserved word in JavaScript. The German word "über" suggested by Douglass Crockford, means more or less the same as "super" and, you have to admit, it sounds uber-cool.

Isolating the inheritance part into a function

Let's move the code that takes care of all of the inheritance details from the last example into a reusable `extend()` function:

```
function extend(Child, Parent) {
var F = function () {};
F.prototype = Parent.prototype;
Child.prototype = new F();
Child.prototype.constructor = Child;
Child.uber = Parent.prototype;
}
```

Using this function (or your own custom version of it) helps you keep your code clean with regard to the repetitive inheritance-related tasks. This way you can inherit by simply using:

```
extend(TwoDShape, Shape);
```

and

```
extend(Triangle, TwoDShape);
```

Let's see a complete example:

```
// inheritance helper
function extend(Child, Parent) {
var F = function () {};
F.prototype = Parent.prototype;
Child.prototype = new F();
Child.prototype.constructor = Child;
Child.uber = Parent.prototype;
}

// define -> augment
function Shape() {}
Shape.prototype.name = 'Shape';
Shape.prototype.toString = function () {
  return this.constructor.uber
    ? this.constructor.uber.toString() + ', ' + this.name
    : this.name;
};

// define -> inherit -> augment
function TwoDShape() {}
extend(TwoDShape, Shape);
TwoDShape.prototype.name = '2D shape';


// define
function Triangle(side, height) {
this.side = side;
this.height = height;
}
// inherit
extend(Triangle, TwoDShape);
// augment
Triangle.prototype.name = 'Triangle';
Triangle.prototype.getArea = function () {
  return this.side * this.height / 2;
};
```

Testing:

```
> new Triangle().toString();
"Shape, 2D shape, Triangle"
```

Copying properties

Now, let's try a slightly different approach. Since inheritance is all about reusing code, can you simply copy the properties you like from one object to another? Or from a parent to a child? Keeping the same interface as the preceding `extend()` function, you can create a function `extend2()` which takes two constructor functions and copies all of the properties from the parent's prototype to the child's prototype. This will, of course, carry over methods too, as methods are just properties that happen to be functions.

```
function extend2(Child, Parent) {
var p = Parent.prototype;
var c = Child.prototype;
for (vari in p) {
c[i] = p[i];
}
c.uber = p;
}
```

As you can see, a simple loop through the properties is all it takes. As with the previous example, you can set an `uber` property if you want to have handy access to parent's methods from the child. Unlike the previous example though, it's not necessary to reset the `Child.prototype.constructor` because here the child prototype is augmented, not overwritten completely, so the `constructor` property points to the initial value.

This method is a little inefficient compared to the previous method because properties of the child prototype are being duplicated instead of simply being looked up via the prototype chain during execution. Bear in mind that this is only true for properties containing primitive types. All objects (including functions and arrays) are not duplicated, because these are passed by reference only.

Let's see an example of using two constructor functions, `Shape()` and `TwoDShape()`. The `Shape()` function's prototype object contains a primitive property, `name`, and a non-primitive one—the `toString()` method:

```
var Shape = function () {};
varTwoDShape = function () {};
Shape.prototype.name = 'Shape';
Shape.prototype.toString = function () {
```

```
    return this.uber
      ? this.uber.toString() + ', ' + this.name
      : this.name;
};
```

If you inherit with `extend()`, neither the objects created with `TwoDShape()` nor its prototype get an own `name` property, but they have access to the one they inherit.

```
> extend(TwoDShape, Shape);
>var td = new TwoDShape();
>td.name;
"Shape"

>TwoDShape.prototype.name;
"Shape"

>td.__proto__.name;
"Shape"

>td.hasOwnProperty('name');
false

> td.__proto__.hasOwnProperty('name');
false
```

But if you inherit with `extend2()`, the prototype of `TwoDShape()` gets its own copy of the `name` property. It also gets its own copy of `toString()`, but it's a reference only, so the function will not be recreated a second time.

```
>extend2(TwoDShape, Shape);
>var td = new TwoDShape();
> td.__proto__.hasOwnProperty('name');
true

> td.__proto__.hasOwnProperty('toString');
true

> td.__proto__.toString === Shape.prototype.toString;
true
```

As you can see, the two `toString()` methods are the same function object. This is good because it means that no unnecessary duplicates of the methods are created.

So, you can say that `extend2()` is less efficient than `extend()` because it recreates the properties of the prototype. But, this is not so bad because only the primitive data types are duplicated. Additionally, this is beneficial during the prototype chain lookups as there are fewer chain links to follow before finding the property.

Take a look at the `uber` property again. This time, for a change, it's set on the `Parent` object's prototype `p`, not on the `Parent` constructor. This is why `toString()` uses it as `this.uber`, as opposed to `this.constructor.uber`. This is just an illustration that you can shape your favorite inheritance pattern in any way you see fit. Let's test it out:

```
>td.toString();
"Shape, Shape"
```

`TwoDShape` didn't redefine the `name` property, hence the repetition. It can do that at any time and (the prototype chain being live) all the instances "see" the update:

```
>TwoDShape.prototype.name = "2D shape";
>td.toString();
"Shape, 2D shape"
```

Heads-up when copying by reference

The fact that objects (including functions and arrays) are copied by reference could sometimes lead to results you don't expect.

Let's create two constructor functions and add properties to the prototype of the first one:

```
> function Papa() {}
>function Wee() {}
>Papa.prototype.name = 'Bear';
>Papa.prototype.owns = ["porridge", "chair", "bed"];
```

Now, let's have `Wee` inherit from `Papa` (either `extend()` or `extend2()` will do):

```
>extend2(Wee, Papa);
```

Using `extend2()`, the `Wee` function's prototype inherited the properties of `Papa.prototype` as its own.

```
>Wee.prototype.hasOwnProperty('name');
true

>Wee.prototype.hasOwnProperty('owns');
true
```

The `name` property is primitive so a new copy of it is created. The property `owns` is an array object so it's copied by reference:

```
>Wee.prototype.owns;
["porridge", "chair", "bed"]
```

```
>Wee.prototype.owns=== Papa.prototype.owns;
true
```

Changing the `Wee` function's copy of `name` doesn't affect `Papa`:

```
>Wee.prototype.name += ', Little Bear';
"Bear, Little Bear"

>Papa.prototype.name;
"Bear"
```

Changing the `Wee` function's `owns` property, however, affects `Papa`, because both properties point to the same array in memory.

```
>Wee.prototype.owns.pop();
"bed"

>Papa.prototype.owns;
["porridge", "chair"]
```

It's a different story when you completely overwrite the `Wee` function's copy of `owns` with another object (as opposed to modifying the existing one). In this case `Papa.owns` keeps pointing to the old object, while `Wee.owns` points to a new one.

```
>Wee.prototype.owns= ["empty bowl", "broken chair"];
>Papa.prototype.owns.push('bed');
>Papa.prototype.owns;
["porridge", "chair", "bed"]
```

Think of an object as something that is created and stored in a physical location in memory. Variables and properties merely point to this location, so when you assign a brand new object to `Wee.prototype.owns` you essentially say, "Hey, forget about this other old object, move your pointer to this new one instead".

The following diagram illustrates what happens if you imagine the memory being a heap of objects (like a wall of bricks) and you point to (refer to) some of these objects.

- A new object is created and A points to it.
- A new variable B is created and made equal to A, meaning it now points to the same place where A is pointing to.
- A property color is changed using the B handle (pointer). The brick is now white. A check for `A.color === "white"` would be true.

- A new object is created and the B variable/pointer is recycled to point to that new object. A and B are now pointing to different parts of the memory pile, they have nothing in common and changes to one of them don't affect the other:

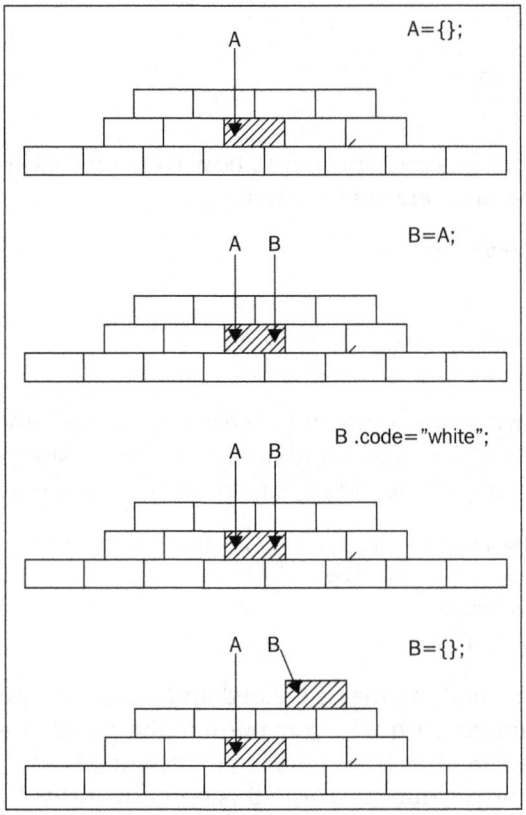

If you want to address the problem that objects are copied by reference, consider a deep copy, described further.

Objects inherit from objects

All of the examples so far in this chapter assume that you create your objects with constructor functions and you want objects created with one constructor to inherit properties that come from another constructor. However, you can also create objects without the help of a constructor function, just by using the object literal and this is, in fact, less typing. So how about inheriting those?

In Java or PHP, you define classes and have them inherit from other classes. That's why you'll see the term *classical*, because the OO functionality comes from the use of classes. In JavaScript, there are no classes, so programmers that come from a classical background resort to constructor functions because constructors are the closest to what they are used to. In addition, JavaScript provides the `new` operator, which can further suggest that JavaScript is like Java. The truth is that, in the end, it all comes down to objects. The first example in this chapter used this syntax:

```
Child.prototype = new Parent();
```

Here, the `Child` constructor (or class, if you will) inherits from `Parent`. But this is done through creating an object using `new Parent()` and inheriting from it. That's why this is also referred to as a *pseudo-classical inheritance pattern*, because it resembles classical inheritance, although it isn't (no classes are involved).

So why not get rid of the middleman (the constructor/class) and just have objects inherit from objects? In `extend2()` the properties of the parent prototype object were copied as properties of the child prototype object. The two prototypes are in essence just objects. Forgetting about prototypes and constructor functions, you can simply take an object and copy all of its properties into another object.

You already know that objects can start as a "blank canvas" without any own properties by using `var o = {};` and then get properties later. But, instead of starting fresh, you can start by copying all of the properties of an existing object. Here's a function that does exactly that: it takes an object and returns a new copy of it.

```
function extendCopy(p) {
var c = {};
for (vari in p) {
c[i] = p[i];
}
c.uber = p;
return c;
}
```

Simply copying all of the properties is a straightforward pattern, and it's widely used. Let's see this function in action. You start by having a base object:

```
var shape = {
name: 'Shape',
toString: function () {
return this.name;
}
};
```

In order to create a new object that builds upon the old one, you can call the function `extendCopy()` which returns a new object. Then, you can augment the new object with additional functionality.

```
vartwoDee = extendCopy(shape);
twoDee.name = '2D shape';
twoDee.toString = function () {
return this.uber.toString() + ', ' + this.name;
};
```

A triangle object that inherits the 2D shape object:

```
var triangle = extendCopy(twoDee);
triangle.name = 'Triangle';
triangle.getArea = function () {
return this.side * this.height / 2;
};
```

Using the triangle:

```
>triangle.side = 5;
>triangle.height = 10;
>triangle.getArea();
25

>triangle.toString();
"Shape, 2D shape, Triangle"
```

A possible drawback of this method is the somewhat verbose way of initializing the new `triangle` object, where you manually set values for `side` and `height`, as opposed to passing them as values to a constructor. But, this is easily resolved by having a function, for example, called `init()` (or `__construct()` if you come from PHP) that acts as a constructor and accepts initialization parameters. Or, have `extendCopy()` accept two parameters: an object to inherit from and another object literal of properties to add to the copy before it's returned, in other words just merge two objects.

Deep copy

The function `extendCopy()`, discussed previously, creates what is called a shallow copy of an object, just like `extend2()` before that. The opposite of a shallow copy would be, naturally, a deep copy. As discussed previously (in the *Heads-up when copying by reference* section), when you copy objects you only copy pointers to the location in memory where the object is stored. This is what happens in a shallow copy. If you modify an object in the copy, you also modify the original. The deep copy avoids this problem.

The deep copy is implemented in the same way as the shallow copy: you loop through the properties and copy them one by one. But, when you encounter a property that points to an object, you call the deep copy function again:

```
function deepCopy(p, c) {
  c = c || {};
  for (vari in p) {
    if (p.hasOwnProperty(i)) {
      if (typeof p[i] === 'object') {
        c[i] = Array.isArray(p[i]) ? [] : {};
deepCopy(p[i], c[i]);
      } else {
        c[i] = p[i];
      }
    }
  }
  return c;
}
```

Let's create an object that has arrays and a sub-object as properties.

```
var parent = {
numbers: [1, 2, 3],
letters: ['a', 'b', 'c'],
obj: {
prop: 1
},
bool: true
};
```

Let's test this by creating a deep copy and a shallow copy. Unlike the shallow copy, when you update the `numbers` property of a deep copy, the original is not affected.

```
>varmydeep = deepCopy(parent);
>varmyshallow = extendCopy(parent);
>mydeep.numbers.push(4,5,6);
6

>mydeep.numbers;
[1, 2, 3, 4, 5, 6]

>parent.numbers;
[1, 2, 3]

>myshallow.numbers.push(10);
4
```

```
>myshallow.numbers;
[1, 2, 3, 10]

>parent.numbers;
[1, 2, 3, 10]

>mydeep.numbers;
[1, 2, 3, 4, 5, 6]
```

Two side notes about the `deepCopy()` function:

- Filtering out non-own properties with `hasOwnProperty()` is always a good idea to make sure you don't carry over someone's additions to the core prototypes.
- `Array.isArray()` exists since ES5 because it's surprisingly hard otherwise to tell real arrays from objects. The best cross-browser solution (if you need to define `isArray()` in ES3 browsers) looks a little hacky, but it works:

```
if (Array.isArray !== "function") {
Array.isArray = function (candidate) {
    return
Object.prototype.toString.call(candidate) ===
'[object Array]';
};
}
```

object()

Based on the idea that objects inherit from objects, Douglas Crockford advocates the use of an `object()` function that accepts an object and returns a new one that has the parent as a prototype.

```
function object(o) {
function F() {}
F.prototype = o;
return new F();
}
```

If you need access to an `uber` property, you can modify the `object()` function like so:

```
function object(o) {
var n;
function F() {}
F.prototype = o;
n = new F();
```

```
n.uber = o;
return n;
}
```

Using this function is the same as using the `extendCopy()`: you take an object such as `twoDee`, create a new object from it and then proceed to augmenting the new object.

```
var triangle = object(twoDee);
triangle.name = 'Triangle';
triangle.getArea = function () {
return this.side * this.height / 2;
};
```

The new triangle still behaves the same way:

```
>triangle.toString();
"Shape, 2D shape, Triangle"
```

This pattern is also referred to as **prototypal inheritance**, because you use a parent object as the prototype of a child object. It's also adopted and built upon in ES5 and called `Object.create()`. For example:

```
>var square = Object.create(triangle);
```

Using a mix of prototypal inheritance and copying properties

When you use inheritance, you will most likely want to take already existing functionality and then build upon it. This means creating a new object by inheriting from an existing object and then adding additional methods and properties. You can do this with one function call, using a combination of the last two approaches just discussed.

You can:

- Use prototypal inheritance to use an existing object as a prototype of a new one
- Copy all of the properties of another object into the newly created one

```
function objectPlus(o, stuff) {
var n;
function F() {}
F.prototype = o;
n = new F();
n.uber = o;

for (vari in stuff) {
```

```
n[i] = stuff[i];
}
return n;
}
```

This function takes an object `o` to inherit from and another object `stuff` that has the additional methods and properties that are to be copied. Let's see this in action.

Start with the base `shape` object:

```
var shape = {
name: 'Shape',
toString: function () {
return this.name;
}
};
```

Create a 2D object by inheriting `shape` and adding more properties. The additional properties are simply created with an object literal.

```
vartwoDee = objectPlus(shape, {
name: '2D shape',
toString: function () {
return this.uber.toString() + ', ' + this.name;
}
});
```

Now, let's create a `triangle` object that inherits from 2D and adds more properties.

```
var triangle = objectPlus(twoDee, {
name: 'Triangle',
getArea: function () {
return this.side * this.height / 2;
},
side: 0,
height: 0
});
```

Testing how it all works by creating a concrete triangle `my` with defined `side` and `height`:

```
var my = objectPlus(triangle, {
side: 4, height: 4
});
>my.getArea();
8
```

```
>my.toString();
"Shape, 2D shape, Triangle, Triangle"
```

The difference here, when executing `toString()`, is that the **Triangle** name is repeated twice. That's because the concrete instance was created by inheriting `triangle`, so there was one more level of inheritance. You could give the new instance a name:

```
>objectPlus(triangle, {
side: 4,
height: 4,
 name: 'My 4x4'
}).toString();
"Shape, 2D shape, Triangle, My 4x4"
```

This `objectPlus()` is even closer to ES5's `Object.create()` only the ES5 one takes the additional properties (the second argument) using something called property descriptors (discussed in *Appendix C, Built-in Objects*).

Multiple inheritance

Multiple inheritance is where a child inherits from more than one parent. Some OO languages support multiple inheritance out of the box, and some don't. You can argue both ways: that multiple inheritance is convenient, or that it's unnecessary, complicates application design, and it's better to use an inheritance chain instead. Leaving the discussion of multiple inheritance's pros and cons for the long, cold winter nights, let's see how you can do it in practice in JavaScript.

The implementation can be as simple as taking the idea of inheritance by copying properties, and expanding it so that it takes an unlimited number of input objects to inherit from.

Let's create a `multi()` function that accepts any number of input objects. You can wrap the loop that copies properties in another loop that goes through all the objects passed as `arguments` to the function.

```
function multi() {
var n = {}, stuff, j = 0, len = arguments.length;
for (j = 0; j <len; j++) {
stuff = arguments[j];
for (vari in stuff) {
      if (stuff.hasOwnProperty(i)) {
n[i] = stuff[i];
      }
}
```

```
}
return n;
}
```

Let's test this by creating three objects: `shape`, `twoDee`, and a third, unnamed object. Then, creating a `triangle` object means calling `multi()` and passing all three objects.

```
var shape = {
name: 'Shape',
toString: function () {
return this.name;
}
};

vartwoDee = {
name: '2D shape',
dimensions: 2
};

var triangle = multi(shape, twoDee, {
name: 'Triangle',
getArea: function () {
return this.side * this.height / 2;
},
side: 5,
height: 10
});
```

Does this work? Let's see. The method `getArea()` should be an own property, `dimensions` should come from `twoDee` and `toString()` from `shape`.

```
>triangle.getArea();
25

>triangle.dimensions;
2

>triangle.toString();
"Triangle"
```

Bear in mind that `multi()` loops through the input objects in the order they appear and if it happens that two of them have the same property, the last one wins.

Mixins

You might come across the term *mixin*. Think of a mixin as an object that provides some useful functionality but is not meant to be inherited and extended by sub-objects. The approach to multiple inheritance outlined previously can be considered an implementation of the mixins idea. When you create a new object you can pick and choose any other objects to mix into your new object. By passing them all to `multi()` you get all their functionality without making them part of the inheritance tree.

Parasitic inheritance

If you like the fact that you can have all kinds of different ways to implement inheritance in JavaScript, and you're hungry for more, here's another one. This pattern, courtesy of Douglas Crockford, is called parasitic inheritance. It's about a function that creates objects by taking all of the functionality from another object into a new one, augmenting the new object, and returning it, "pretending that it has done all the work".

Here's an ordinary object, defined with an object literal, and unaware of the fact that it's soon going to fall victim to parasitism:

```
vartwoD = {
name: '2D shape',
dimensions: 2
};
```

A function that creates triangle objects could:

- Use `twoD` object as a prototype of an object called `that` (similar to `this` for convenience). This can be done in any way you saw previously, for example using the `object()` function or copying all the properties.
- Augment `that` with more properties.
- Return `that`.

```
function triangle(s, h) {
var that = object(twoD);
that.name ='Triangle';
that.getArea = function () {
return this.side * this.height / 2;
};
that.side = s;
that.height = h;
return that;
}
```

Because `triangle()` is a normal function, not a constructor, it doesn't require the `new` operator. But because it returns an object, calling it with `new` by mistake works too.

```
>var t = triangle(5, 10);
>t.dimensions;
2

>var t2 = new triangle(5,5);
>t2.getArea();
12.5
```

Note, that `that` is just a name; it doesn't have a special meaning, the way `this` does.

Borrowing a constructor

One more way of implementing inheritance (the last one in the chapter, I promise) has to do again with constructor functions, and not the objects directly. In this pattern the constructor of the child calls the constructor of the parent using either `call()` or `apply()` methods. This can be called *stealing a constructor*, or *inheritance by borrowing a constructor* if you want to be more subtle about it.

`call()` and `apply()` were discussed in *Chapter 4, Objects* but here's a refresher: they allow you to call a function and pass an object that the function should bind to its `this` value. So for inheritance purposes, the child constructor calls the parent's constructor and binds the child's newly-created `this` object as the parent's `this`.

Let's have this parent constructor `Shape()`:

```
function Shape(id) {
this.id = id;
}
Shape.prototype.name = 'Shape';
Shape.prototype.toString = function () {
return this.name;
};
```

Now, let's define `Triangle()` which uses `apply()` to call the `Shape()` constructor, passing `this` (an instance created with `new Triangle()`) and any additional arguments.

```
function Triangle() {
Shape.apply(this, arguments);
}
Triangle.prototype.name = 'Triangle';
```

Note, that both `Triangle()` and `Shape()` have added some extra properties to their prototypes.

Now, let's test this by creating a new triangle object:

```
>var t = new Triangle(101);
>t.name;
"Triangle"
```

The new triangle object inherits the `id` property from the parent, but it doesn't inherit anything added to the parent's prototype:

```
>t.id;
101

>t.toString();
"[object Object]"
```

The triangle failed to get the `Shape` function's prototype properties because there was never a `new Shape()` instance created, so the prototype was never used. But, you saw how to do this at the beginning of this chapter. You can redefine `Triangle` like this:

```
function Triangle() {
Shape.apply(this, arguments);
}
Triangle.prototype = new Shape();
Triangle.prototype.name = 'Triangle';
```

In this inheritance pattern, the parent's own properties are recreated as the child's own properties. If a child inherits an array or other object, it's a completely new value (not a reference) and modifying it won't affect the parent.

The drawback is that the parent's constructor gets called twice: once with `apply()` to inherit own properties and once with `new` to inherit the prototype. In fact the own properties of the parent are inherited twice. Let's take this simplified scenario:

```
function Shape(id) {
this.id = id;
}
function Triangle() {
Shape.apply(this, arguments);
}
Triangle.prototype = new Shape(101);
```

Creating a new instance:

```
>var t = new Triangle(202);
>t.id;
202
```

There's an own property `id`, but there's also one that comes down the prototype chain, ready to shine through:

```
>t.__proto__.id;
101

> delete t.id;
true

>t.id;
101
```

Borrow a constructor and copy its prototype

The problem of the double work performed by calling the constructor twice can easily be corrected. You can call `apply()` on the parent constructor to get all own properties and then copy the prototype's properties using a simple iteration (or `extend2()` as discussed previously).

```
function Shape(id) {
this.id = id;
}
Shape.prototype.name = 'Shape';
Shape.prototype.toString = function () {
return this.name;
};

function Triangle() {
Shape.apply(this, arguments);
}
extend2(Triangle, Shape);
Triangle.prototype.name = 'Triangle';
```

Testing:

```
>var t = new Triangle(101);
>t.toString();
"Triangle"
>t.id;
101
```

No double inheritance:

```
>typeoft.__proto__.id;
"undefined"
```

`extend2()` also gives access to `uber` if needed:

```
>t.uber.name;
"Shape"
```

Summary

In this chapter you learned quite a few ways (patterns) for implementing inheritance and the following table summarizes them. The different types can roughly be divided into:

- Patterns that work with constructors
- Patterns that work with objects

You can also classify the patterns based on whether they:

- Use the prototype
- Copy properties
- Do both (copy properties of the prototype)

#	Name	Example	Classification	Notes
1	Prototype chaining (pseudo-classical)	`Child.prototype = new Parent();`	• Works with constructors • Uses the prototype chain	• The default mechanism. • Tip: move all properties/ methods that are meant to be reused to the prototype, add the non-reusable as own properties.

#	Name	Example	Classification	Notes
2	Inherit only the prototype	`Child.prototype = Parent.prototype;`	• Works with constructors • Copies the prototype (no prototype chain, all share the same prototype object)	• More efficient, no new instances are created just for the sake of inheritance. • Prototype chain lookup during runtime- is fast, since there's no chain. • Drawback: children can modify parents' functionality.

3	Temporary constructor	`function extend(Child, Parent) {`
		`var F = function(){};`
		`F.prototype = Parent.prototype;`
		`Child.prototype = new F();`
		`Child.prototype.constructor = Child;`
		`Child.uber = Parent.prototype;`
		`}`
			• Works with constructors
			• Uses the prototype chain
				• Unlike #1, it only inherits properties of the prototype. Own properties (created with this inside the constructor) are not inherited.
				• Provides convenient access to the parent (through uber).

4	Copying the prototype properties	`function extend2(Child, Parent) {`
		`var p = Parent.prototype;`
		`var c = Child.prototype;`
		`for (vari in p) {`
		`c[i] = p[i];`
		`}`
		`c.uber = p;`
		`}`
			• Works with constructors
			• Copies properties
			• Uses the prototype chain
				• All properties of the parent prototype become properties of the child prototype
				• No need to create a new object only for inheritance purposes
				• Shorter prototype chains

#	Name	Example	Classification	Notes
5	Copy all properties (shallow copy)	`function extendCopy(p) { var c = {}; for (vari in p) { c[i] = p[i]; } c.uber = p; return c; }`	• Works with objects • Copies properties	• Simple • Doesn't use prototypes
6	Deep copy	Same as above, but recurse into objects	• Works with objects • Copies properties	Same as #5 but clones objects and arrays
7	Prototypal inheritance	`function object(o) { function F() {} F.prototype = o; return new F(); }`	• Works with objects • Uses the prototype chain	• No pseudo-classes, objects inherit from objects • Leverages the benefits of the prototype
8	Extend and augment	`function objectPlus(o, stuff) { var n; function F() {} F.prototype = o; n = new F(); n.uber = o; for (vari in stuff) { n[i] = stuff[i]; } return n; }`	• Works with objects • Uses the prototype chain • Copies properties	• Mix of prototypal inheritance (#7) and copying properties (#5) • One function call to inherit and extend at the same time

#	Name	Example	Classification	Notes

9	Multiple inheritance	`function multi() {`
		`var n = {}, stuff, j = 0,`
		`len = arguments.length;`
		`for (j = 0; j <len; j++) {`
		`stuff = arguments[j];`
		`for (vari in stuff) {`
		`n[i] = stuff[i];`
		`}`
		`}`
		`return n;`
		`}`
			• Works with objects
			• Copies properties
				• A mixin-style implementation
				• Copies all the properties of all the parent objects in the order of appearance

10	Parasitic inheritance	`function parasite(victim) {`
		`var that = object(victim);`
		`that.more = 1;`
		`return that;`
		`}`
			• Works with objects
			• Uses the prototype chain
				• Constructor-like function creates objects
				• Copies an object, augments and returns the copy

11	Borrowing constructors	`function Child() {`
		`Parent.apply(this, arguments);`
		`}`
			Works with constructors	• Inherits only own properties
				• Can be combined with #1 to inherit the prototype too
				• Convenient way to deal with the issues when a child inherits a property that is an object (and therefore passed by reference)

12	Borrow a constructor and copy the prototype	`function Child() {`
		`Parent.apply(this, arguments);`
		`}`
		
		`extend2(Child, Parent);`
			• Works with constructors
			• Uses the prototype chain
			• Copies properties
				• Combination of #11 and #4
				• Allows you to inherit both own properties and prototype properties without calling the parent constructor twice

Given so many options, you must be wondering: which is the right one? That depends on your style and preferences, your project, task, and team. Are you more comfortable thinking in terms of classes? Then pick one of the methods that work with constructors. Are you going to need just one or a few instances of your "class"? Then choose an object-based pattern.

Are these the only ways of implementing inheritance? No. You can chose a pattern from the preceding table or you can mix them, or you can think of your own. The important thing is to understand and be comfortable with objects, prototypes, and constructors; the rest is just pure joy.

Case study – drawing shapes

Let's finish off this chapter with a more practical example of using inheritance. The task is to be able to calculate the area and the perimeter of different shapes, as well as to draw them, while reusing as much code as possible.

Analysis

Let's have one `Shape` constructor that contains all of the common parts. From there, let's have `Triangle`, `Rectangle`, and `Square` constructors, all inheriting from `Shape`. A square is really a rectangle with the same-length sides, so let's reuse `Rectangle` when building the `Square`.

In order to define a shape, you'll need points with `x` and `y` coordinates. A generic shape can have any number of points. A triangle is defined with three points, a rectangle (to keep it simpler)—with one point and the lengths of the sides. The perimeter of any shape is the sum of its sides' lengths. Calculating the area is shape-specific and will be implemented by each shape.

The common functionality in `Shape` would be:

- A `draw()` method that can draw any shape given the points
- A `getParameter()` method
- A property that contains an array of `points`
- Other methods and properties as needed

For the drawing part let's use a `<canvas>` tag. It's not supported in early IEs, but hey, this is just an exercise.

Let's have two other helper constructors—`Point` and `Line`. `Point` will help when defining shapes; `Line` will make calculations easier, as it can give the length of the line connecting any two given points.

You can play with a working example here: `http://www.phpied.com/files/canvas/`. Just open your console and start creating new shapes as you'll see in a moment.

Implementation

Let's start by adding a canvas tag to a blank HTML page:

```
<canvas height="600" width="800" id="canvas" />
```

Then, put the JavaScript code inside `<script>` tags:

```
<script>
// ... code goes here
</script>
```

Now, let's take a look at what's in the JavaScript part. First, the helper `Point` constructor. It just can't get any more trivial than this:

```
function Point(x, y) {
this.x = x;
this.y = y;
}
```

Bear in mind that the coordinates of the points on the canvas start from x=0, y=0, which is the top left. The bottom right will be x = 800, y = 600:

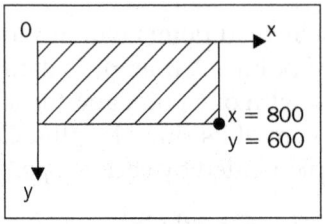

Next, the `Line` constructor. It takes two points and calculates the length of the line between them, using the Pythagorean Theorem a2 + b2 = c2 (imagine a right-angled triangle where the hypotenuse connects the two given points).

```
function Line(p1, p2) {
this.p1 = p1;
this.p2 = p2;
this.length = Math.sqrt(
Math.pow(p1.x - p2.x, 2) +
Math.pow(p1.y - p2.y, 2)
);
}
```

Next, comes the `Shape` constructor. The shapes will have their points (and the lines that connect them) as own properties. The constructor also invokes an initialization method, `init()`, that will be defined in the prototype.

```
function Shape() {
this.points = [];
this.lines= [];
this.init();
}
```

Now the big part: the methods of `Shape.prototype`. Let's define all of these methods using the object literal notation. Refer to the comments for guidelines as to what each method does.

```
Shape.prototype = {
  // reset pointer to constructor
  constructor: Shape,

  // initialization, sets this.context to point
  // to the context if the canvas object
init: function () {
    if (this.context === undefined) {
var canvas = document.getElementById('canvas');
Shape.prototype.context = canvas.getContext('2d');
    }
  },

  // method that draws a shape by looping through this.points
  draw: function () {
vari, ctx = this.context;
ctx.strokeStyle = this.getColor();
ctx.beginPath();
ctx.moveTo(this.points[0].x, this.points[0].y);
    for (i = 1; i<this.points.length; i++) {
ctx.lineTo(this.points[i].x, this.points[i].y);
    }
ctx.closePath();
ctx.stroke();
  },

  // method that generates a random color
getColor: function () {
vari, rgb = [];
    for (i = 0; i< 3; i++) {
rgb[i] = Math.round(255 * Math.random());
```

```
    }
    return 'rgb(' + rgb.join(',') + ')';
  },

  // method that loops through the points array,
  // creates Line instances and adds them to this.lines
getLines: function () {
    if (this.lines.length> 0) {
      return this.lines;
    }
vari, lines = [];
    for (i = 0; i<this.points.length; i++) {
      lines[i] = new Line(this.points[i],
this.points[i + 1] || this.points[0]);
    }
this.lines = lines;
    return lines;
  },

  // shell method, to be implemented by children
getArea: function () {},

  // sums the lengths of all lines
getPerimeter: function () {
vari, perim = 0, lines = this.getLines();
    for (i = 0; i<lines.length; i++) {
perim += lines[i].length;
    }
    return perim;
  }
};
```

Now, the children constructor functions. `Triangle` first:

```
function Triangle(a, b, c) {
this.points = [a, b, c];

this.getArea = function () {
var p = this.getPerimeter(),
        s = p / 2;
    return Math.sqrt(
      s
      * (s - this.lines[0].length)
      * (s - this.lines[1].length)
      * (s - this.lines[2].length));
  };
}
```

The `Triangle` constructor takes three point objects and assigns them to `this.points` (its own collection of points). Then it implements the `getArea()` method, using Heron's formula:

```
Area = s(s-a)(s-b)(s-c)
```

`s` is the semi-perimeter (perimeter divided by two).

Next, comes the `Rectangle` constructor. It receives one point (the upper-left point) and the lengths of the two sides. Then, it populates its `points` array starting from that one point.

```
function Rectangle(p, side_a, side_b){
this.points = [
p,
new Point(p.x + side_a, p.y),// top right
new Point(p.x + side_a, p.y + side_b), // bottom right
new Point(p.x, p.y + side_b)// bottom left
];
this.getArea = function () {
return side_a * side_b;
};
}
```

The last child constructor is `Square`. A square is a special case of a rectangle, so it makes sense to reuse `Rectangle`. The easiest thing to do here is to borrow the constructor.

```
function Square(p, side){
Rectangle.call(this, p, side, side);
}
```

Now that all constructors are done, let's take care of inheritance. Any pseudo-classical pattern (one that works with constructors as opposed to objects) will do. Let's try using a modified and simplified version of the prototype-chaining pattern (the first method described in this chapter). This pattern calls for creating a new instance of the parent and setting it as the child's prototype. In this case, it's not necessary to have a new instance for each child—they can all share it.

```
(function () {
var s = new Shape();
Triangle.prototype = s;
Rectangle.prototype = s;
Square.prototype = s;
})();
```

Testing

Let's test this by drawing shapes. First, define three points for a triangle:

```
>varp1 = new Point(100, 100);
>varp2 = new Point(300, 100);
>varp3 = new Point(200, 0);
```

Now, you can create a triangle by passing the three points to the `Triangle` constructor:

```
>var t = new Triangle(p1, p2, p3);
```

You can call the methods to draw the triangle on the canvas and get its area and perimeter:

```
>t.draw();
>t.getPerimeter();
482.842712474619

>t.getArea();
10000.000000000002
```

Now, let's play with a rectangle instance:

```
>var r = new Rectangle(new Point(200, 200), 50, 100);
>r.draw();
>r.getArea();
5000

>r.getPerimeter();
300
```

And finally, a square:

```
>var s = new Square(new Point(130, 130), 50);
>s.draw();
>s.getArea();
2500

>s.getPerimeter();
200
```

It's fun to draw these shapes. You can also be as lazy as the following example, which draws another square, reusing a triangle's point:

```
> new Square(p1, 200).draw();
```

The result of the tests will be something like this:

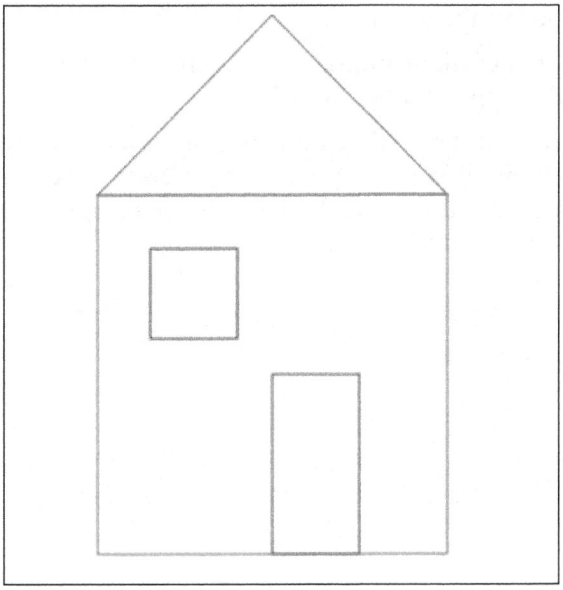

Exercises

1. Implement multiple inheritance but with a prototypal inheritance pattern, not property copying. For example:

   ```
   var my = objectMulti(obj, another_obj, a_third, {
   additional: "properties"
   });
   ```

   The property `additional` should be an own property, all the rest should be mixed into the prototype.

2. Use the canvas example to practice. Try out different things, for example:
    - Draw a few triangles, squares, and rectangles.
    - Add constructors for more shapes, such as `Trapezoid`, `Rhombus`, `Kite`, and `Pentagon`. If you want to learn more about the canvas tag, create a `Circle` constructor too. It will need to overwrite the `draw()` method of the parent.
    - Can you think of another way to approach the problem and use another type of inheritance?
    - Pick one of the methods that uses `uber` as a way for a child to access its parent. Add functionality where the parents can keep track of who their children are. Perhaps by using a property that contains a `children` array?

7

The Browser Environment

You know that JavaScript programs need a host environment. Most of what you learned so far in this book was related to core ECMAScript/JavaScript and can be used in many different host environments. Now, let's shift the focus to the browser, since this is the most popular and natural host environment for JavaScript programs. In this chapter, you will learn about the following elements:

- The **Browser Object Model (BOM)**
- The **Document Object Model (DOM)**
- Browser events
- The `XMLHttpRequest` object

Including JavaScript in an HTML page

To include JavaScript in an HTML page, you need to use the `<script>` tag as follows:

```
<!DOCTYPE>
<html>
  <head>
    <title>JS test</title>
    <script src="somefile.js"></script>
  </head>
  <body>
    <script>
      var a = 1;
      a++;
    </script>
  </body>
</html>
```

In this example, the first `<script>` tag includes an external file, `somefile.js`, which contains JavaScript code. The second `<script>` tag includes the JavaScript code directly in the HTML code of the page. The browser executes the JavaScript code in the sequence it finds it on the page and all the code in all tags share the same global namespace. This means that when you define a variable in `somefile.js`, it also exists in the second `<script>` block.

BOM and DOM – an overview

The JavaScript code in a page has access to a number of objects. These objects can be divided into the following types:

- **Core ECMAScript objects**: All the objects mentioned in the previous chapters
- **DOM**: Objects that have to do with the currently loaded page (the page is also called the document)
- **BOM**: Objects that deal with everything outside the page (the browser window and the desktop screen)

DOM stands for Document Object Model and BOM for Browser Object Model.

The DOM is a standard, governed by the **World Wide Web Consortium** (**W3C**) and has different versions, called levels, such as DOM Level 1, DOM Level 2, and so on. Browsers in use today have different degrees of compliance with the standard but in general, they almost all completely implement DOM Level 1. The DOM was standardized post-factum, after the browser vendors had each implemented their own ways to access the document. The legacy part (from before the W3C took over) is still around and is referred to as DOM 0, although no real DOM Level 0 standard exists. Some parts of DOM 0 have become de-facto standards as all major browsers support them. Some of these were added to the DOM Level 1 standard. The rest of DOM 0 that didn't find its way to DOM 1 is too browser-specific and won't be discussed here.

BOM historically has not been a part of any standard. Similar to DOM 0, it has a subset of objects that is supported by all major browsers, and another subset that is browser-specific. The HTML5 standard codifies common behavior among browsers, and it includes common BOM objects. Additionally, mobile devices come with their specific objects (and HTML5 aims to standardize those as well) which traditionally have not been necessary for desktop computers, but make sense in a mobile world, for example, geolocation, camera access, vibration, touch events, telephony, and SMS.

This chapter discusses only cross-browser subsets of BOM and DOM Level 1 (unless noted otherwise in the text). Even these safe subsets constitute a large topic, and a full reference is beyond the scope of this book. You can also consult the following references:

- Mozilla DOM reference (`http://developer.mozilla.org/en/docs/Gecko_DOM_Reference`)
- Mozilla's HTML5 wiki (`https://developer.mozilla.org/en-US/docs/HTML/HTML5`)
- Microsoft's documentation for Internet Explorer (`http://msdn2.microsoft.com/en-us/library/ms533050(vs.85).aspx`)
- W3C's DOM specifications (`http://www.w3.org/DOM/DOMTR`)

BOM

The Browser Object Model (BOM) is a collection of objects that give you access to the browser and the computer screen. These objects are accessible through the global object `window`.

The window object revisited

As you know already, in JavaScript there's a global object provided by the host environment. In the browser environment, this global object is accessible using `window`. All global variables are also accessible as properties of the `window` object as follows:

```
> window.somevar = 1;
  1

> somevar;
  1
```

Also, all of the core JavaScript functions (discussed in *Chapter 2, Primitive Data Types, Arrays, Loops, and Conditions*) are methods of the global object. Have a look at the following code snippet:

```
> parseInt('123a456');
  123

> window.parseInt('123a456');
  123
```

In addition to being a reference to the global object, the `window` object also serves a second purpose providing information about the browser environment. There's a `window` object for every frame, iframe, pop up, or browser tab.

Let's see some of the browser-related properties of the `window` object. Again, these can vary from one browser to another, so let's only consider the properties that are implemented consistently and reliably across all major browsers.

window.navigator

The `navigator` is an object that has some information about the browser and its capabilities. One property is `navigator.userAgent`, which is a long string of browser identification. In Firefox, you'll get the following output:

```
> window.navigator.userAgent;
```

"Mozilla/5.0 (Macintosh; Intel Mac OS X 10_8_3) AppleWebKit/536.28.10 (KHTML, like Gecko) Version/6.0.3 Safari/536.28.10"

The `userAgent` string in Microsoft Internet Explorer would be something like the following:

"Mozilla/5.0 (compatible; MSIE 10.0; Windows NT 6.1; Trident/6.0)"

Because the browsers have different capabilities, developers have been using the `userAgent` string to identify the browser and provide different versions of the code. For example, the following code searches for the presence of the string `MSIE` to identify Internet Explorer:

```
if (navigator.userAgent.indexOf('MSIE') !== -1) {
  // this is IE
} else {
  // not IE
}
```

It's better not to rely on the user agent string, but to use feature sniffing (also called capability detection) instead. The reason for this is that it's hard to keep track of all browsers and their different versions. It's much easier to simply check if the feature you intend to use is indeed available in the user's browser. For example have a look at the following code:

```
if (typeof window.addEventListener === 'function') {
  // feature is supported, let's use it
} else {
  // hmm, this feature is not supported, will have to
  // think of another way
}
```

Another reason to avoid user agent sniffing is that some browsers allow users to modify the string and pretend they are using a different browser.

Your console is a cheat sheet

The console lets you inspect what's in an object and this includes all the BOM and DOM properties. Just type the following code:

```
> navigator;
```

Then click on the result. The result is a list of properties and their values, as shown in the following screenshot:

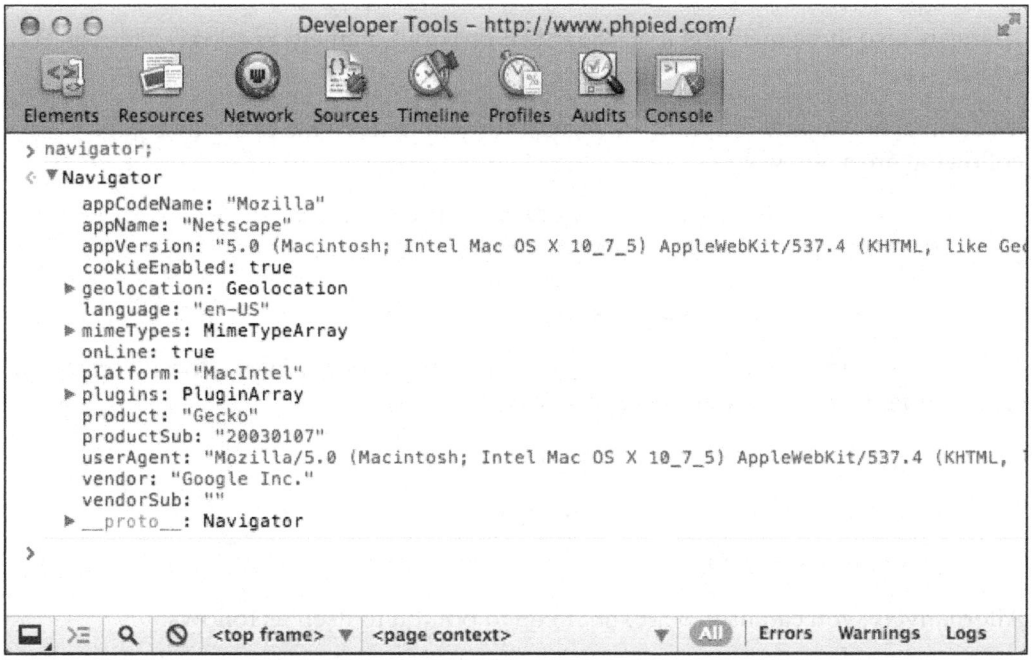

window.location

The `location` property points to an object that contains information about the URL of the currently loaded page. For example, `location.href` is the full URL and `location.hostname` is only the domain. With a simple loop, you can see the full list of properties of the `location` object.

Imagine you're on a page with a URL `http://search.phpied.com:8080/search?q=java&what=script#results`.

```
for (var i in location) {
  if (typeof location[i] === "string") {
    console.log(i + ' = "' + location[i] + '"');
  }
```

```
}
    href = "http://search.phpied.com:8080/search?q=java&what=script#results"
    hash = "#results"
    host = "search.phpied.com:8080"
    hostname = "search.phpied.com"
    pathname = "/search"
    port = «8080»
    protocol = «http:»
    search = "?q=java&what=script"
```

There are also three methods that `location` provides, namely `reload()`, `assign()`, and `replace()`.

It's curious how many different ways exist for you to navigate to another page. Following are a few ways:

```
> window.location.href = 'http://www.packtpub.com';
> location.href = 'http://www.packtpub.com';
> location = 'http://www.packtpub.com';
> location.assign('http://www.packtpub.com');
```

`replace()` is almost the same as `assign()`. The difference is that it doesn't create an entry in the browser's history list as follows:

```
> location.replace('http://www.yahoo.com');
```

To reload a page you can use the following code:

```
> location.reload();
```

Alternatively, you can use `location.href` to point it to itself as follows:

```
> window.location.href = window.location.href;
```

Or, simply use the following code:

```
> location = location;
```

window.history

`window.history` allows limited access to the previously visited pages in the same browser session. For example, you can see how many pages the user has visited before coming to your page as follows:

```
> window.history.length;
  5
```

You cannot see the actual URLs though. For privacy reasons this doesn't work. See the following code:

```
> window.history[0];
```

You can, however, navigate back and forth through the user's session as if the user had clicked on the Back/Forward browser buttons as follows:

```
> history.forward();
> history.back();
```

You can also skip pages back and forth with `history.go()`. This is the same as calling `history.back()`. Code for history go() is as follows:

```
> history.go(-1);
```

For going two pages back use the following code:

```
> history.go(-2);
```

Reload the current page using the following code:

```
> history.go(0);
```

More recent browsers also support HTML5 History API, which lets you change the URL without reloading the page. This is perfect for dynamic pages because they can allow users to bookmark a specific URL, which represents the state of the application, and when they come back (or share with their friends) the page can restore the application state based on the URL. To get a sense of the history API, go to any page and write the following code in the console:

```
> history.pushState({a: 1}, "", "hello");

> history.pushState({b: 2}, "", "hello-you-too");

> history.state;
```

Notice how the URL changes, but the page is the same. Now, experiment with Back and Forward buttons in the browser and inspect the `history.state` again.

window.frames

`window.frames` is a collection of all of the frames in the current page. It doesn't distinguish between frames and iframes (inline frames). Regardless of whether there are frames on the page or not, `window.frames` always exists and points to `window` as follows:

```
> window.frames === window;
  true
```

Let's consider an example where you have a page with one iframe as follows:

```
<iframe name="myframe" src="hello.html" />
```

In order to tell if there are any frames on the page, you can check the `length` property. In case of one iframe, you'll see the following output:

```
> frames.length
  1
```

Each frame contains another page, which has its own global `window` object.

To get access to the iframe's `window`, you can do any of the following:

```
> window.frames[0];
> window.frames[0].window;
> window.frames[0].window.frames;
> frames[0].window;
> frames[0];
```

From the parent page, you can access properties of the child frame also. For example, you can reload the frame as follows:

```
> frames[0].window.location.reload();
```

From inside the child you can access the parent as follows:

```
> frames[0].parent === window;
  true
```

Using a property called `top`, you can access the top-most page (the one that contains all the other frames) from within any frame as follows:

```
> window.frames[0].window.top === window;
  true

> window.frames[0].window.top === window.top;
  true

> window.frames[0].window.top === top;
  true
```

In addition, `self` is the same as `window` as follows:

```
> self === window;
  true

> frames[0].self == frames[0].window;
  true
```

If a frame has a `name` attribute, you can not only access the frame by name, but also by index as follows:

```
> window.frames['myframe'] === window.frames[0];
  true
```

Or, alternatively you can use the following code:

```
> frames.myframe === window.frames[0];
  true
```

window.screen

`screen` provides information about the environment outside the browser. For example, the property `screen.colorDepth` contains the color bit-depth (the color quality) of the monitor. This is mostly used for statistical purposes. Have a look at the following code:

```
> window.screen.colorDepth;
  32
```

You can also check the available screen real estate (the resolution):

```
> screen.width;
  1440

> screen.availWidth;
  1440

> screen.height;
  900

> screen.availHeight;
  847
```

The difference between `height` and `availHeight` is that the `height` is the whole screen, while `availHeight` subtracts any operating system menus such as the Windows task bar. The same is the case for `width` and `availWidth`.

Somewhat related is the property mentioned in the following code:

```
> window.devicePixelRatio;
  1
```

It tells you the difference (ratio) between physical pixels and device pixels in the retina displays in mobile devices (for example, value 2 in iPhone).

window.open()/close()

Having explored some of the most common cross-browser properties of the `window` object, let's move to some of the methods. One such method is `open()`, which allows you to open new browser windows (pop ups). Various browser policies and user settings may prevent you from opening a pop up (due to abuse of the technique for marketing purposes), but generally you should be able to open a new window if it was initiated by the user. Otherwise, if you try to open a pop up as the page loads, it will most likely be blocked, because the user didn't initiate it explicitly.

`window.open()` accepts the following parameters:

- URL to load in the new window
- Name of the new window, which can be used as the value of a form's `target` attribute
- Comma-separated list of features. They are as follows:
  - `resizable`: Should the user be able to resize the new window
  - `width`, `height`: Width and height of the pop up
  - `status`: Should the status bar be visible

`window.open()` returns a reference to the `window` object of the newly created browser instance. Following is an example:

```
var win = window.open('http://www.packtpub.com', 'packt',
                      'width=300,height=300,resizable=yes');
```

`win` points to the `window` object of the pop up. You can check if `win` has a falsy value, which means that the pop up was blocked.

`win.close()` closes the new window.

It's best to stay away from opening new windows for accessibility and usability reasons. If you don't like sites popping up windows to you, why do it to your users? There are legitimate purposes, such as providing help information while filling out a form, but often the same can be achieved with alternative solutions, such as using a floating `<div>` inside the page.

window.moveTo() and window.resizeTo()

Continuing with the shady practices from the past, following are more methods to irritate your users, provided their browser and personal settings allow you to.

- `window.moveTo(100, 100)` moves the browser window to screen location `x = 100` and `y = 100` (counted from the top-left corner)

- `window.moveBy(10, -10)` moves the window 10 pixels to the right and 10 pixels up from its current location
- `window.resizeTo(x, y)` and `window.resizeBy(x, y)` accept the same parameters as the move methods but they resize the window as opposed to moving it

Again, try to solve the problem you're facing without resorting to these methods.

window.alert(), window.prompt(), and window.confirm()

Chapter 2, *Primitive Data Types, Arrays, Loops, and Conditions*, talked about the function `alert()`. Now you know that global functions are accessible as methods of the global object so `alert('Watch out!')` and `window.alert('Watch out!')` are exactly the same.

`alert()` is not an ECMAScript function, but a BOM method. In addition to it, two other BOM methods allow you to interact with the user through system messages. Following are the methods:

- `confirm()` gives the user two options, **OK** and **Cancel**
- `prompt()` collects textual input

See how this works as follows:

```
> var answer = confirm('Are you cool?');
> answer;
```

It presents you with a window similar to the following screenshot (the exact look depends on the browser and the operating system):

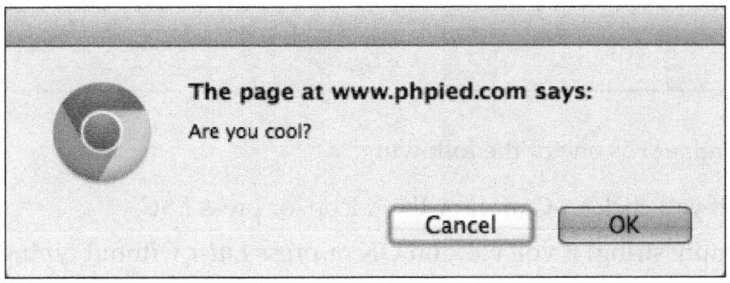

You'll notice the following things:

- Nothing gets written to the console until you close this message, this means that any JavaScript code execution freezes, waiting for the user's answer
- Clicking on **OK** returns **true**, clicking on **Cancel** or closing the message using the **X** icon (or the *ESC* key) returns **false**

This is handy for confirming user actions as follows:

```
if (confirm('Sure you want to delete this?')) {
  // delete
} else {
  // abort
}
```

Make sure you provide an alternative way to confirm user actions for people who have disabled JavaScript (or for search engine spiders).

`window.prompt()` presents the user with a dialog to enter text as follows:

```
> var answer = prompt('And your name was?');
> answer;
```

This results in the following dialog box (Chrome, MacOS):

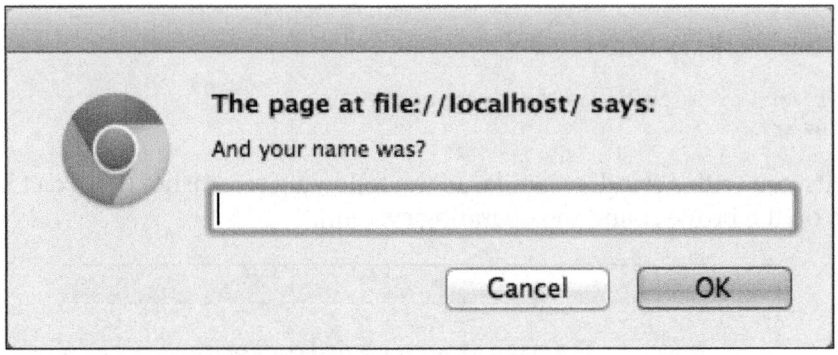

The value of `answer` is one of the following:

- **null** if you click on **Cancel** or the **X** icon, or press *ESC*
- "" (empty string) if you click on **OK** or press *Enter* without typing anything
- A text string if you type something and then click on **OK** (or press *Enter*)

The function also takes a string as a second parameter and displays it as a default value prefilled into the input field.

window.setTimeout() and window.setInterval()

`setTimeout()` and `setInterval()` allow for scheduling the execution of a piece of code. `setTimeout()` attempts to execute the given code once after a specified number of milliseconds. `setInterval()` attempts to execute it repeatedly after a specified number of milliseconds has passed.

This shows an alert after approximately 2 seconds (2000 milliseconds):

```
> function boo() { alert('Boo!'); }
> setTimeout(boo, 2000);
  4
```

As you can see the function returned an integer (in this case **4**) representing the ID of the timeout. You can use this ID to cancel the timeout using `clearTimeout()`. In the following example, if you're quick enough, and clear the timeout before 2 seconds have passed, the alert will never be shown as you can see in the following code:

```
> var id = setTimeout(boo, 2000);
> clearTimeout(id);
```

Let's change `boo()` to something less intrusive as follows:

```
> function boo() { console.log('boo'); }
```

Now, using `setInterval()` you can schedule `boo()` to execute every 2 seconds, until you cancel the scheduled execution with `clearInterval()`:

```
> var id = setInterval(boo, 2000);
  boo
  boo
  boo
  boo
  boo
  boo
> clearInterval(id);
```

Note, that both functions accept a pointer to a callback function as a first parameter. They can also accept a string which is evaluated with `eval()` but as you know, `eval()` is evil, so it should be avoided. And what if you want to pass arguments to the function? In such cases, you can just wrap the function call inside another function.

The following code is valid, but not recommended:

```
// bad idea
var id = setInterval("alert('boo, boo')", 2000);
```

This alternative is preferred:

```
var id = setInterval(
  function () {
    alert('boo, boo');
  },
  2000
);
```

Be aware that scheduling a function in some amount of milliseconds is not a guarantee that it will execute exactly at that time. One reason is that most browsers don't have millisecond resolution time. If you schedule something in 3 milliseconds, it will execute after a minimum of 15 in older IEs and sooner in more modern browsers, but most likely not in 1 millisecond. The other reason is that browsers maintain a queue of what you request them to do. 100 milliseconds timeout means add to the queue after 100 milliseconds. But if the queue is delayed by something slow happening, your function will have to wait and execute after, say, 120 milliseconds.

More recent browsers implement the `requestAnimationFrame()` function. It's preferable to the timeout functions because you're asking the browser to call your function whenever it has available resources, not after a predefined time in milliseconds. Try the following in your console:

```
function animateMe() {
  webkitRequestAnimationFrame(function(){
    console.log(new Date());
    animateMe();
  });
}

animateMe();
```

window.document

`window.document` is a BOM object that refers to the currently loaded document (page). Its methods and properties fall into the DOM category of objects. Take a deep breath (and maybe first look at the BOM exercises at the end of the chapter) and let's dive into the DOM.

DOM

The Document Object Model (DOM) represents an XML or an HTML document as a tree of nodes. Using DOM methods and properties, you can access any element on the page, modify or remove elements, or add new ones. The DOM is a language-independent API (Application Programming Interface) and can be implemented not only in JavaScript, but also in any other language. For example, you can generate pages on the server-side with PHP's DOM implementation (`http://php.net/dom`).

Take a look at this example HTML page:

```
<!DOCTYPE html>
<html>
  <head>
    <title>My page</title>
  </head>
  <body>
    <p class="opener">first paragraph</p>
    <p><em>second</em> paragraph</p>
    <p id="closer">final</p>
    <!-- and that's about it -->
  </body>
</html>
```

Consider the second paragraph (`<p><em>second</em> paragraph</p>`). You see that it's a `<p>` tag and it's contained in the `<body>` tag. If you think in terms of family relationships, you can say that `<body>` is the parent of `<p>` and `<p>` is the child. The first and the third paragraphs would also be children of the `<body>`, and at the same time siblings of the second paragraph. The `<em>` tag is a child of the second `<p>`, so `<p>` is its parent. The parent-child relationships can be represented graphically in an ancestry tree, called the DOM tree:

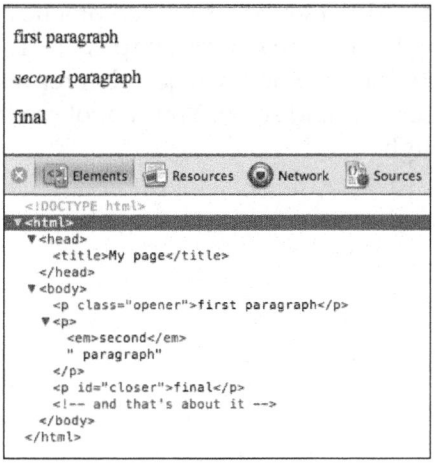

The previous screenshot shows what you'll see in the webkit console's **Elements** tab after you expand each node.

You can see how all of the tags are shown as expandable nodes on the tree. Although not shown, there exists the so-called text nodes, for example, the text inside the `<em>` (the word second) is a text node. Whitespace is also considered a text node. Comments inside the HTML code are also nodes in the tree, the `<!-- and that's about it -->` comment in the HTML source is a comment node in the tree.

Every node in the DOM tree is an object and the **Properties** section on the right lists all of the properties and methods you can use to work with these objects, following the inheritance chain of how this object was created:

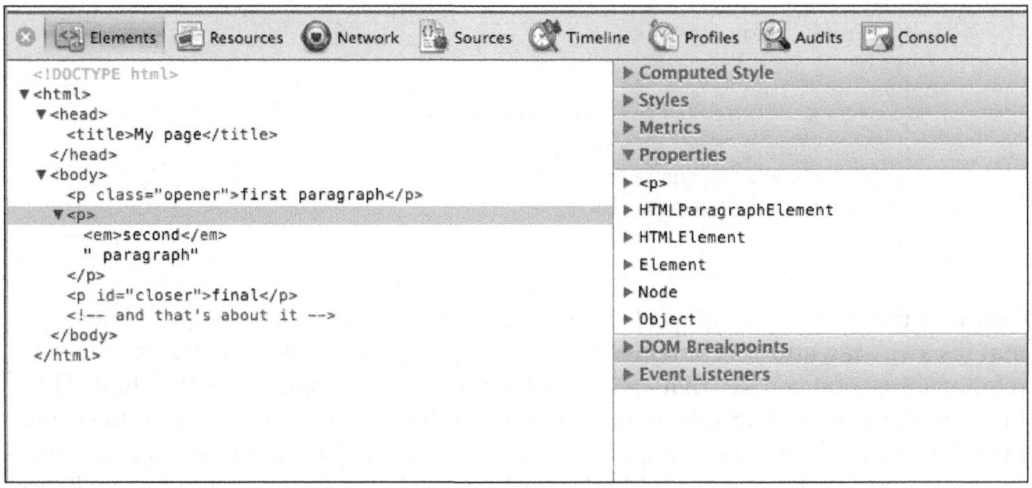

You can also see the constructor function that was used behind the scenes to create each of these objects. Although this is not too practical for day-to-day tasks, it may be interesting to know that, for example, `<p>` is created by the `HTMLParagraphElement()` constructor, the object that represents the `head` tag is created by `HTMLHeadElement()`, and so on. You cannot create objects using these constructors directly, though.

Core DOM and HTML DOM

One last diversion before moving on to more practical examples. As you now know, the DOM represents both XML documents and HTML documents. In fact, HTML documents are XML documents, but a little more specific. Therefore, as part of DOM Level 1, there is a Core DOM specification that is applicable to all XML documents, and there is also an HTML DOM specification, which extends and builds upon the core DOM. Of course, the HTML DOM doesn't apply to all XML documents, but only to HTML documents. Let's see some examples of Core DOM and HTML DOM constructors:

Constructor	Inherits from	Core or HTML	Comment
`Node`		Core	Any node on the tree.
`Document`	`Node`	Core	The `document` object, the main entry point to any XML document.
`HTMLDocument`	`Document`	HTML	This is `window.document` or simply `document`, the HTML-specific version of the previous object, which you'll use extensively.
`Element`	`Node`	Core	Every tag in the source is represented by an element. That's why you say "the P element" meaning "the `<p></p>` tag".
`HTMLElement`	`Element`	HTML	General-purpose constructor, all constructors for HTML elements inherit from it.
`HTMLBodyElement`	`HTMLElement`	HTML	Element representing the `<body>` tag.
`HTMLLinkElement`	`HTMLElement`	HTML	An A element (an `<a href="...">/a>` tag).
and other such constructors.	`HTMLElement`	HTML	All the rest of the HTML elements.
`CharacterData`	`Node`	Core	General-purpose constructor for dealing with texts.
`Text`	`CharacterData`	Core	Text node inside a tag. In `<em>second</em>` you have the element node EM and the text node with value second.
`Comment`	`CharacterData`	Core	`<!-- any comment -->`

Constructor	Inherits from	Core or HTML	Comment
`Attr`	`Node`	Core	Represents an attribute of a tag, in `<p id="closer">` the `id` attribute is a DOM object created by the `Attr()` constructor.
`NodeList`		Core	A list of nodes, an array-like object that has a `length` property.
`NamedNodeMap`		Core	Same as `NodeList` but the nodes can be accessed by name, not only by numeric index.
`HTMLCollection`		HTML	Similar to `NamedNodeMap` but specific for HTML.

These are by no means all of the Core DOM and HTML DOM objects. For the full list consult `http://www.w3.org/TR/DOM-Level-1/`.

Now that this bit of DOM theory is behind you, let's focus on the practical side of working with the DOM. In the following sections, you'll learn how to do the following things:

- Access DOM nodes
- Modify nodes
- Create new nodes
- Remove nodes

Accessing DOM nodes

Before you can validate the user input in a form on a page or swap an image, you need to get access to the element you want to inspect or modify. Luckily, there are many ways to get to any element, either by navigating around traversing the DOM tree or by using a shortcut.

It's best if you start experimenting with all of the new objects and methods. The examples you'll see use the same simple document that you saw at the beginning of the DOM section, and which you can access at `http://www.phpied.com/files/jsoop/ch7.html`. Open your console, and let's get started.

The document node

`document` gives you access to the current document. To explore this object, you can use your console as a cheat sheet. Type `console.dir(document)` and click on the result:

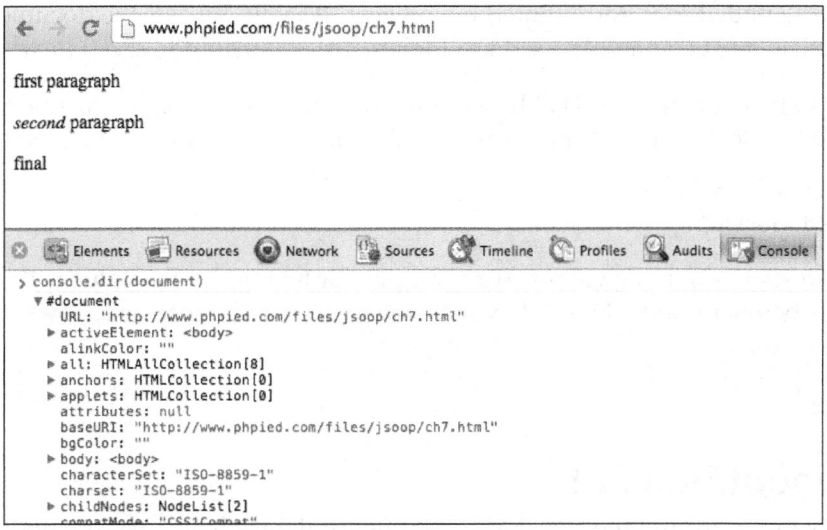

Alternatively, you can you can browse all of the properties and methods of the `document` object DOM properties in the **Elements** panel:

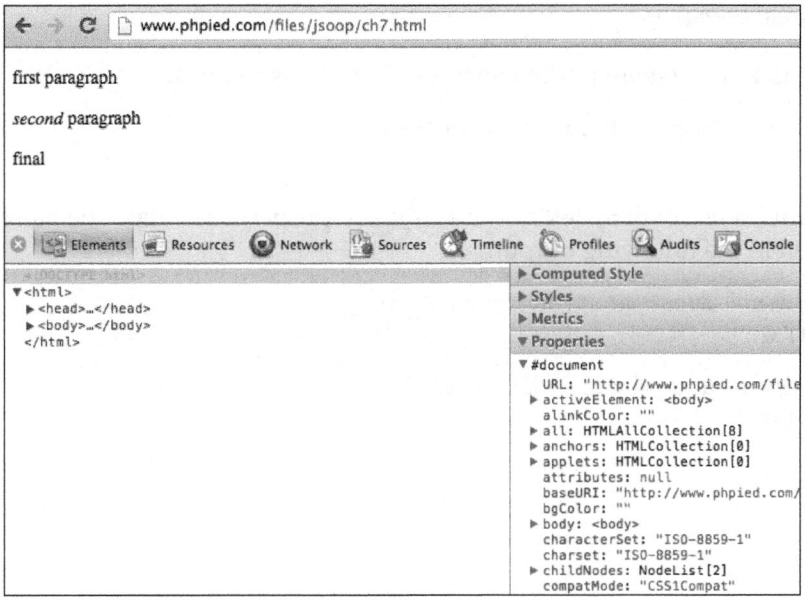

All nodes (this also includes the document node, text nodes, element nodes, and attribute nodes) have `nodeType`, `nodeName`, and `nodeValue` properties:

```
> document.nodeType;
  9
```

There are 12 node types, represented by integers. As you can see, the document node type is **9**. The most commonly used are 1 (element), 2 (attribute), and 3 (text).

Nodes also have names. For HTML tags the node name is the tag name (`tagName` property). For text nodes, it's **#text**, and for document nodes the name is as follows:

```
> document.nodeName;
  "#document"
```

Nodes can also have node values. For example, for text nodes the value is the actual text. The document node doesn't have a value which can be seen as follows:

```
> document.nodeValue;
  null
```

documentElement

Now, let's move around the tree. XML documents always have one root node that wraps the rest of the document. For HTML documents, the root is the `<html>` tag. To access the root, you use the `documentElement` property of the `document` object:

```
> document.documentElement;
  <html>...</html>
```

`nodeType` is **1** (an element node) which can be seen as follows:

```
> document.documentElement.nodeType;
  1
```

For element nodes, both `nodeName` and `tagName` properties contain the name of the tag, as seen in the following output:

```
> document.documentElement.nodeName;
  "HTML"

> document.documentElement.tagName;
  "HTML"
```

Child nodes

In order to tell if a node has any children you use `hasChildNodes()` as follows:

```
> document.documentElement.hasChildNodes();
  true
```

The HTML element has three children, the `head` and the `body` elements and the whitespace between them (whitespace is counted in most, but not all browsers). You can access them using the `childNodes` array-like collection as follows:

```
> document.documentElement.childNodes.length;
  3

> document.documentElement.childNodes[0];
  <head>...</head>

> document.documentElement.childNodes[1];
  #text

> document.documentElement.childNodes[2];
  <body>...</body>
```

Any child has access to its parent through the `parentNode` property, as seen in the following code:

```
> document.documentElement.childNodes[1].parentNode;
  <html>...</html>
```

Let's assign a reference to `body` to a variable as follows:

```
> var bd = document.documentElement.childNodes[2];
```

How many children does the `body` element have?

```
> bd.childNodes.length;
  9
```

As a refresher, here again is the `body` of the document:

```
<body>
  <p class="opener">first paragraph</p>
  <p><em>second</em> paragraph</p>
  <p id="closer">final</p>
  <!-- and that's about it -->
</body>
```

How come `body` has **9** children? Well, three paragraphs plus one comment makes four nodes. The whitespace between these four nodes makes three more text nodes. This makes a total of seven so far. The whitespace between `<body>` and the first `<p>` is the eighth node. The whitespace between the comment and the closing `</body>` is another text node. This makes a total of nine child nodes. Just type `bd.childNodes` in the console to inspect them all.

Attributes

Because the first child of the body is a whitespace, the second child (index 1) is the first paragraph. Refer to the following piece of code:

```
> bd.childNodes[1];
  <p class="opener">first paragraph</p>
```

You can check whether an element has attributes using `hasAttributes()` as follows:

```
> bd.childNodes[1].hasAttributes();
  true
```

How many attributes? In this example, one is the `class` attribute which can be seen as follows:

```
> bd.childNodes[1].attributes.length;
  1
```

You can access the attributes by index and by name. You can also get the value using the `getAttribute()` method as follows:

```
> bd.childNodes[1].attributes[0].nodeName;
  "class"

> bd.childNodes[1].attributes[0].nodeValue;
  "opener"

> bd.childNodes[1].attributes['class'].nodeValue;
  "opener"

> bd.childNodes[1].getAttribute('class');
  "opener"
```

Accessing the content inside a tag

Let's take a look at the first paragraph:

```
> bd.childNodes[1].nodeName;
  "P"
```

You can get the text contained in the paragraph by using the `textContent` property. `textContent` doesn't exist in older IEs, but another property called `innerText` returns the same value, as seen in the following output:

```
> bd.childNodes[1].textContent;
  "first paragraph"
```

There is also the `innerHTML` property. It's a relatively new addition to the DOM standard despite the fact that it previously existed in all major browsers. It returns (or sets) HTML code contained in a node. You can see how this is a little inconsistent as DOM treats the document as a tree of nodes, not as a string of tags. But `innerHTML` is so convenient to use that you'll see it everywhere. Refer to the following code:

```
> bd.childNodes[1].innerHTML;
  "first paragraph"
```

The first paragraph contains only text, so `innerHTML` is the same as `textContent` (or `innerText` in IE). However, the second paragraph does contain an `em` node, so you can see the difference as follows:

```
> bd.childNodes[3].innerHTML;
  "<em>second</em> paragraph"

> bd.childNodes[3].textContent;
  "second paragraph"
```

Another way to get the text contained in the first paragraph is by using the `nodeValue` of the text node contained inside the `p` node as follows:

```
> bd.childNodes[1].childNodes.length;
  1

> bd.childNodes[1].childNodes[0].nodeName;
  "#text"

> bd.childNodes[1].childNodes[0].nodeValue;
  "first paragraph"
```

DOM access shortcuts

By using `childNodes`, `parentNode`, `nodeName`, `nodeValue`, and `attributes` you can navigate up and down the tree and do anything with the document. But the fact that whitespace is a text node makes this a fragile way of working with the DOM. If the page changes, your script may no longer work correctly. Also, if you want to get to a node deeper in the tree, it could take a bit of code before you get there. That's why you have shortcut methods, namely, `getElementsByTagName()`, `getElementsByName()`, and `getElementById()`.

`getElementsByTagName()` takes a tag name (the name of an element node) and returns an HTML collection (array-like object) of nodes with the matching tag name. For example, the following example asks "give me a count of all paragraphs" which is given as follows:

```
> document.getElementsByTagName('p').length;
  3
```

You can access an item in the list by using the brackets notation, or the method `item()`, and passing the index (0 for the first element). Using `item()` is discouraged as array brackets are more consistent and also shorter to type. Refer to the following piece of code:

```
> document.getElementsByTagName('p')[0];
  <p class="opener">first paragraph</p>

> document.getElementsByTagName('p').item(0);
  <p class="opener">first paragraph</p>
```

Getting the contents of the first `p` can be done as follows:

```
> document.getElementsByTagName('p')[0].innerHTML;
  "first paragraph"
```

Accessing the last `p` can be done as follows:

```
> document.getElementsByTagName('p')[2];
  <p id="closer">final</p>
```

To access the attributes of an element, you can use the `attributes` collection or `getAttribute()` as shown previously. But a shorter way is to use the attribute name as a property of the element you're working with. So to get the value of the `id` attribute, you just use `id` as a property as follows:

```
> document.getElementsByTagName('p')[2].id;
  "closer"
```

Getting the `class` attribute of the first paragraph won't work though. It's an exception, because it just happens so that class is a reserved word in ECMAScript. You can use `className` instead as follows:

```
> document.getElementsByTagName('p')[0].className;
  "opener"
```

Using `getElementsByTagName()` you can get all of the elements on the page as follows:

```
> document.getElementsByTagName('*').length;
  8
```

In earlier versions of IE before IE7, `*` is not acceptable as a tag name. To get all elements you can use IE's proprietary `document.all` collection, although selecting every element is rarely needed.

The other shortcut mentioned is `getElementById()`. This is probably the most common way of accessing an element. You just assign IDs to the elements you plan to play with and they'll be easy to access later on, as seen in the following code:

```
> document.getElementById('closer');
<p id="closer">final</p>
```

Additional shortcut methods in more recent browsers include the following:

- `getElementByClassName()`: This method finds elements using their `class` attribute
- `querySelector()`: This method finds an element using a CSS selector string
- `querySelectorAll()`: This method is the same as the previous one but returns all matching elements not just the first

Siblings, body, first, and last child

`nextSibling` and `previousSibling` are two other convenient properties to navigate the DOM tree, once you have a reference to one element:

```
> var para = document.getElementById('closer');
> para.nextSibling;
  #text

> para.previousSibling;
  #text

> para.previousSibling.previousSibling;
  <p>...</p>

> para.previousSibling.previousSibling.previousSibling;
  #text

> para.previousSibling.previousSibling.nextSibling.nextSibling;
  <p id="closer">final</p>
```

The `body` element is used so often that it has its own shortcut:

```
> document.body;
  <body>...</body>

> document.body.nextSibling;
  null

> document.body.previousSibling.previousSibling;
  <head>...</head>
```

`firstChild` and `lastChild` are also convenient. `firstChild` is the same as `childNodes[0]` and `lastChild` is the same as `childNodes[childNodes.length - 1]`:

```
> document.body.firstChild;
  #text

> document.body.lastChild;
  #text

> document.body.lastChild.previousSibling;
  <!-- and that's about it -->

> document.body.lastChild.previousSibling.nodeValue;
  " and that's about it "
```

The following screenshot shows the family relationships between the body and three paragraphs in it. For simplicity, all the whitespace text nodes are removed from the screenshot:

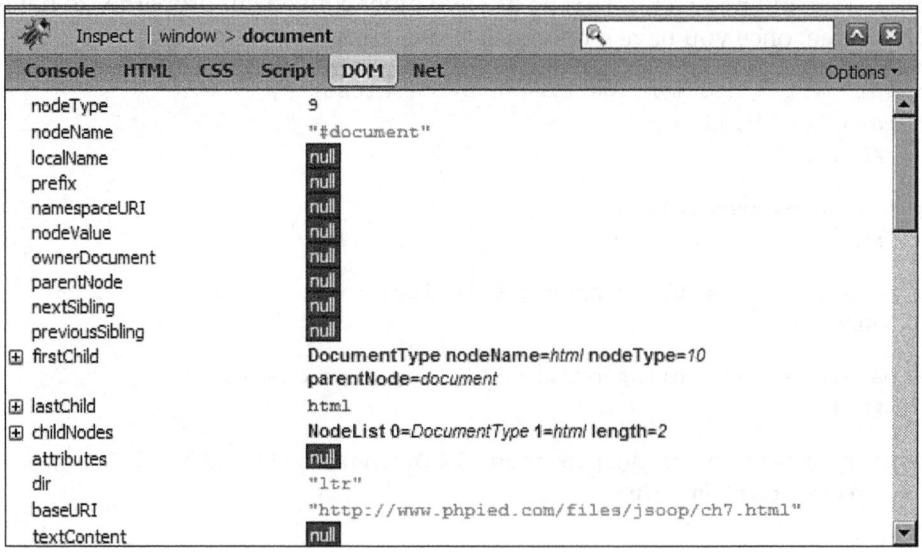

Walk the DOM

To wrap up, here's a function that takes any node and walks through the DOM tree recursively, starting from the given node:

```
function walkDOM(n) {
  do {
    console.log(n);
    if (n.hasChildNodes()) {
      walkDOM(n.firstChild);
    }
  } while (n = n.nextSibling);
}
```

You can test the function as follows:

```
> walkDOM(document.documentElement);
> walkDOM(document.body);
```

Modifying DOM nodes

Now that you know a whole lot of methods for accessing any node of the DOM tree and its properties, let's see how you can modify these nodes.

Let's assign a pointer to the last paragraph to the variable `my` as follows:

```
> var my = document.getElementById('closer');
```

Now, changing the text of the paragraph can be as easy as changing the `innerHTML` value:

```
> my.innerHTML = 'final!!!';
  "final!!!"
```

Because `innerHTML` accepts a string of HTML source code, you can also create a new `em` node in the DOM tree as follows:

```
> my.innerHTML = '<em>my</em> final';
  "<em>my</em> final"
```

The new `em` node becomes a part of the tree:

```
> my.firstChild;
  <em>my</em>

> my.firstChild.firstChild;
  "my"
```

Another way to change text is to get the actual text node and change its `nodeValue` as follows:

```
> my.firstChild.firstChild.nodeValue = 'your';
  "your"
```

Modifying styles

Often you don't change the content of a node but its presentation. The elements have a `style` property, which in turn has a property mapped to each CSS property. For example, changing the style of the paragraph to add a red border:

```
> my.style.border = "1px solid red";
  "1px solid red"
```

CSS properties often have dashes, but dashes are not acceptable in JavaScript identifiers. In such cases, you skip the dash and uppercase the next letter. So `padding-top` becomes `paddingTop`, `margin-left` becomes `marginLeft`, and so on. Have a look at the following code:

```
> my.style.fontWeight = 'bold';
  "bold"
```

You also have access to `cssText` property of `style`, which lets you work with styles as strings:

```
> my.style.cssText;
  "border: 1px solid red; font-weight: bold;"
```

And modifying styles is a string manipulation:

```
> my.style.cssText += " border-style: dashed;"
"border: 1px dashed red; font-weight: bold; border-style: dashed;"
```

Fun with forms

As mentioned earlier, JavaScript is great for client-side input validation and can save a few round-trips to the server. Let's practice form manipulations and play a little bit with a form located on a popular page `www.google.com`:

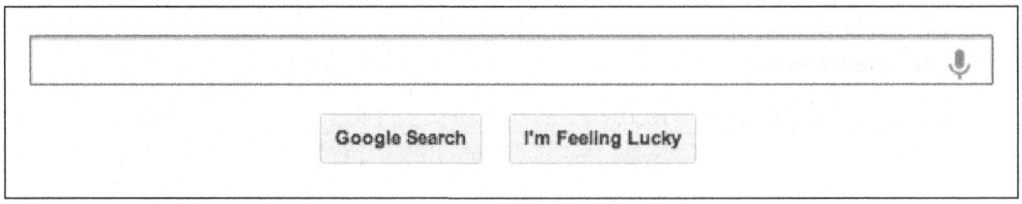

Finding the first text input using the `querySelector()` method and a CSS selector string is as follows:

```
> var input = document.querySelector('input[type=text]');
```

Accessing the search box:

```
> input.name;
  "q"
```

Changing the search query by setting the text contained in the `value` attribute is done as follows:

```
> input.value = 'my query';
  "my query"
```

Now, let's have some fun. Changing the word **Lucky** with **Tricky** in the button:

```
> var feeling = document.querySelectorAll("button")[2];
> feeling.textContent = feelingtextContent.replace(/Lu/, 'Tri');
  "I'm Feeling Tricky"
```

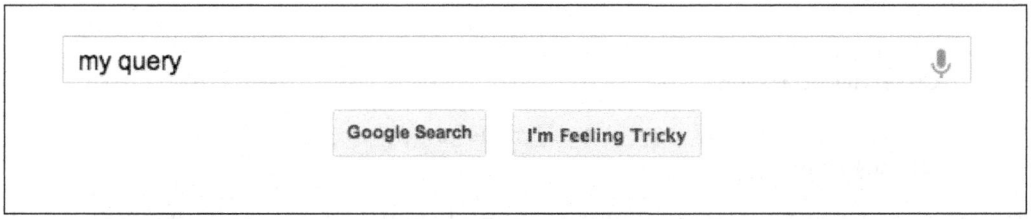

Now, let's implement the tricky part and make that button show and hide for one second. You can do this with a simple function. Let's call it `toggle()`. Every time you call the function, it checks the value of the CSS property `visibility` and sets it to visible if it's hidden and vice versa using following code:

```
function toggle() {
  var st = document.querySelectorAll('button')[2].style;
  st.visibility = (st.visibility === 'hidden')
    ? 'visible'
    : 'hidden';
}
```

Instead of calling the function manually, let's set an interval and call it every second:

```
> var myint = setInterval(toggle, 1000);
```

The result? The button starts blinking (making it trickier to click). When you're tired of chasing it, just remove the timeout interval:

```
> clearInterval(myint);
```

Creating new nodes

To create new nodes, you can use the methods `createElement()` and `createTextNode()`. Once you have the new nodes, you add them to the DOM tree using `appendChild()` (or `insertBefore()`, or `replaceChild()`).

Reload `http://www.phpied.com/files/jsoop/ch7.html` and let's play.

Creating a new `p` element and set its `innerHTML`, as shown in the following code:

```
> var myp = document.createElement('p');
> myp.innerHTML = 'yet another';
  "yet another"
```

The new element automatically gets all the default properties, such as `style`, which you can modify:

```
> myp.style;
  CSSStyleDeclaration

> myp.style.border = '2px dotted blue';
  "2px dotted blue"
```

Using `appendChild()` you can add the new node to the DOM tree. Calling this method on the `document.body` node means creating one more child node right after the last child:

```
> document.body.appendChild(myp);
  <p style="border: 2px dotted blue;">yet another</p>
```

Here's an illustration of how the page looks like after the new node is appended:

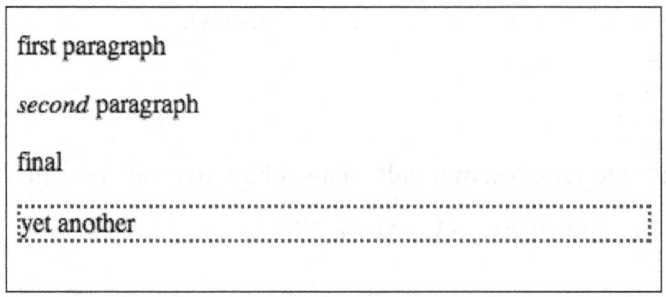

DOM-only method

`innerHTML` gets things done a little more quickly than using pure DOM. In pure DOM you need to perform the following steps:

1. Create a new text node containing yet another text
2. Create a new paragraph node
3. Append the text node as a child to the paragraph
4. Append the paragraph as a child to the body

This way you can create any number of text nodes and elements and nest them however you like. Let's say you want to add the following HTML to the end of the body:

```
<p>one more paragraph<strong>bold</strong></p>
```

Presenting this as a hierarchy would be something like the following:

```
P element
    text node with value "one more paragraph"
    STRONG element
        text node with value "bold"
```

The code that accomplishes this is as follows:

```
// create P
var myp = document.createElement('p');
// create text node and append to P
var myt = document.createTextNode('one more paragraph');
myp.appendChild(myt);
// create STRONG and append another text node to it
var str = document.createElement('strong');
str.appendChild(document.createTextNode('bold'));
// append STRONG to P
myp.appendChild(str);
// append P to BODY
document.body.appendChild(myp);
```

cloneNode()

Another way to create nodes is by copying (or cloning) existing ones. The method `cloneNode()` does this and accepts a boolean parameter (`true` = deep copy with all the children, `false` = shallow copy, only this node). Let's test the method.

Getting a reference to the element you want to clone can be done as follows:

```
> var el = document.getElementsByTagName('p')[1];
```

Now, `el` refers to the second paragraph on the page that looks like the following code:

```
<p><em>second</em> paragraph</p>
```

Let's create a shallow clone of `el` and append it to the body:

```
> document.body.appendChild(el.cloneNode(false));
```

You won't see a difference on the page, because the shallow copy only copied the P node, without any children. This means that the text inside the paragraph (which is a text node child) was not cloned. The line above would be equivalent to the following:

```
> document.body.appendChild(document.createElement('p'));
```

But if you create a deep copy, the whole DOM subtree starting from P is copied, and this includes text nodes and the EM element. This line copies (visually too) the second paragraph to the end of the document:

```
> document.body.appendChild(el.cloneNode(true));
```

You can also copy only the EM if you want as follows:

```
> document.body.appendChild(el.firstChild.cloneNode(true));
  <em>second</em>
```

Or, only the text node with value second:

```
> document.body.appendChild(
    el.firstChild.firstChild.cloneNode(false));
  "second"
```

insertBefore()

Using `appendChild()`, you can only add new children at the end of the selected element. For more control over the exact location there is `insertBefore()`. This is the same as `appendChild()`, but accepts an extra parameter specifying where (before which element) to insert the new node. For example, the following code inserts a text node at the end of the `body`:

```
> document.body.appendChild(document.createTextNode('boo!'));
```

And this creates another text node and adds it as the first child of the `body`:

```
document.body.insertBefore(
  document.createTextNode('first boo!'),
  document.body.firstChild
);
```

Removing nodes

To remove nodes from the DOM tree, you can use the method `removeChild()`. Again, let's start fresh with the same page with the body:

```
<body>
  <p class="opener">first paragraph</p>
  <p><em>second</em> paragraph</p>
  <p id="closer">final</p>
  <!-- and that's about it -->
</body>
```

Here's how you can remove the second paragraph:

```
> var myp = document.getElementsByTagName('p')[1];
> var removed = document.body.removeChild(myp);
```

The method returns the removed node if you want to use it later. You can still use all the DOM methods even though the element is no longer in the tree:

```
> removed;
  <p>...</p>

> removed.firstChild;
  <em>second</em>
```

There's also the `replaceChild()` method that removes a node and puts another one in its place.

After removing the node, the tree looks like the following:

```
<body>
  <p class="opener">first paragraph</p>
  <p id="closer">final</p>
  <!-- and that's about it -->
</body>
```

Now, the second paragraph is the one with the ID "closer":

```
> var p = document.getElementsByTagName('p')[1];
> p;
  <p id="closer">final</p>
```

Let's replace this paragraph with the one in the `removed` variable:

```
> var replaced = document.body.replaceChild(removed, p);
```

Just like `removeChild()`, `replaceChild()` returns a reference to the node that is now out of the tree:

```
> replaced;
  <p id="closer">final</p>
```

Now, the body looks like the following:

```
<body>
  <p class="opener">first paragraph</p>
  <p><em>second</em> paragraph</p>
  <!-- and that's about it -->
</body>
```

A quick way to wipe out all of the content of a subtree is to set the `innerHTML` to a blank string. This removes all of the children of the BODY:

```
> document.body.innerHTML = '';
  ""
```

Testing is done as follows:

```
> document.body.firstChild;
  null
```

Removing with `innerHTML` is fast and easy. The DOM-only way would be to go over all of the child nodes and remove each one individually. Here's a little function that removes all nodes from a given start node:

```
function removeAll(n) {
  while (n.firstChild) {
    n.removeChild(n.firstChild);
  }
}
```

If you want to delete all BODY children and leave the page with an empty `<body></body>` use the following code:

```
> removeAll(document.body);
```

HTML-only DOM objects

As you know already, the Document Object Model applies to both XML and HTML documents. What you've learned above about traversing the tree and then adding, removing, or modifying nodes applies to any XML document. There are, however, some HTML-only objects and properties.

`document.body` is one such HTML-only object. It's so common to have a `<body>` tag in HTML documents and it's accessed so often, that it makes sense to have an object that's shorter and friendlier than the equivalent `document.getElementsByTagName('body')[0]`.

`document.body` is one example of a legacy object inherited from the prehistoric DOM Level 0 and moved to the HTML extension of the DOM specification. There are other objects similar to `document.body`. For some of them there is no core DOM equivalent, for others there is an equivalent, but the DOM0 original was ported anyway for simplicity and legacy purposes. Let's see some of those objects.

Primitive ways to access the document

Unlike the DOM, which gives you access to any element (and even comments and whitespace), initially JavaScript had only limited access to the elements of an HTML document. This was done mainly through a number of collections:

- `document.images`: This is a collection of all of the images on the page. The Core DOM equivalent is `document.getElementsByTagName('img')`
- `document.applets`: This is the same as `document.getElementsByTagName('applet')`
- `document.links`
- `document.anchors`
- `document.forms`

`document.links` contains a list of all `<a href="..."></a>` tags on the page, meaning the `<a>` tags that have an `href` attribute. `document.anchors` contain all links with a `name` attribute (`<a name="..."></a>`).

One of the most widely used collections is `document.forms`, which contains a list of `<form>` elements.

Let's play with a page that contains a form and an input, `http://www.phpied.com/files/jsoop/ch7-form.html`. The following gives you access to the first form on the page:

```
> document.forms[0];
```

It's the same as the following:

```
> document.getElementsByTagName('forms')[0];
```

The `document.forms` collection contains collections of input fields and buttons, accessible through the `elements` property. Here's how to access the first input of the first form on the page:

```
> document.forms[0].elements[0];
```

Once you have access to an element, you can access its attributes as object properties. The first field of the first form in the test page is this:

```
<input name="search" id="search" type="text" size="50"
       maxlength="255" value="Enter email..." />
```

You can change the text in the field (the value of the `value` attribute) by using the following code:

```
> document.forms[0].elements[0].value = 'me@example.org';
  "me@example.org"
```

If you want to disable the field dynamically use the following code:

```
> document.forms[0].elements[0].disabled = true;
```

When forms or form elements have a `name` attribute, you can access them by name too as in the following code:

```
> document.forms[0].elements['search']; // array notation
> document.forms[0].elements.search;    // object property
```

document.write()

The method `document.write()` allows you to insert HTML into the page while the page is being loaded. You can have something like the following code:

```
<p>It is now
  <script>
    document.write("<em>" + new Date() + "</em>");
  </script>
</p>
```

This is the same as if you had the date directly in the source of the HTML document as follows:

```
<p>It is now
  <em>Fri Apr 26 2013 16:55:16 GMT-0700 (PDT)</em>
</p>
```

Note, that you can only use `document.write()` while the page is being loaded. If you try it after page load, it will replace the content of the whole page.

It's rare that you would need `document.write()`, and if you think you do, try an alternative approach. The ways to modify the contents of the page provided by DOM Level 1 are preferred and are much more flexible.

Cookies, title, referrer, domain

The four additional properties of `document` you'll see in this section are also ported from DOM Level 0 to the HTML extension of DOM Level 1. Unlike the previous ones, for these properties there are no core DOM equivalents.

`document.cookie` is a property that contains a string. This string is the content of the cookies exchanged between the server and the client. When the server sends a page to the browser, it may include the `Set-Cookie` HTTP header. When the client sends a request to the server, it sends the cookie information back with the `Cookie` header. Using `document.cookie` you can alter the cookies the browser sends to the server. For example, visiting `cnn.com` and typing `document.cookie` in the console gives you the following output:

```
> document.cookie;
  "mbox=check#true#1356053765|session#1356053704195-121286#1356055565;...
```

`document.title` allows you to change the title of the page displayed in the browser window. For example, see the following code:

```
> document.title = 'My title';
  "My title"
```

Note, that this doesn't change the value of the `<title>` element, but only the display in the browser window, so it's not equivalent to `document.querySelector('title')`.

`document.referrer` tells you the URL of the previously-visited page. This is the same value the browser sends in the `Referer` HTTP header when requesting the page. (Note, that `Referer` is misspelled in the HTTP headers, but is correct in JavaScript's `document.referrer`). If you've visited the CNN page by searching on Yahoo first, you can see something like the following:

```
> document.referrer;
  "http://search.yahoo.com/search?p=cnn&ei=UTF-8&fr=moz2"
```

`document.domain` gives you access to the domain name of the currently loaded page. This is commonly used when you need to perform so-called domain relaxation. Imagine your page is `www.yahoo.com` and inside it you have an iframe hosted on `music.yahoo.com` subdomain. These are two separate domains so the browser's security restrictions won't allow the page and the iframe to communicate. To resolve this you can set `document.domain` on both pages to `yahoo.com` and they'll be able to talk to each other.

Note, that you can only set the domain to a less-specific one, for example, you can change `www.yahoo.com` to `yahoo.com`, but you cannot change `yahoo.com` to `www.yahoo.com` or any other non-yahoo domain.

```
> document.domain;
  "www.yahoo.com"

> document.domain = 'yahoo.com';
  "yahoo.com"

> document.domain = 'www.yahoo.com';
  Error: SecurityError: DOM Exception 18

> document.domain = 'www.example.org';
  Error: SecurityError: DOM Exception 18
```

Previously in this chapter, you saw the `window.location` object. Well, the same functionality is also available as `document.location`:

```
> window.location === document.location;
  true
```

Events

Imagine you are listening to a radio program and they announce, "Big event! Huge! Aliens have landed on Earth!" You might think "Yeah, whatever", some other listeners might think "They come in peace" and some "We're all gonna die!". Similarly, the browser broadcasts events and your code could be notified should it decide to tune in and listen to the events as they happen. Some example events include:

- The user clicks a button
- The user types a character in a form field
- The page finishes loading

You can attach a JavaScript function (called an event listener or event handler) to a specific event and the browser will invoke your function as soon the event occurs. Let's see how this is done.

Inline HTML attributes

Adding specific attributes to a tag is the laziest (but the least maintainable) way, for example:

```
<div onclick="alert('Ouch!')">click</div>
```

In this case when the user clicks on the `<div>`, the click event fires and the string of JavaScript code contained in the `onclick` attribute is executed. There's no explicit function that listens to the click event, but behind the scenes a function is still created and it contains the code you specified as a value of the `onclick` attribute.

Element Properties

Another way to have some code executed when a click event fires is to assign a function to the `onclick` property of a DOM node element. For example:

```
<div id="my-div">click</div>
<script>
  var myelement = document.getElementById('my-div');
  myelement.onclick = function () {
    alert('Ouch!');
    alert('And double ouch!');
  };
</script>
```

This way is better because it helps you keep your `<div>` clean of any JavaScript code. Always keep in mind that HTML is for content, JavaScript for behavior, and CSS for formatting, and you should keep these three separate as much as possible.

This method has the drawback that you can attach only one function to the event, as if the radio program has only one listener. It's true that you can have a lot happening inside the same function, but this is not always convenient, as if all the radio listeners are in the same room.

DOM event listeners

The best way to work with browser events is to use the event listener approach outlined in DOM Level 2, where you can have many functions listening to an event. When the event fires, all functions are executed. All of the listeners don't need to know about each other and can work independently. They can tune in and out at any time without affecting the other listeners.

Let's use the same simple markup from the previous section (available for you to play with at `http://www.phpied.com/files/jsoop/ch7.html`). It has this piece of markup as follows:

```
<p id="closer">final</p>
```

Your JavaScript code can assign listeners to the click event using the `addEventListener()` method. Let's attach two listeners as follows:

```
var mypara = document.getElementById('closer');
mypara.addEventListener('click', function () {
  alert('Boo!');
}, false);
mypara.addEventListener(
  'click', console.log.bind(console), false);
```

As you can see, `addEventListeners()` is a method called on the node object and accepts the type of event as its first parameter and a function pointer as its second. You can use anonymous functions such as `function () { alert('Boo!'); }` or existing functions such as `console.log`. The listener functions you specify are called when the event happens and an argument is passed to them. This argument is an event object. If you run the preceding code and click on the last paragraph, you can see event objects being logged to the console. Clicking on an event object allows you to see its properties:

```
Elements   Resources   Network   Sources
▼MouseEvent {webkitMovementY: 0, webkitMovementX: 0
  altKey: false
  bubbles: true
  button: 0
  cancelBubble: false
  cancelable: true
  charCode: 0
  clientX: 19
  clientY: 92
  clipboardData: undefined
  ctrlKey: false
  currentTarget: null
  dataTransfer: null
  defaultPrevented: false
  detail: 1
  eventPhase: 0
  fromElement: null
  keyCode: 0
  layerX: 19
  layerY: 92
  metaKey: false
  offsetX: 11
  offsetY: 8
  pageX: 19
  pageY: 92
  relatedTarget: null
  returnValue: true
  screenX: 254
  screenY: 186
  shiftKey: false
  ▶srcElement: <p>
  ▶target: <p>
  timeStamp: 1356056143153
  ▶toElement: <p>
  type: "click"
  ▶view: Window
  webkitMovementX: 0
  webkitMovementY: 0
  which: 1
  x: 19
  y: 92
  ▶__proto__: MouseEvent
>
```

Capturing and bubbling

In the calls to `addEventListener()`, there was a third parameter, `false`. Let's see what is it for.

Say you have a link inside an unordered list as follows:

```
<body>
  <ul>
    <li><a href="http://phpied.com">my blog</a></li>
  </ul>
</body>
```

When you click on the link, you're actually also clicking on the list item `<li>`, the list `<ul>`, the `<body>`, and eventually the document as a whole. This is called event propagation. A click on a link can also be seen as click on the document. The process of propagating an event can be implemented in two ways:

- Event capturing: The click happens on the document first, then it propagates down to the body, the list, the list item, and finally to the link
- Event bubbling: The click happens on the link and then bubbles up to the document

DOM Level 2 events specification suggests that the events propagate in three phases, namely, capturing, at target, and bubbling. This means that the event propagates from the document to the link (target) and then bubbles back up to the document. The event objects have an `eventPhase` property, which reflects the current phase:

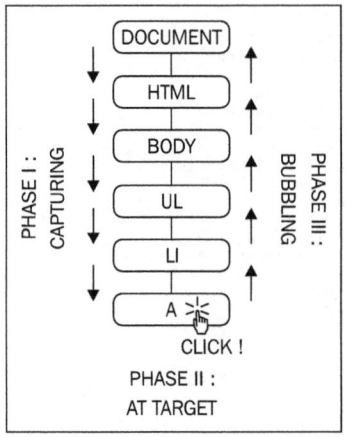

Historically, IE and Netscape (working on their own and without a standard to follow) implemented the exact opposites. IE implemented only bubbling, Netscape only capturing. Today, long after the DOM specification, modern browsers implement all three phases.

The practical implications related to the event propagation are as follows:

- The third parameter to `addEventListener()` specifies whether or not capturing should be used. In order to have your code more portable across browsers, it's better to always set this parameter to `false` and use bubbling only.
- You can stop the propagation of the event in your listeners so that it stops bubbling up and never reaches the document. To do this you can call the `stopPropagation()` method of the event object (there is an example in the next section).
- You can also use event delegation. If you have ten buttons inside a `<div>`, you can always attach ten event listeners, one for each button. But a smarter thing to do is to attach only one listener to the wrapping `<div>` and once the event happens, check which button was the target of the click.

As a side note, there is a way to use event capturing in old IEs too (using `setCapture()` and `releaseCapture()` methods) but only for mouse events. Capturing any other events (keystroke events for example) is not supported.

Stop propagation

Let's see an example of how you can stop the event from bubbling up. Going back to the test document, there is this piece of code:

```
<p id="closer">final</p>
```

Let's define a function that handles clicks on the paragraph:

```
function paraHandler() {
  alert('clicked paragraph');
}
```

Now, let's attach this function as a listener to the click event:

```
var para = document.getElementById('closer');
para.addEventListener('click', paraHandler, false);
```

Let's also attach listeners to the click event on the body, the document, and the browser window:

```
document.body.addEventListener('click', function () {
  alert('clicked body');
}, false);
document.addEventListener('click', function () {
  alert('clicked doc');
```

```
}, false);
window.addEventListener('click', function () {
  alert('clicked window');
}, false);
```

Note, that the DOM specifications don't say anything about events on the window. And why would they, since DOM deals with the document and not the browser. So browsers implement window events inconsistently.

Now, if you click on the paragraph, you'll see four alerts saying:

- clicked paragraph
- clicked body
- clicked doc
- clicked window

This illustrates how the same single click event propagates (bubbles up) from the target all the way up to the window.

The opposite of `addEventLister()` is `removeEventListener()` and it accepts exactly the same parameters. Let's remove the listener attached to the paragraph.

```
> para.removeEventListener('click', paraHandler, false);
```

If you try now, you'll see alerts only for the click event on the body, document, and window, but not on the paragraph.

Now, let's stop the propagation of the event. The function you add as a listener receives the event object as a parameter and you can call the `stopPropagation()` method of that event object as follows:

```
function paraHandler(e) {
  alert('clicked paragraph');
  e.stopPropagation();
}
```

Adding the modified listener is done as follows:

```
para.addEventListener('click', paraHandler, false);
```

Now, when you click on the paragraph you see only one alert because the event doesn't bubble up to the body, the document, or the window.

Note, that when you remove a listener, you have to pass a pointer to the same function you previously attached. Otherwise doing the following does not work because the second argument is a new function, not the same you passed when adding the event listener, even if the body is exactly the same:

```
document.body.removeEventListener('click',
  function () {
    alert('clicked body');
  },
false); //  does NOT remove the handler
```

Prevent default behavior

Some browser events have a predefined behavior. For example, clicking a link causes the browser to navigate to another page. You can attach listeners to clicks on a link and you can also disable the default behavior by calling the method `preventDefault()` on the event object.

Let's see how you can annoy your visitors by asking "Are you sure you want to follow this link?" every time they click a link. If the user clicks on **Cancel** (causing `confirm()` to return `false`), the `preventDefault()` method is called as follows:

```
// all links
var all_links = document.getElementsByTagName('a');
for (var i = 0; i < all_links.length; i++) { // loop all links
  all_links[i].addEventListener(
    'click',        // event type
    function (e) { // handler
      if (!confirm('Sure you want to follow this link?')) {
        e.preventDefault();
      }
    },
    false // don't use capturing
  );
}
```

Note, that not all events allow you to prevent the default behavior. Most do, but if you want to be sure, you can check the `cancellable` property of the event object.

Cross-browser event listeners

As you already know, most modern browsers almost fully implement the DOM Level 1 specification. However, the events were not standardized until DOM 2. As a result, there are quite a few differences in how IE before version 9 implements this functionality compared to modern browsers.

Check out an example that causes the `nodeName` of a clicked element (the target element) to be written to the console:

```
document.addEventListener('click', function (e) {
  console.log(e.target.nodeName);
}, false);
```

Now, let's take a look at how IE is different:

- In IE there's no `addEventListener()` method, although since IE Version 5 there is an equivalent `attachEvent()`. For earlier versions, your only choice is accessing the property (such as `onclick`) directly.
- `click` event becomes `onclick` when using `attachEvent()`.
- If you listen to events the old-fashioned way (for example, by setting a function value to the `onclick` property), when the callback function is invoked, it doesn't get an event object passed as a parameter. But, regardless of how you attach the listener in IE, there is always a global object `window.event` that points to the latest event.
- In IE the event object doesn't get a `target` attribute telling you the element on which the event fired, but it does have an equivalent property called `srcElement`.
- As mentioned before, event capturing doesn't apply to all events, so only bubbling should be used.
- There's no `stopPropagation()` method, but you can set the IE-only `cancelBubble` property to `true`.
- There's no `preventDefault()` method, but you can set the IE-only `returnValue` property to `false`.
- To stop listening to an event, instead of `removeEventListener()` in IE you'll need `detachEvent()`.

So, here's the revised version of the previous code that works across browsers:

```
function callback(evt) {
  // prep work
  evt = evt || window.event;
```

```
    var target = evt.target || evt.srcElement;

    // actual callback work
    console.log(target.nodeName);
  }

  //  start listening for click events
  if (document.addEventListener) { // Modern browsers
    document.addEventListener('click', callback, false);
  } else if (document.attachEvent) { // old IE
    document.attachEvent('onclick', callback);
  } else {
    document.onclick = callback; // ancient
  }
```

Types of events

Now you know how to handle cross-browser events. But all of the examples above used only click events. What other events are happening out there? As you can probably guess, different browsers provide different events. There is a subset of cross-browser events and some browser-specific ones. For a full list of events, you should consult the browser's documentation, but here's a selection of cross-browser events:

- Mouse events
  - mouseup, mousedown, click (the sequence is mousedown-up-click), dblclick
  - mouseover (mouse is over an element), mouseout (mouse was over an element but left it), mousemove
- Keyboard events
  - keydown, keypress, keyup (occur in this sequence)
- Loading/window events
  - load (an image or a page and all of its components are done loading), unload (user leaves the page), beforeunload (the script can provide the user with an option to stop the unload)
  - abort (user stops loading the page or an image in IE), error (a JavaScript error, also when an image cannot be loaded in IE)
  - resize (the browser window is resized), scroll (the page is scrolled), contextmenu (the right-click menu appears)

- Form events
  - focus (enter a form field), blur (leave the form field)
  - change (leave a field after the value has changed), select (select text in a text field)
  - reset (wipe out all user input), submit (send the form)

Additionally, modern browsers provide drag events (dragstart, dragend, drop, and others) and touch devices provide touchstart, touchmove, and touchend.

This concludes the discussion of events. Refer to the exercise section at the end of this chapter for a little challenge of creating your own event utility to handle cross-browser events.

XMLHttpRequest

`XMLHttpRequest()` is an object (a constructor function) that allows you to send HTTP requests from JavaScript. Historically, `XMLHttpRequest` (or XHR for short) was introduced in IE and was implemented as an ActiveX object. Starting with IE7 it's a native browser object, the same way as it's in the other browsers. The common implementation of this object across browsers gave birth to the so-called Ajax applications, where it's no longer necessary to refresh the whole page every time you need new content. With JavaScript, you can make an HTTP request to the server, get the response, and update only a part of the page. This way you can build much more responsive and desktop-like web pages.

Ajax stands for **Asynchronous JavaScript and XML**.

- Asynchronous because after sending an HTTP request your code doesn't need to wait for the response, but it can do other stuff and be notified (through an event) when the response arrives.
- JavaScript because it's obvious that XHR objects are created with JavaScript.
- XML because initially developers were making HTTP requests for XML documents and were using the data contained in them to update the page. This is no longer a common practice, though, as you can request data in plain text, in the much more convenient JSON format, or simply as HTML ready to be inserted into the page.

There are two steps to using the `XMLHttpRequest`:

- **Send the request**: This includes creating an `XMLHttpRequest` object and attaching an event listener
- **Process the response**: Your event listener gets notified that the response has arrived and your code gets busy doing something amazing with the response

Sending the request

In order to create an object you simply use the following code (let's deal with browser inconsistencies in just a bit):

```
var xhr = new XMLHttpRequest();
```

The next thing is to attach an event listener to the `readystatechange` event fired by the object:

```
xhr.onreadystatechange = myCallback;
```

Then, you need to call the `open()` method, as follows:

```
xhr.open('GET', 'somefile.txt', true);
```

The first parameter specifies the type of HTTP request (`GET`, `POST`, `HEAD`, and so on). `GET` and `POST` are the most common. Use `GET` when you don't need to send much data with the request and your request doesn't modify (write) data on the server, otherwise use `POST`. The second parameter is the URL you are requesting. In this example, it's the text file `somefile.txt` located in the same directory as the page. The last parameter is a boolean specifying whether the request is asynchronous (`true`, always prefer this) or not (`false`, blocks all the JavaScript execution and waits until the response arrives).

The last step is to fire off the request which is done as follows:

```
xhr.send('');
```

The method `send()` accepts any data you want to send with the request. For `GET` requests, this is an empty string, because the data is in the URL. For `POST` request, it's a query string in the form `key=value&key2=value2`.

At this point, the request is sent and your code (and the user) can move on to other tasks. The callback function `myCallback` will be invoked when the response comes back from the server.

Processing the response

A listener is attached to the `readystatechange` event. So what exactly is the ready state and how does it change?

There is a property of the XHR object called `readyState`. Every time it changes, the `readystatechange` event fires. The possible values of the `readyState` property are as follows:

- 0-uninitialized
- 1-loading
- 2-loaded
- 3-interactive
- 4-complete

When `readyState` gets the value of 4, it means the response is back and ready to be processed. In `myCallback` after you make sure `readyState` is 4, the other thing to check is the status code of the HTTP request. You might have requested a non-existing URL for example and get a 404 (File not found) status code. The interesting code is the 200 (OK) code, so `myCallback` should check for this value. The status code is available in the `status` property of the XHR object.

Once `xhr.readyState` is 4 and `xhr.status` is 200, you can access the contents of the requested URL using the `xhr.responseText` property. Let's see how `myCallback` could be implemented to simply `alert()` the contents of the requested URL:

```
function myCallback() {

  if (xhr.readyState < 4) {
    return; // not ready yet
  }

  if (xhr.status !== 200) {
    alert('Error!'); // the HTTP status code is not OK
    return;
  }

  //  all is fine, do the work
  alert(xhr.responseText);
}
```

Once you've received the new content you requested, you can add it to the page, or use it for some calculations, or for any other purpose you find suitable.

Overall, this two-step process (send request and process response) is the core of the whole XHR/Ajax functionality. Now that you know the basics, you can move on to building the next Gmail. Oh yes, let's have a look at some minor browser inconsistencies.

Creating XMLHttpRequest objects in IE prior to Version 7

In Internet Explorer prior to version 7, the `XMLHttpRequest` object was an ActiveX object, so creating an XHR instance is a little different. It goes like the following:

```
var xhr = new ActiveXObject('MSXML2.XMLHTTP.3.0');
```

MSXML2.XMLHTTP.3.0 is the identifier of the object you want to create. There are several versions of the `XMLHttpRequest` object and if your page visitor doesn't have the latest one installed, you can try two older ones, before you give up.

For a fully-cross-browser solution, you should first test to see if the user's browser supports `XMLHttpRequest` as a native object, and if not, try the IE way. Therefore, the whole process of creating an XHR instance could be like this:

```
var ids = ['MSXML2.XMLHTTP.3.0',
           'MSXML2.XMLHTTP',
           'Microsoft.XMLHTTP'];

var xhr;
if (XMLHttpRequest) {
  xhr = new XMLHttpRequest();
} else {
  // IE: try to find an ActiveX object to use
  for (var i = 0; i < ids.length; i++) {
    try {
      xhr = new ActiveXObject(ids[i]);
      break;
    } catch (e) {}
  }
}
```

What is this doing? The array `ids` contains a list of ActiveX program IDs to try. The variable `xhr` points to the new XHR object. The code first checks to see if `XMLHttpRequest` exists. If so, this means that the browser supports `XMLHttpRequest()` natively (so the browser is relatively modern). If it is not, the code loops through `ids` trying to create an object. `catch(e)` quietly ignores failures and the loop continues. As soon as an `xhr` object is created, you `break` out of the loop.

As you can see, this is quite a bit of code so it's best to abstract it into a function. Actually, one of the exercises at the end of the chapter prompts you to create your own Ajax utility.

A is for Asynchronous

Now you know how to create an XHR object, give it a URL and handle the response to the request. What happens when you send two requests asynchronously? What if the response to the second request comes before the first?

In the example above, the XHR object was global and `myCallback` was relying on the presence of this global object in order to access its `readyState`, `status`, and `responseText` properties. Another way, which prevents you from relying on global variables, is to wrap the callback in a closure. Let's see how:

```
var xhr = new XMLHttpRequest();

xhr.onreadystatechange = (function (myxhr) {
  return function () {
    myCallback(myxhr);
  };
}(xhr));

xhr.open('GET', 'somefile.txt', true);
xhr.send('');
```

In this case `myCallback()` receives the XHR object as a parameter and is not going to look for it in the global space. This also means that at the time the response is received, the original `xhr` might have been reused for a second request. The closure keeps pointing to the original object.

X is for XML

Although these days JSON (discussed in the next chapter) is preferred over XML as a data transfer format, XML is still an option. In addition to the `responseText` property, the XHR objects also have another property called `responseXML`. When you send an HTTP request for an XML document, `responseXML` points to an XML DOM document object. To work with this document, you can use all of the core DOM methods discussed previously in this chapter, such as `getElementsByTagName()`, `getElementById()`, and so on.

An example

Let's wrap up the different XHR topics with an example. You can visit the page located at `http://www.phpied.com/files/jsoop/xhr.html` to work on the example yourself:

The main page, `xhr.html`, is a simple static page that contains nothing but three `<div>` tags.

```
<div id="text">Text will be here</div>
<div id="html">HTML will be here</div>
<div id="xml">XML will be here</div>
```

Using the console, you can write code that requests three files and loads their respective contents into each `<div>`.

The three files to load are:

- `content.txt`: a simple text file containing the text "I am a text file"
- `content.html`: a file containing HTML code `"I am <strong>formatted</strong> <em>HTML</em>"`
- `content.xml`: an XML file, containing the following code:

```
<?xml version="1.0" ?>
<root>
    I'm XML data.
</root>
```

All of the files are stored in the same directory as `xhr.html`.

For security reasons you can only use the original `XMLHttpRequest` to request files that are on the same domain. However, modern browsers support XHR2 which lets you make cross-domain requests, provided that the appropriate Access-Control-Allow-Origin HTTP header is in place.

First, let's create a function to abstract the request/response part:

```
function request(url, callback) {
  var xhr = new XMLHttpRequest();
  xhr.onreadystatechange = (function (myxhr) {
    return function () {
      if (myxhr.readyState === 4 && myxhr.status === 200) {
        callback(myxhr);
      }
    };
```

```
    }(xhr));
    xhr.open('GET', url, true);
    xhr.send('');
  }
```

This function accepts a URL to request and a callback function to call once the response arrives. Let's call the function three times, once for each file, as follows:

```
request(
  'http://www.phpied.com/files/jsoop/content.txt',
  function (o) {
    document.getElementById('text').innerHTML =
      o.responseText;
  }
);
request(
  'http://www.phpied.com/files/jsoop/content.html',
  function (o) {
    document.getElementById('html').innerHTML =
      o.responseText;
  }
);
request(
  'http://www.phpied.com/files/jsoop/content.xml',
  function (o) {
    document.getElementById('xml').innerHTML =
      o.responseXML
       .getElementsByTagName('root')[0]
       .firstChild
       .nodeValue;
  }
);
```

The callback functions are defined inline. The first two are identical. They just replace the HTML of the corresponding `<div>` with the contents of the requested file. The third one is a little different as it deals with the XML document. First, you access the XML DOM object as `o.responseXML`. Then, using `getElementsByTagName()` you get a list of all `<root>` tags (there is only one). The `firstChild` of `<root>` is a text node and `nodeValue` is the text contained in it ("I'm XML data"). Then just replace the HTML of `<div id="xml">` with the new content. The result is shown on the following screenshot:

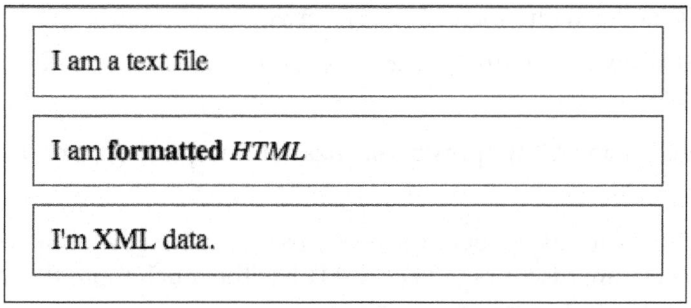

When working with the XML document, you can also use `o.responseXML.documentElement` to get to the `<root>` element, instead of `o.responseXML.getElementsByTagName('root')[0]`. Remember that `documentElement` gives you the root node of an XML document. The root in HTML documents is always the `<html>` tag.

Summary

You learned quite a bit in this chapter. You have learned some cross-browser BOM (Browser Object Model) objects:

- Properties of the global `window` object such as `navigator`, `location`, `history`, `frames`, `screen`
- Methods such as `setInterval()` and `setTimeout()`; `alert()`, `confirm()` and `prompt()`; `moveTo/By()` and `resizeTo/By()`

Then you learned about the DOM (Document Object Model), an API to represent an HTML (or XML) document as a tree structure where each tag or text is a node on the tree. You also learned how to do the following actions:

- Access nodes
  - Using parent/child relationship properties `parentNode`, `childNodes`, `firstChild`, `lastChild`, `nextSibling`, and `previousSibling`
  - Using `getElementsById()`, `getElementsByTagName()`, `getElementsByName()`, and `querySelectorAll()`
- Modify nodes:
  - Using `innerHTML` or `innerText/textContent`
  - Using `nodeValue` or `setAttribute()` or just using attributes as object properties

- Remove nodes with `removeChild()` or `replaceChild()`
- And add new ones with `appendChild()`, `cloneNode()`, and `insertBefore()`

You also learned some DOM0 (prestandardization) properties, ported to DOM Level 1:

- Collections such as `document.forms`, `images`, `links`, `anchors`, `applets`. Using these are discouraged as DOM1 has the much more flexible method `getElementsByTagName()`.
- `document.body` which gives you convenient access to `<body>`.
- `document.title`, `cookie`, `referrer`, and `domain`.

Next, you learned about how the browser broadcasts events that you can listen to. It's not straightforward to do this in a cross-browser manner, but it's possible. Events bubble up, so you can use event delegation to listen to events more globally. You can also stop the propagation of events and interfere with the default browser behavior.

Finally, you learned about the `XMLHttpRequest` object that allows you to build responsive web pages that do the following tasks:

- Make HTTP requests to the server to get pieces of data
- Process the response to update portions of the page

Exercises

In the previous chapters, the solutions to the exercises could be found in the text of the chapter. This time, some of the exercises require you to do some more reading (or experimentation) outside this book.

1. BOM: As a BOM exercise, try coding something wrong, obtrusive, user-unfriendly, and all in all, very Web 1.0, the shaking browser window. Try implementing code that opens a 200 x 200 pop up window and then resizes it slowly and gradually to 400 x 400. Next, move the window around as if there's an earthquake. All you'll need is one of the `move*()` functions, one or more calls to `setInterval()`, and maybe one to `setTimeout()`/`clearInterval()` to stop the whole thing. Or here's an easier one, print the current date/time in the `document.title` and update it every second, like a clock.
2. DOM:
    - Implement `walkDOM()` differently. Also make it accept a callback function instead of hard coding `console.log()`

- Removing content with `innerHTML` is easy (`document.body.innerHTML = ''`), but not always best. The problem will be when there are event listeners attached to the removed elements, they won't be removed in IE causing the browser to leak memory, because it stores references to something that doesn't exist. Implement a general-purpose function that deletes DOM nodes, but removes any event listeners first. You can loop through the attributes of a node and check if the value is a function. If it is, it's most likely an attribute like `onclick`. You need to set it to `null` before removing the element from the tree.
- Create a function called `include()` that includes external scripts on demand. This means you need to create a new `<script>` tag dynamically, set its `src` attribute and append to the document's `<head>`. Test by using the following code:

```
> include('somescript.js');
```

3. Events:

   Create an event utility (object) called `myevent` which has the following methods working cross-browser:

   - `addListener(element, event_name, callback)` where `element` could also be an array of elements
   - `removeListener(element, event_name, callback)`
   - `getEvent(event)` just to check for a `window.event` for older versions of IE
   - `getTarget(event)`
   - `stopPropagation(event)`
   - `preventDefault(event)`

   Usage example:

```
function myCallback(e) {
  e = myevent.getEvent(e);
  alert(myevent.getTarget(e).href);
  myevent.stopPropagation(e);
  myevent.preventDefault(e);
}
myevent.addListener(document.links, 'click', myCallback);
```

   The result of the example code should be that all of the links in the document lead nowhere but only alert the `href` attribute.

Create an absolutely positioned `<div>`, say at `x = 100px`, `y = 100px`. Write the code to be able to move the div around the page using the arrow keys or the keys *J* (left), *K* (right), *M* (down), and *I* (up). Reuse your own event utility from 3.1.

4. XMLHttpRequest

   Create your own XHR utility (object) called `ajax`. For example, have a look at the following code:

```
function myCallback(xhr) {
  alert(xhr.responseText);
}
ajax.request('somefile.txt', 'get', myCallback);
ajax.request('script.php', 'post', myCallback,
             'first=John&last=Smith');
```

8

Coding and Design Patterns

Now that you know all about the objects in JavaScript, you've mastered prototypes and inheritance, and you have seen some practical examples of using browser-specific objects, let's move forward, or rather move a level up. Let's have a look at some common JavaScript patterns.

But first, what's pattern? In short, a pattern is a good solution to a common problem.

Sometimes when you're facing a new programming problem, you may recognize right away that you've previously solved another, suspiciously similar problem. In such cases, it's worth isolating this class of problems and searching for a common solution. A pattern is a proven and reusable solution (or an approach to a solution) to a class of problems.

There are cases where a pattern is nothing more than an idea or a name. Sometimes just using a name helps you think more clearly about a problem. Also, when working with other developers in a team, it's much easier to communicate when everybody uses the same terminology to discuss a problem or a solution.

Other times you may come across a unique problem that doesn't look like anything you've seen before and doesn't readily fit into a known pattern. Blindly applying a pattern just for the sake of using a pattern is not a good idea. It's preferable to not use any known pattern than to try to tweak your problem so that it fits an existing solution.

This chapter talks about two types of patterns:

- **Coding patterns**: These are mostly JavaScript-specific best practices
- **Design patterns**: These are language-independent patterns, popularized by the famous "Gang of Four" book

Coding patterns

Let's start with some patterns that reflect JavaScript's unique features. Some patterns aim to help you organize your code (for example, namespacing), others are related to improving performance (such as lazy definitions and init-time branching), and some make up for missing features such as private properties. The patterns discussed in this section include:

- Separating behavior
- Namespaces
- Init-time branching
- Lazy definition
- Configuration objects
- Private variables and methods
- Privileged methods
- Private functions as public methods
- Immediate functions
- Chaining
- JSON

Separating behavior

As discussed previously, the three building blocks of a web page are as follows:

- Content (HTML)
- Presentation (CSS)
- Behavior (JavaScript)

Content

HTML is the content of the web page, the actual text. Ideally, the content should be marked up using the least amount of HTML tags that sufficiently describe the semantic meaning of that content. For example, if you're working on a navigation menu it's a good idea to use `<ul>` and `<li>` since a navigation menu is in essence just a list of links.

Your content (HTML) should be free from any formatting elements. Visual formatting belongs to the presentation layer and should be achieved through the use of **Cascading Style Sheets** (**CSS**). This means the following:

- The `style` attribute of HTML tags should not be used, if possible.
- Presentational HTML tags such as `<font>` should not be used at all.
- Tags should be used for their semantic meaning, not because of how browsers render them by default. For instance, developers sometimes use a `<div>` tag where a `<p>` would be more appropriate. It's also favorable to use `<strong>` and `<em>` instead of `<b>` and `<i>` as the latter describe the visual presentation rather than the meaning.

Presentation

A good approach to keep presentation out of the content is to reset, or nullify all browser defaults. For example, using `reset.css` from the Yahoo! UI library. This way the browser's default rendering won't distract you from consciously thinking about the proper semantic tags to use.

Behavior

The third component of a web page is the behavior. Behavior should be kept separate from both the content and the presentation. Behavior is usually added by using JavaScript that is isolated to `<script>` tags, and preferably contained in external files. This means not using any inline attributes such as `onclick`, `onmouseover`, and so on. Instead, you can use the `addEventListener/attachEvent` methods from the previous chapter.

The best strategy for separating behavior from content is as follows:

- Minimize the number of `<script>` tags
- Avoid inline event handlers
- Do not use CSS expressions
- Dynamically add markup that has no purpose if JavaScript is disabled by the user
- Towards the end of your content when you are ready to close the `<body>` tag, insert a single `external.js` file

Example of separating behavior

Let's say you have a search form on a page and you want to validate the form with JavaScript. So, you go ahead and keep the form tags free from any JavaScript, and then immediately before the closing the `</body>` tag you insert a `<script>` tag which links to an external file as follows:

```
<body>
  <form id="myform" method="post" action="server.php">
  <fieldset>
    <legend>Search</legend>
    <input
      name="search"
      id="search"
      type="text"
    />
    <input type="submit" />
    </fieldset>
  </form>
  <script src="behaviors.js"></script>
</body>
```

In `behaviors.js` you attach an event listener to the submit event. In your listener, you check to see if the text input field was left blank and if so, stop the form from being submitted. This way you save a round trip between the server and the client and make the application immediately responsive.

The content of `behaviors.js` is given in the following code. It assumes that you've created your `myevent` utility from the exercise at the end of the previous chapter:

```
// init
myevent.addListener('myform', 'submit', function (e) {
  // no need to propagate further
  e = myevent.getEvent(e);
  myevent.stopPropagation(e);
  // validate
  var el = document.getElementById('search');
  if (!el.value) { // too bad, field is empty
    myevent.preventDefault(e); // prevent the form submission
    alert('Please enter a search string');
  }
});
```

Asynchronous JavaScript loading

You noticed how the script was loaded at the end of the HTML right before closing the body. The reason is that JavaScript blocks the DOM construction of the page and in some browsers even the downloads of the other components that follow. By moving the scripts to the bottom of the page you ensure the script is out of the way and when it arrives, it simply enhances the already usable page.

Another way to prevent external JavaScript files from blocking the page is to load them asynchronously. This way you can start loading them earlier. HTML5 has the `defer` attribute for this purpose:

```
<script defer src="behaviors.js"></script>
```

Unfortunately, the `defer` attribute is not supported by older browsers, but luckily, there is a solution that works across browsers, old and new. The solution is to create a script node dynamically and append it to the DOM. In other words you use a bit of inline JavaScript to load the external JavaScript file. You can have this script loader snippet at the top of your document so that the download has an early start:

```
...
<head>
(function () {
  var s = document.createElement('script');
  s.src = 'behaviors.js';
  document.getElementsByTagName('head')[0].appendChild(s);
}());
</head>
...
```

Namespaces

Global variables should be avoided in order to reduce the possibility of variable naming collisions. You can minimize the number of globals by namespacing your variables and functions. The idea is simple, you create only one global object and all your other variables and functions become properties of that object.

An Object as a namespace

Let's create a global object called `MYAPP`:

```
// global namespace
var MYAPP = MYAPP || {};
```

Now, instead of having a global `myevent` utility (from the previous chapter), you can have it as an `event` property of the `MYAPP` object as follows:

```
// sub-object
MYAPP.event = {};
```

Adding the methods to the `event` utility is still the same:

```
// object together with the method declarations
MYAPP.event = {
  addListener: function (el, type, fn) {
    // .. do the thing
  },
  removeListener: function (el, type, fn) {
    // ...
  },
  getEvent: function (e) {
    // ...
  }
  // ... other methods or properties
};
```

Namespaced constructors

Using a namespace doesn't prevent you from creating constructor functions. Here is how you can have a DOM utility that has an `Element` constructor, which allows you to create DOM elements easier:

```
MYAPP.dom = {};
MYAPP.dom.Element = function (type, properties) {
  var tmp = document.createElement(type);
  for (var i in properties) {
    if (properties.hasOwnProperty(i)) {
      tmp.setAttribute(i, properties[i]);
    }
  }
  return tmp;
};
```

Similarly, you can have a `Text` constructor to create text nodes:

```
MYAPP.dom.Text = function (txt) {
  return document.createTextNode(txt);
};
```

Using the constructors to create a link at the bottom of a page can be done as follows:

```
var link = new MYAPP.dom.Element('a',
  {href: 'http://phpied.com', target: '_blank'});
var text = new MYAPP.dom.Text('click me');
link.appendChild(text);
document.body.appendChild(link);
```

A namespace() method

You can create a namespace utility that makes your life easier so that you can use more convenient syntax:

```
MYAPP.namespace('dom.style');
```

Instead of the more verbose syntax as follows:

```
MYAPP.dom = {};
MYAPP.dom.style = {};
```

Here's how you can create such a `namespace()` method. First, you create an array by splitting the input string using the period (.) as a separator. Then, for every element in the new array, you add a property to your global object, if one doesn't already exist as follows:

```
var MYAPP = {};
MYAPP.namespace = function (name) {
  var parts = name.split('.');
  var current = MYAPP;
  for (var i = 0; i < parts.length; i++) {
    if (!current[parts[i]]) {
      current[parts[i]] = {};
    }
    current = current[parts[i]];
  }
};
```

Testing the new method is done as follows:

```
MYAPP.namespace('event');
MYAPP.namespace('dom.style');
```

The result of the preceding code is the same as if you did the following:

```
var MYAPP = {
  event: {},
  dom: {
    style: {}
  }
};
```

Init-time branching

In the previous chapter you noticed that sometimes different browsers have different implementations for the same or similar functionalities. In such cases, you need to branch your code depending on what's supported by the browser currently executing your script. Depending on your program this branching can happen far too often and, as a result, may slow down the script execution.

You can mitigate this problem by branching some parts of the code during initialization, when the script loads, rather than during runtime. Building upon the ability to define functions dynamically, you can branch and define the same function with a different body depending on the browser. Let's see how.

First, let's define a namespace and placeholder method for the `event` utility:

```
var MYAPP = {};
MYAPP.event = {
  addListener: null,
  removeListener: null
};
```

At this point, the methods to add or remove a listener are not implemented. Based on the results from feature sniffing, these methods can be defined differently as follows:

```
if (window.addEventListener) {
  MYAPP.event.addListener = function (el, type, fn) {
    el.addEventListener(type, fn, false);
  };
  MYAPP.event.removeListener = function (el, type, fn) {
    el.removeEventListener(type, fn, false);
  };
} else if (document.attachEvent) { // IE
  MYAPP.event.addListener = function (el, type, fn) {
    el.attachEvent('on' + type, fn);
  };
  MYAPP.event.removeListener = function (el, type, fn) {
```

```
      el.detachEvent('on' + type, fn);
    };
  } else { // older browsers
    MYAPP.event.addListener = function (el, type, fn) {
      el['on' + type] = fn;
    };
    MYAPP.event.removeListener = function (el, type) {
      el['on' + type] = null;
    };
  }
```

After this script executes, you have the `addListener()` and `removeListener()` methods defined in a browser-dependent way. Now, every time you invoke one of these methods there's no more feature-sniffing and it results in less work and faster execution.

One thing to watch out for when sniffing features is not to assume too much after checking for one feature. In the previous example this rule is broken because the code only checks for `addEventListener` support but then defines both `addListener()` and `removeListener()`. In this case it's probably safe to assume that if a browser implements `addEventListener()` it also implements `removeEventListener()`. But, imagine what happens if a browser implements `stopPropagation()` but not `preventDefault()` and you haven't checked for these individually. You have assumed that because `addEventListener()` is not defined, the browser must be an old IE and write your code using your knowledge and assumptions of how IE works. Remember that all of your knowledge is based on the way a certain browser works today, but not necessarily the way it will work tomorrow. So to avoid many rewrites of your code as new browser versions are shipped, it's best to individually check for features you intend to use and don't generalize on what a certain browser supports.

Lazy definition

The lazy definition pattern is similar to the previous init-time branching pattern. The difference is that the branching happens only when the function is called for the first time. When the function is called, it redefines itself with the best implementation. Unlike the init-time branching where the if happens once, during loading, here it may not happen at all in cases when the function is never called. The lazy definition also makes the initialization process lighter as there's no init-time branching work to be done.

Let's see an example that illustrates this via the definition of an `addListener()` function. The function is first defined with a generic body. It checks which functionality is supported by the browser when it's called for the first time and then redefines itself using the most suitable implementation. At the end of the first call, the function calls itself so that the actual event attaching is performed. The next time you call the same function it will be defined with its new body and be ready for use, so no further branching is necessary. Following is the code snippet:

```
var MYAPP = {};
MYAPP.myevent = {
  addListener: function (el, type, fn) {
    if (el.addEventListener) {
      MYAPP.myevent.addListener = function (el, type, fn) {
        el.addEventListener(type, fn, false);
      };
    } else if (el.attachEvent) {
      MYAPP.myevent.addListener = function (el, type, fn) {
        el.attachEvent('on' + type, fn);
      };
    } else {
      MYAPP.myevent.addListener = function (el, type, fn) {
        el['on' + type] = fn;
      };
    }
    MYAPP.myevent.addListener(el, type, fn);
  }
};
```

Configuration object

This pattern is convenient when you have a function or method that accepts a lot of optional parameters. It's up to you to decide how many constitutes a lot. But generally, a function with more than three parameters is not convenient to call because you have to remember the order of the parameters, and it is even more inconvenient when some of the parameters are optional.

Instead of having many parameters, you can use one parameter and make it an object. The properties of the object are the actual parameters. This is suitable for passing configuration options because these tend to be numerous and optional (with smart defaults). The beauty of using a single object as opposed to multiple parameters is described as follows:

- The order doesn't matter
- You can easily skip parameters that you don't want to set

- It's easy to add more optional configuration attributes
- It makes the code more readable because the configuration object's properties are present in the calling code along with their names

Imagine you have some sort of UI widget constructor you use to create fancy buttons. It accepts the text to put inside the button (the `value` attribute of the `<input>` tag) and an optional parameter of the `type` of button. For simplicity let's say the fancy button takes the same configuration as a regular button. Have a look at the following code:

```
// a constructor that creates buttons
MYAPP.dom.FancyButton = function (text, type) {
  var b = document.createElement('input');
  b.type = type || 'submit';
  b.value = text;
  return b;
};
```

Using the constructor is simple; you just give it a string. Then you can add the new button to the body of the document:

```
document.body.appendChild(
  new MYAPP.dom.FancyButton('puuush')
);
```

This is all well and works fine, but then you decide you also want to be able to set some of the style properties of the button such as colors and fonts. You can end up with a definition like the following:

```
MYAPP.dom.FancyButton =
  function (text, type, color, border, font) {
  // ...
};
```

Now, using the constructor can become a little inconvenient, especially when you want to set the third and fifth parameter, but not the second or the fourth:

```
new MYAPP.dom.FancyButton(
  'puuush', null, 'white', null, 'Arial');
```

A better approach is to use one config object parameter for all the settings. The function definition can become something like the following:

```
MYAPP.dom.FancyButton = function (text, conf) {
  var type = conf.type || 'submit';
  var font = conf.font || 'Verdana';
  // ...
};
```

Using the constructor is given as follows:

```
var config = {
  font: 'Arial, Verdana, sans-serif',
  color: 'white'
};
new MYAPP.dom.FancyButton('puuush', config);
```

Another usage example is as follows:

```
document.body.appendChild(
  new MYAPP.dom.FancyButton('dude', {color: 'red'})
);
```

As you can see, it's easy to set only some of the parameters and to switch around their order. In addition, the code is friendlier and easier to understand when you see the names of the parameters at the same place where you call the method.

A drawback of this pattern is the same as its strength. It's trivial to keep adding more parameters, which means trivial to abuse the technique. Once you have an excuse to add to this free-for-all bag of properties, you will find it tempting to keep adding some that are not entirely optional or some that are dependent on other properties.

As a rule of thumb, all these properties should be independent and optional. If you have to check all possible combinations inside your function ("oh, A is set, but A is only used if B is also set") this is a recipe for a large function body, which quickly becomes confusing and difficult, if not impossible, to test, because of all the combinations.

Private properties and methods

JavaScript doesn't have the notion of access modifiers, which set the privileges of the properties in an object. Other languages often have access modifiers such as:

- Public—all users of an object can access these properties (or methods)
- Private—only the object itself can access these properties
- Protected—only objects inheriting the object in question can access these properties

JavaScript doesn't have a special syntax to denote private properties or methods, but as discussed in *Chapter 3, Functions*, you can use local variables and methods inside a function and achieve the same level of protection.

Continuing with the example of the `FancyButton` constructor, you can have a local variable styles which contains all the defaults, and a local `setStyle()` function. These are invisible to the code outside of the constructor. Here's how `FancyButton` can make use of the local private properties:

```
var MYAPP = {};
MYAPP.dom = {};
MYAPP.dom.FancyButton = function (text, conf) {
  var styles = {
    font: 'Verdana',
    border: '1px solid black',
    color: 'black',
    background: 'grey'
  };
  function setStyles(b) {
    var i;
    for (i in styles) {
      if (styles.hasOwnProperty(i)) {
        b.style[i] = conf[i] || styles[i];
      }
    }
  }
  conf = conf || {};
  var b = document.createElement('input');
  b.type = conf.type || 'submit';
  b.value = text;
  setStyles(b);
  return b;
};
```

In this implementation, `styles` is a private property and `setStyle()` is a private method. The constructor uses them internally (and they can access anything inside the constructor), but they are not available to code outside of the function.

Privileged methods

Privileged methods (this term was coined by Douglas Crockford) are normal public methods that can access private methods or properties. They can act like a bridge in making some of the private functionality accessible but in a controlled manner, wrapped in a privileged method.

Private functions as public methods

Let us say you've defined a function that you absolutely need to keep intact, so you make it private. But, you also want to provide access to the same function so that outside code can also benefit from it. In this case, you can assign the private function to a publicly available property.

Let's define `_setStyle()` and `_getStyle()` as private functions, but then assign them to the public `setStyle()` and `getStyle()`:

```
var MYAPP = {};
MYAPP.dom = (function () {
  var _setStyle = function (el, prop, value) {
    console.log('setStyle');
  };
  var _getStyle = function (el, prop) {
    console.log('getStyle');
  };
  return {
    setStyle: _setStyle,
    getStyle: _getStyle,
    yetAnother: _setStyle
  };
}());
```

Now, when you call `MYAPP.dom.setStyle()`, it invokes the private `_setStyle()` function. You can also overwrite `setStyle()` from the outside:

```
MYAPP.dom.setStyle = function () {alert('b');};
```

Now, the result is as follows:

- `MYAPP.dom.setStyle` points to the new function
- `MYAPP.dom.yetAnother` still points to `_setStyle()`
- `_setStyle()` is always available when any other internal code relies on it to be working as intended, regardless of the outside code

When you expose something private, keep in mind that objects (and functions and arrays are objects too) are passed by reference and, therefore, can be modified from the outside.

Immediate functions

Another pattern that helps you keep the global namespace clean is to wrap your code in an anonymous function and execute that function immediately. This way any variables inside the function are local (as long as you use the `var` statement) and are destroyed when the function returns, if they aren't part of a closure. This pattern was discussed in more detail in *Chapter 3, Functions*. Have a look at the following code:

```
(function () {
  // code goes here...
}());
```

This pattern is especially suitable for on-off initialization tasks performed when the script loads.

The immediate (self-executing) function pattern can be extended to create and return objects. If the creation of these objects is more complicated and involves some initialization work, then you can do this in the first part of the self-executable function and return a single object, which can access and benefit from any private properties in the top portion as follows:

```
var MYAPP = {};
MYAPP.dom = (function () {
  // initialization code...
  function _private() {
    // ...
  }
  return {
    getStyle: function (el, prop) {
      console.log('getStyle');
      _private();
    },
    setStyle: function (el, prop, value) {
      console.log('setStyle');
    }
  };
}());
```

Modules

Combining several of the previous patterns, gives you a new pattern, commonly referred to as a module pattern. The concept of modules in programming is convenient as it allows you to code separate pieces or libraries and combine them as needed just like pieces of a puzzle.

Two notable facts beyond the scope of this chapter

JavaScript doesn't have a built-in concept of modules, although this is planned for the future via `export` and `import` declarations. There is also the module specification from `http://www.commonjs.org`, which defines a `require()` function and an `exports` object.

The module pattern includes:

- Namespaces to reduce naming conflicts among modules
- An immediate function to provide a private scope and initialization
- Private properties and methods
- Returning an object that has the public API of the module as follows:

```
namespace('MYAPP.module.amazing');

MYAPP.module.amazing = (function () {

  // short names for dependencies
  var another = MYAPP.module.another;

  // local/private variables
  var i, j;

  // private functions
  function hidden() {}

  // public API
  return {
    hi: function () {
      return "hello";
    }
  };
}());
```

And using the following module:

```
MYAPP.module.amazing.hi(); // "hello"
```

Chaining

Chaining is a pattern that allows you to invoke multiple methods on one line as if the methods are the links in a chain. This is convenient when calling several related methods. You invoke the next method on the result of the previous without the use of an intermediate variable.

Say you've created a constructor that helps you work with DOM elements. The code to create a new `<span>` and add it to the `<body>` could look something like the following:

```
var obj = new MYAPP.dom.Element('span');
obj.setText('hello');
obj.setStyle('color', 'red');
obj.setStyle('font', 'Verdana');
document.body.appendChild(obj);
```

As you know, constructors return the object referred to as `this` that they create. You can make your methods such as `setText()` and `setStyle()` also return `this`, which allows you to call the next method on the instance returned by the previous one. This way you can chain method calls:

```
var obj = new MYAPP.dom.Element('span');
obj.setText('hello')
   .setStyle('color', 'red')
   .setStyle('font', 'Verdana');
document.body.appendChild(obj);
```

You don't even need the `obj` variable if you don't plan on using it after the new element has been added to the tree, so the code looks like the following:

```
document.body.appendChild(
  new MYAPP.dom.Element('span')
    .setText('hello')
    .setStyle('color', 'red')
    .setStyle('font', 'Verdana')
);
```

A drawback of this pattern is that it makes it a little harder to debug when an error occurs somewhere in a long chain and you don't know which link is to blame because they are all on the same line.

JSON

Let's wrap up the coding patterns section of this chapter with a few words about JSON. JSON is not technically a coding pattern, but you can say that using JSON is a good pattern.

JSON is a popular lightweight format for exchanging data. It's often preferred over XML when using `XMLHttpRequest()` to retrieve data from the server. **JSON** stands for **JavaScript Object Notation** and there's nothing specifically interesting about it other than the fact that it's extremely convenient. The JSON format consists of data defined using object, and array literals. Here is an example of a JSON string that your server could respond with after an XHR request:

```
{
  'name':   'Stoyan',
  'family': 'Stefanov',
  'books':  ['OOJS', 'JSPatterns', 'JS4PHP']
}
```

An XML equivalent of this would be something like the following:

```
<?xml version="1.1" encoding="iso-8859-1"?>
<response>
  <name>Stoyan</name>
  <family>Stefanov</family>
  <books>
    <book>OOJS</book>
    <book>JSPatterns</book>
    <book>JS4PHP</book>
  </books>
</response>
```

First, you can see how JSON is lighter in terms of the number of bytes. But, the main benefit is not the smaller byte size but the fact that it's trivial to work with JSON in JavaScript. Let's say you've made an XHR request and have received a JSON string in the `responseText` property of the XHR object. You can convert this string of data into a working JavaScript object by simply using `eval()`:

```
// warning: counter-example
var response = eval('(' + xhr.responseText + ')');
```

Now, you can access the data in obj as object properties:

```
console.log(response.name); // "Stoyan"
console.log(response.books[2]); // "JS4PHP"
```

The problem is that `eval()` is insecure, so it's best if you use the JSON object to parse the JSON data (a fallback for older browsers is available from `http://json.org/`). Creating an object from a JSON string is still trivial:

```
var response = JSON.parse(xhr.responseText);
```

To do the opposite, that is, to convert an object to a JSON string, you use the method `stringify()`:

```
var str = JSON.stringify({hello: "you"});
```

Due to its simplicity, JSON has quickly become popular as a language-independent format for exchanging data and you can easily produce JSON on the server side using your preferred language. In PHP, for example, there are the functions `json_encode()` and `json_decode()` that let you serialize a PHP array or object into a JSON string and vice versa.

Design patterns

The second part of this chapter presents a JavaScript approach to a subset of the design patterns introduced by the book called *Design Patterns: Elements of Reusable Object-Oriented Software*, an influential book most commonly referred to as the *Book of Four* or the *Gang of Four*, or *GoF* (after its four authors). The patterns discussed in the *GoF* book are divided into three groups:

- Creational patterns that deal with how objects are created (instantiated)
- Structural patterns that describe how different objects can be composed in order to provide new functionality
- Behavioral patterns that describe ways for objects to communicate with each other

There are 23 patterns in the *Book of Four* and more patterns have been identified since the book's publication. It's way beyond the scope of this book to discuss all of them, so the remainder of the chapter demonstrates only four, along with examples of their implementation in JavaScript. Remember that the patterns are more about interfaces and relationships rather than implementation. Once you have an understanding of a design pattern, it's often not difficult to implement it, especially in a dynamic language such as JavaScript.

The patterns discussed through the rest of the chapter are:

- Singleton
- Factory
- Decorator
- Observer

Singleton

Singleton is a creational design pattern meaning that its focus is on creating objects. It helps when you want to make sure there is only one object of a given kind (or class). In a classical language this would mean that an instance of a class is only created once and any subsequent attempts to create new objects of the same class would return the original instance.

In JavaScript, because there are no classes, a singleton is the default and most natural pattern. Every object is a singleton object.

The most basic implementation of the singleton in JavaScript is the object literal:

```
var single = {};
```

That was easy, right?

Singleton 2

If you want to use class-like syntax and still implement the singleton pattern, things become a bit more interesting. Let's say you have a constructor called `Logger()` and you want to be able to do something like the following:

```
var my_log = new Logger();
my_log.log('some event');

// ... 1000 lines of code later in a different scope ...

var other_log = new Logger();
other_log.log('some new event');
console.log(other_log === my_log); // true
```

The idea is that although you use `new`, only one instance needs to be created, and this instance is then returned in consecutive calls.

Global variable

One approach would be to use a global variable to store the single instance. Your constructor could look like this:

```
function Logger() {
  if (typeof global_log === "undefined") {
    global_log = this;
  }
  return global_log;
}
```

Using this constructor gives the expected result:

```
var a = new Logger();
var b = new Logger();
console.log(a === b); // true
```

The drawback is, obviously, the use of a global variable. It can be overwritten at any time, even accidentally, and you lose the instance. The opposite, your global variable overwriting someone else's is also possible.

Property of the Constructor

As you know, functions are objects and they have properties. You can assign the single instance to a property of the constructor function as follows:

```
function Logger() {
  if (Logger.single_instance) {
    Logger.single_instance = this;
  }
  return Logger.single_instance;
}
```

If you write `var a = new Logger()`, `a` points to the newly created `Logger.single_instance` property. A subsequent call `var b = new Logger()` results in `b` pointing to the same `Logger.single_instance` property, which is exactly what you want.

This approach certainly solves the global namespace issue because no global variables are created. The only drawback is that the property of the `Logger` constructor is publicly visible, so it can be overwritten at any time. In such cases, the single instance can be lost or modified. Of course, you can only provide so much protection against fellow programmers shooting themselves in the foot. After all, if someone can mess with the single instance property, they can mess up the `Logger` constructor directly, as well.

In a private property

The solution to the problem of overwriting the publicly visible property is not to use a public property but a private one. You already know how to protect variables with a closure, so as an exercise you can implement this approach to the singleton pattern.

Factory

The factory is another creational design pattern as it deals with creating objects. The factory can help when you have similar types of objects and you don't know in advance which one you want to use. Based on user input or other criteria, your code determines the type of object it needs on the fly.

Let's say you have three different constructors, which implement similar functionality. All the objects they create take a URL but do different things with it. One creates a text DOM node, the second creates a link, and the third an image as follows:

```
var MYAPP = {};
MYAPP.dom = {};
MYAPP.dom.Text = function (url) {
  this.url = url;
  this.insert = function (where) {
    var txt = document.createTextNode(this.url);
    where.appendChild(txt);
  };
};
MYAPP.dom.Link = function (url) {
  this.url = url;
  this.insert = function (where) {
    var link = document.createElement('a');
    link.href = this.url;
    link.appendChild(document.createTextNode(this.url));
    where.appendChild(link);
  };
};
MYAPP.dom.Image = function (url) {
  this.url = url;
  this.insert = function (where) {
    var im = document.createElement('img');
    im.src = this.url;
    where.appendChild(im);
  };
};
```

Using the three different constructors is exactly the same, pass the `url` and call the `insert()` method:

```
var url = 'http://www.phpied.com/images/covers/oojs.jpg';

var o = new MYAPP.dom.Image(url);
o.insert(document.body);

var o = new MYAPP.dom.Text(url);
o.insert(document.body);

var o = new MYAPP.dom.Link(url);
o.insert(document.body);
```

Imagine your program doesn't know in advance which type of object is required. The user decides, during runtime, by clicking on a button for example. If `type` contains the required type of object, you'll need to use an `if` or a `switch`, and do something like this:

```
var o;
if (type === 'Image') {
  o = new MYAPP.dom.Image(url);
}
if (type === 'Link') {
  o = new MYAPP.dom.Link(url);
}
if (type === 'Text') {
  o = new MYAPP.dom.Text(url);
}
o.url = 'http://...';
o.insert();
```

This works fine, but if you have a lot of constructors, the code becomes too lengthy and hard to maintain. Also, if you are creating a library or a framework that allows extensions or plugins, you don't even know the exact names of all the constructor functions in advance. In such cases, it's convenient to have a factory function that takes care of creating an object of the dynamically determined type:

Let's add a factory method to the `MYAPP.dom` utility:

```
MYAPP.dom.factory = function (type, url) {
  return new MYAPP.dom[type](url);
};
```

Now, you can replace the three `if` functions with the simpler code as follows:

```
var image = MYAPP.dom.factory("Image", url);
image.insert(document.body);
```

The example `factory()` method in the previous code was simple, but in a real life scenario you'd want to do some validation against the `type` value (for example, check if `MYAPP.dom[type]` exists) and optionally do some setup work common to all object types (for example, setup the URL all constructors use).

Decorator

The Decorator design pattern is a structural pattern; it doesn't have much to do with how objects are created but rather how their functionality is extended. Instead of using inheritance where you extend in a linear way (parent-child-grandchild), you can have one base object and a pool of different decorator objects that provide extra functionality. Your program can pick and choose which decorators it wants and in which order. For a different program or code path, you might have a different set of requirements and pick different decorators out of the same pool. Take a look at how the usage part of the decorator pattern could be implemented:

```
var obj = {
  doSomething: function () {
    console.log('sure, asap');
  }
  // ...
};
obj = obj.getDecorator('deco1');
obj = obj.getDecorator('deco13');
obj = obj.getDecorator('deco5');
obj.doSomething();
```

You can see how you can start with a simple object that has a `doSomething()` method. Then you can pick one of the decorator objects you have lying around and can be identified by name. All decorators provide a `doSomething()` method which first calls the same method of the previous decorator and then proceeds with its own code. Every time you add a decorator, you overwrite the base `obj` with an improved version of it. At the end, when you are finished adding decorators, you call `doSomething()`. As a result all of the `doSomething()` methods of all the decorators are executed in sequence. Let's see an example.

Decorating a Christmas tree

Let's illustrate the decorator pattern with an example of decorating a Christmas tree. You start with the `decorate()` method as follows:

```
var tree = {};
tree.decorate = function () {
  alert('Make sure the tree won\'t fall');
};
```

Now, let's implement a `getDecorator()` method which adds extra decorators. The decorators will be implemented as constructor functions, and they'll all inherit from the base `tree` object:

```
tree.getDecorator = function (deco) {
  tree[deco].prototype = this;
  return new tree[deco];
};
```

Now, let's create the first decorator, `RedBalls()`, as a property of `tree` (in order to keep the global namespace cleaner). The red ball objects also provide a `decorate()` method, but they make sure they call their parent's `decorate()` first:

```
tree.RedBalls = function () {
  this.decorate = function () {
    this.RedBalls.prototype.decorate();
    alert('Put on some red balls');
  };
};
```

Similarly, implementing `BlueBalls()` and `Angel()` decorators:

```
tree.BlueBalls = function () {
  this.decorate = function () {
    this.BlueBalls.prototype.decorate();
    alert('Add blue balls');
  };
};
tree.Angel = function () {
  this.decorate = function () {
    this.Angel.prototype.decorate();
    alert('An angel on the top');
  };
};
```

Now, let's add all of the decorators to the base object:

```
tree = tree.getDecorator('BlueBalls');
tree = tree.getDecorator('Angel');
tree = tree.getDecorator('RedBalls');
```

Finally, running the `decorate()` method:

```
tree.decorate();
```

This single call results in the following alerts (in this order):

- Make sure the tree won't fall
- Add blue balls
- An angel on the top
- Add some red balls

As you see, this functionality allows you to have as many decorators as you like, and to choose and combine them in any way you like.

Observer

The observer pattern (also known as the subscriber-publisher pattern) is a behavioral pattern, which means that it deals with how different objects interact and communicate with each other. When implementing the observer pattern you have the following objects:

- One or more publisher objects that announce when they do something important.
- One or more subscribers tuned in to one or more publishers. They listen to what the publishers announce and then act appropriately.

The observer pattern may look familiar to you. It sounds similar to the browser events discussed in the previous chapter, and rightly so, because the browser events are one example application of this pattern. The browser is the publisher, it announces the fact that an event (such as a click) has happened. Your event listener functions that are subscribed to (listen to) this type of event will be notified when the event happens. The browser-publisher sends an event object to all of the subscribers. In your custom implementations you can send any type of data you find appropriate.

There are two subtypes of the observer pattern, push and pull. Push is where the publishers are responsible for notifying each subscriber, and pull is where the subscribers monitor for changes in a publisher's state.

Let's take a look at an example implementation of the push model. Let's keep the observer-related code into a separate object and then use this object as a mix-in, adding its functionality to any other object that decides to be a publisher. In this way any object can become a publisher and any function can become a subscriber. The observer object will have the following properties and methods:

- An array of `subscribers` that are just callback functions
- `addSubscriber()` and `removeSubscriber()` methods that add to, and remove from, the subscribers collection
- A `publish()` method that takes data and calls all subscribers, passing the data to them
- A `make()` method that takes any object and turns it into a publisher by adding all of the methods mentioned previously to it

Here's the observer mix-in object, which contains all the subscription-related methods and can be used to turn any object into a publisher:

```
var observer = {
  addSubscriber: function (callback) {
    if (typeof callback === "function") {
      this.subscribers[this.subscribers.length] = callback;
    }
  },
  removeSubscriber: function (callback) {
    for (var i = 0; i < this.subscribers.length; i++) {
      if (this.subscribers[i] === callback) {
        delete this.subscribers[i];
      }
    }
  },
  publish: function (what) {
    for (var i = 0; i < this.subscribers.length; i++) {
      if (typeof this.subscribers[i] === 'function') {
        this.subscribers[i](what);
      }
    }
  },
  make: function (o) { // turns an object into a publisher
    for (var i in this) {
      if (this.hasOwnProperty(i)) {
        o[i] = this[i];
        o.subscribers = [];
      }
    }
  }
};
```

Now, let's create some publishers. A publisher can be any object and its only duty is to call the `publish()` method whenever something important occurs. Here's a `blogger` object which calls `publish()` every time a new blog posting is ready:

```
var blogger = {
  writeBlogPost: function() {
    var content = 'Today is ' + new Date();
    this.publish(content);
  }
};
```

Another object could be the LA Times newspaper which calls `publish()` when a new newspaper issue is out:

```
var la_times = {
  newIssue: function() {
    var paper = 'Martians have landed on Earth!';
    this.publish(paper);
  }
};
```

Turning these objects into publishers:

```
observer.make(blogger);
observer.make(la_times);
```

Now, let's have two simple objects `jack` and `jill`:

```
var jack = {
  read: function(what) {
    console.log("I just read that " + what)
  }
};
var jill = {
  gossip: function(what) {
    console.log("You didn't hear it from me, but " + what)
  }
};
```

`jack` and `jill` can subscribe to the `blogger` object by providing the callback methods they want to be called when something is published:

```
blogger.addSubscriber(jack.read);
blogger.addSubscriber(jill.gossip);
```

What happens now when the `blogger` writes a new post? The result is that `jack` and `jill` get notified:

```
> blogger.writeBlogPost();
```

I just read that Today is Fri Jan 04 2013 19:02:12 GMT-0800 (PST)
You didn't hear it from me, but Today is Fri Jan 04 2013 19:02:12 GMT-0800 (PST)

At any time, `jill` may decide to cancel her subscription. Then, when writing another blog post, the unsubscribed object is no longer notified:

```
> blogger.removeSubscriber(jill.gossip);
> blogger.writeBlogPost();
```

I just read that Today is Fri Jan 04 2013 19:03:29 GMT-0800 (PST)

`jill` may decide to subscribe to LA Times as an object can be a subscriber to many publishers:

```
> la_times.addSubscriber(jill.gossip);
```

Then, when LA Times publishes a new issue, `jill` gets notified and `jill.gossip()` is executed:

```
> la_times.newIssue();
```

You didn't hear it from me, but Martians have landed on Earth!

Summary

In this chapter, you learned about common JavaScript coding patterns and learned how to make your programs cleaner, faster, and better at working with other programs and libraries. Then you saw a discussion and sample implementations of a handful of the design patterns from the *Book of Four*. You can see how JavaScript is a fully featured dynamic programming language and that implementing classical patterns in a dynamic loosely typed language is pretty easy. The patterns are, in general, a large topic and you can join the author of this book in a further discussion of the JavaScript patterns at the website `JSPatterns.com` or take a look at the book appropriately named "JavaScript Patterns".

A
Reserved Words

This appendix provides two lists of reserved keywords as defined in ECMAScript 5 (ES5). The first one is the current list of words, and the second is the list of words reserved for future implementations.

There's also a list of words that are no longer reserved, although they used to be in ES3.

You cannot use reserved words as variable names:

```
var break = 1; // syntax error
```

If you use these words as object properties, you have to quote them:

```
var o = {break: 1};    // OK in many browsers, error in IE
var o = {"break": 1}; // Always OK
alert(o.break);        // error in IE
alert(o["break"]);     // OK
```

Keywords

The list of words currently reserved in ES5 is as follows:

`break`

`case`

`catch`

`continue`

`debugger`

`default`

`delete`

```
do
else
finally
for
function
if
in
instanceof
new
return
switch
this
throw
try
typeof
var
void
while
with
```

Future reserved words

These keywords are not currently used, but are reserved for future versions of the language.

- `class`
- `const`
- `enum`
- `export`
- `extends`
- `implements`

- `import`
- `interface`
- `let`
- `package`
- `private`
- `protected`
- `public`
- `static`
- `super`
- `yield`

Previously reserved words

These words are no longer reserved starting with ES5, but best to stay away for the sake of older browsers.

- `abstract`
- `boolean`
- `byte`
- `char`
- `double`
- `final`
- `float`
- `goto`
- `int`
- `long`
- `native`
- `short`
- `synchronized`
- `throws`
- `transient`
- `volatile`

B

Built-in Functions

This appendix contains a list of the built-in functions (methods of the global object), discussed in *Chapter 3, Functions*.

Function	Description

`parseInt()`	Takes two parameters: an input object and radix; then tries to return an integer representation of the input. Doesn't handle exponents in the input. The default radix is `10` (a decimal number). Returns `NaN` on failure. Omitting the radix may lead to unexpected results (for example for inputs such as `08`), so it's best to always specify it.
	`> parseInt('10e+3');`
	10
	`> parseInt('FF');`
	NaN
	`> parseInt('FF', 16);`
	255

`parseFloat()`	Takes a parameter and tries to return a floating-point number representation of it. Understands exponents in the input.
	`> parseFloat('10e+3');`
	10000
	`> parseFloat('123.456test');`
	123.456

Function	Description

`isNaN()`	Abbreviated from "Is Not a Number". Accepts a parameter and returns `true` if the parameter is not a valid number, `false` otherwise. Attempts to convert the input to a number first.
	`> isNaN(NaN);`
	true
	`> isNaN(123);`
	false
	`> isNaN(parseInt('FF'));`
	true
	`> isNaN(parseInt('FF', 16));`
	false

`isFinite()`	Returns `true` if the input is a number (or can be converted to a number), but is not the number `Infinity` or `-Infinity`. Returns `false` for infinity or non-numeric values.
	`> isFinite(1e+1000);`
	false
	`> isFinite(-Infinity);`
	false
	`> isFinite("123");`
	true

`encodeURIComponent()`	Converts the input into a URL-encoded string. For more details on how URL encoding works, refer to the Wikipedia article at `http://en.wikipedia.org/wiki/Url_encode`.
	`> encodeURIComponent ('http://phpied.com/');`
	"http%3A%2F%2Fphpied.com%2F"
	`> encodeURIComponent ('some script?key=v@lue');`
	"some%20script%3Fkey%3Dv%40lue"

`decodeURIComponent()`	Takes a URL-encoded string and decodes it. `> decodeURIComponent('%20%40%20');` **" @ "**

Function	Description

`encodeURI()`	URL-encodes the input, but assumes a full URL is given, so returns a valid URL by not encoding the protocol (for example, `http://`) and hostname (for example, `www.phpied.com`).
	`> encodeURI('http://phpied.com/');`
	"http://phpied.com/"
	`> encodeURI('some script?key=v@lue');`
	"some%20script?key=v@lue"

`decodeURI()`	Opposite of `encodeURI()`. `> decodeURI("some%20script?key=v@lue");` **"some script?key=v@lue"**

`eval()`	Accepts a string of JavaScript code and executes it. Returns the result of the last expression in the input string.
	To be avoided where possible.
	`> eval('1 + 2');`
	3
	`> eval('parseInt("123")');`
	123
	`> eval('new Array(1, 2, 3)');`
	[1, 2, 3]
	`> eval('new Array(1, 2, 3); 1 + 2;');`
	3

C
Built-in Objects

This Appendix lists the built-in constructor functions outlined in the **ECMAScript (ES)** standard, together with the properties and methods of the objects created by these constructors. ES5-specific APIs are listed separately.

Object

`Object()` is a constructor that creates objects, for example:

```
> var o = new Object();
```

This is the same as using the object literal:

```
> var o = {}; // recommended
```

You can pass anything to the constructor and it will try to guess what it is and use a more appropriate constructor. For example, passing a string to `new Object()` will be the same as using the `new String()` constructor. This is not a recommended practice (it's better to be explicit than let guesses creep in), but still possible.

```
> var o = new Object('something');
> o.constructor;
function String() { [native code] }

> var o = new Object(123);
> o.constructor;
function Number() { [native code] }
```

All other objects, built-in or custom, inherit from `Object`. So, the properties and methods listed in the following sections apply to all types of objects.

Members of the Object constructor

Have a look at the following table:

Property/method	Description

`Object.prototype`	The prototype of all objects (also an object itself). Anything you add to this prototype will be inherited by all other objects, so be careful.
	`> var s = new String('noodles');`
	`> Object.prototype.custom = 1;`
	1
	`> s.custom;`
	1

The Object.prototype members

Have a look at the following table:

Property/method	Description

`constructor`	Points back to the constructor function used to create the object, in this case, `Object`.
	`> Object.prototype.constructor === Object;`
	true
	`> var o = new Object();`
	`> o.constructor === Object;`
	true

`toString(radix)`	Returns a string representation of the object. If the object happens to be a `Number` object, the radix parameter defines the base of the returned number. The default radix is `10`.
	`> var o = {prop: 1};`
	`> o.toString();`
	"[object Object]"
	`> var n = new Number(255);`
	`> n.toString();`
	"255"
	`> n.toString(16);`
	"ff"

Property/method	Description
`toLocaleString()`	The same as `toString()`, but matching the current locale. Meant to be customized by objects, such as `Date()`, `Number()`, and `Array()` and provide locale-specific values, such as different date formatting. In the case of `Object()` instances as with most other cases, it just calls `toString()`. In browsers, you can figure out the language using the property `language` (or `userLanguage` in IE) of the navigator BOM object: `> navigator.language;` **"en-US"**

`valueOf()`	Returns a primitive representation of `this`, if applicable. For example, `Number` objects return a primitive number and `Date` objects return a timestamp. If no suitable primitive makes sense, it simply returns `this`.
	
	`> var o = {};`
	`> typeof o.valueOf();`
	"object"
	`> o.valueOf() === o;`
	true
	`> var n = new Number(101);`
	`> typeof n.valueOf();`
	"number"
	`> n.valueOf() === n;`
	false
	`> var d = new Date();`
	`> typeof d.valueOf();`
	"number"
	`> d.valueOf();`
	1357840170137

Property/method	Description

`hasOwnProperty(prop)`	Returns `true` if a property is an own property of the object, or `false` if it was inherited from the prototype chain. Also returns `false` if the property doesn't exist.
	`> var o = {prop: 1};`
	`> o.hasOwnProperty('prop');`
	true
	`> o.hasOwnProperty('toString');`
	false
	`> o.hasOwnProperty('fromString');`
	false

`isPrototypeOf(obj)`	Returns `true` if an object is used as a prototype of another object. Any object from the prototype chain can be tested, not only the direct creator.
	`> var s = new String('');`
	`> Object.prototype.isPrototypeOf(s);`
	true
	`> String.prototype.isPrototypeOf(s);`
	true
	`> Array.prototype.isPrototypeOf(s);`
	false

`propertyIsEnumerable(prop)`	Returns `true` if a property shows up in a `for-in` loop.
	`> var a = [1, 2, 3];`
	`> a.propertyIsEnumerable('length');`
	false
	`> a.propertyIsEnumerable(0);`
	true

ECMAScript 5 additions to Object

In ECMAScript 3 all object properties can be changed, added, or deleted at any time, except for a few built-in properties (for example, `Math.PI`). In ES5 you have the ability to define properties that cannot be changed or deleted—a privilege previously reserved for built-ins. ES5 introduces the concept of **property descriptors** that give you tighter control over the properties you define.

Think of a property descriptor as an object that specifies the features of a property. The syntax to describe these features is a regular object literal, so property descriptors have properties and methods of their own, but let's call them **attributes** to avoid confusion. The attributes are:

- `value` - what you get when you access the property
- `writable` - can you change this property
- `enumerable` - should it appear in `for-in` loops
- `configurable` - can you delete it
- `set()` - a function called any time you update the value
- `get()` - called when you access the value of the property

Further, there's a distinction between **data descriptors** (you define the properties `enumerable`, `configurable`, `value`, and `writable`) and **accessor descriptors** (you define `enumerable`, `configurable`, `set()`, and `get()`). If you define `set()` or `get()`, the descriptor is considered an accessor and attempting to define value or writable will raise an error.

Defining a regular old school ES3-style property:

```
var person = {};
person.legs = 2;
```

The same using an ES5 data descriptor:

```
var person = {};
Object.defineProperty(person, "legs", {
  value: 2,
  writable: true,
  configurable: true,
  enumerable: true
});
```

The value of `value` if set to `undefined` by default, all others are `false`. So, you need to set them to `true` explicitly if you want to be able to change this property later.

Or, the same property using an ES5 accessor descriptor:

```
var person = {};
Object.defineProperty(person, "legs", {
  set: function (v) {this.value = v;},
  get: function (v) {return this.value;},
  configurable: true,
  enumerable: true
});
person.legs = 2;
```

As you can see property descriptors are a lot more code, so you only use them if you really want to prevent someone from mangling your property, and also you forget about backwards compatibility with ES3 browsers because, unlike additions to `Array.prototype` for example, you cannot "shim" this feature in old browsers.

And the power of the descriptors in action (defining a nonmalleable property):

```
> var person = {};
> Object.defineProperty(person, 'heads', {value: 1});
> person.heads = 0;
0

> person.heads;
1

> delete person.heads;
false

> person.heads;
1
```

The following is a list of all ES5 additions to `Object`:

Property/method	Description

`Object.getPrototypeOf(obj)`	While in ES3 you have to guess what is the prototype of a given object using the method `Object.prototype.isPrototypeOf()`, in ES5 you can directly ask "Who is your prototype?"
	`> Object.getPrototypeOf([]) ===`
	`Array.prototype;`
	true

Property/method	Description

`Object.create(obj, descr)`	Discussed in *Chapter 6, Inheritance*. Creates a new object, sets its prototype and defines properties of that object using property descriptors (discussed earlier).
	`> var parent = {hi: 'Hello'};`
	`> var o = Object.create(parent, {`
	`  prop: {`
	`  value: 1`
	`  }`
	`  });`
	`> o.hi;`
	"Hello"
	It even lets you create a completely blank object, something you cannot do in ES3.
	`> var o = Object.create(null);`
	`> typeof o.toString;`
	"undefined"

`Object.getOwnPropertyDescriptor(obj, property)`	Allows you to inspect how a property was defined. You can even peek into the built-ins and see all these previously hidden attributes.
	`> Object.getOwnPropertyDescriptor(`
	`  Object.prototype, 'toString');`
	Object
	configurable: true
	enumerable: false
	value: function toString() { [native code] }
	writable: true

`Object.getOwnPropertyNames(obj)`	Returns an array of all own property names (as strings), enumerable or not. Use `Object.keys()` to get only enumerable ones.
	`> Object.getOwnPropertyNames(`
	`  Object.prototype);`
	["constructor", "toString", "toLocaleString", "valueOf",...

`Object.defineProperty(obj, descriptor)`	Defines a property of an object using a property descriptor. See the discussion preceding this table.

Property/method	Description

`Object.defineProperties(obj, descriptors)`	The same as `defineProperty()`, but lets you define multiple properties at once.
	`> var glass = Object.defineProperties({}, {`
	`"color": {`
	`value: "transparent",`
	`writable: true`
	`},`
	`"fullness": {`
	`value: "half",`
	`writable: false`
	`}`
	`});`
	`> glass.fullness;`
	"half"

`Object.preventExtensions(obj)`
 	
`Object.isExtensible(obj)`
	`preventExtensions()` disallows adding further properties to an object and `isExtensible()` checks whether you can add properties.
	`> var deadline = {};`
	`> Object.isExtensible(deadline);`
	true
	`> deadline.date = "yesterday";`
	"yesterday"
	`> Object.preventExtensions(deadline);`
	`> Object.isExtensible(deadline);`
	false
	`> deadline.date = "today";`
	"today"
	`> deadline.date;`
	"today"
	Attempting to add properties to a non-extensible object is not an error, but simply doesn't work:
	`> deadline.report = true;`
	`> deadline.report;`
	undefined

Property/method	Description

`Object.seal(obj)`
 	
`Object.isSealed(obj)`
	`seal()` does the same as `preventExtensions ()` and additionally makes all existing properties non-configurable.
	
	This means you *can* change the value of an existing property, but you *cannot* delete it or reconfigure it (using `defineProperty()` won't work). So you cannot, for example, make an enumerable property non-enumerable.

`Object.freeze(obj)`
 	
`Object.isFrozen(obj)`
	Everything that `seal()` does plus prevents changing the values of properties.
	
	`> var deadline = Object.freeze(`
	`  {date: "yesterday"});`
	`> deadline.date = "tomorrow";`
	`> deadline.excuse = "lame";`
	`> deadline.date;`
	"yesterday"
	`> deadline.excuse;`
	undefined
	`> Object.isSealed(deadline);`
	true

`Object.keys(obj)`	An alternative to a `for-in` loop. Returns only own properties (unlike `for-in`). The properties need to be enumerable in order to show up (unlike `Object.getOwnPropertyNames()`). The return value is an array of strings.
	
	`> Object.prototype.customProto = 101;`
	`> Object.getOwnPropertyNames(`
	`  Object.prototype);`
	["constructor", "toString", ..., "customProto"]
	`> Object.keys(Object.prototype);`
	["customProto"]
	`> var o = {own: 202};`
	`> o.customProto;`
	`101`
	`> Object.keys(o);`
	["own"]

Array

The `Array` constructor creates array objects:

```
> var a = new Array(1, 2, 3);
```

This is the same as the array literal:

```
> var a = [1, 2, 3]; //recommended
```

When you pass only one numeric value to the `Array` constructor, it's assumed to be the array length.

```
> var un = new Array(3);
> un.length;
3
```

You get an array with the desired length and if you ask for the value of each of the array elements, you get `undefined`.

```
> un;
[undefined, undefined, undefined]
```

There is a subtle difference between an array full of elements and an array with no elements, but just length:

```
> '0' in a;
true

> '0' in un;
false
```

This difference in the `Array()` constructor's behavior when you specify one versus more parameters can lead to unexpected behavior. For example, the following use of the array literal is valid:

```
> var a = [3.14];
> a;
[3.14]
```

However, passing the floating-point number to the `Array` constructor is an error:

```
> var a = new Array(3.14);
Range Error: invalid array length
```

The Array.prototype members

Property/method	Description
`length`	The number of elements in the array. `> [1, 2, 3, 4].length;` **4**
`concat(i1, i2, i3,...)`	Merges arrays together. `> [1, 2].concat([3, 5], [7, 11]);` **[1, 2, 3, 5, 7, 11]**

`join(separator)`	Turns an array into a string. The separator parameter is a string with comma as the default value.
	`> [1, 2, 3].join();`
	"1,2,3"
	`> [1, 2, 3].join('|');`
	"1|2|3"
	`> [1, 2, 3].join(' is less than ');`
	"1 is less than 2 is less than 3"

`pop()`	Removes the last element of the array and returns it.
	`> var a = ['une', 'deux', 'trois'];`
	`> a.pop();`
	"trois"
	`> a;`
	["une", "deux"]

`push(i1, i2, i3,...)`	Appends elements to the end of the array and returns the length of the modified array.
	`> var a = [];`
	`> a.push('zig', 'zag', 'zebra','zoo');`
	4

`reverse()`	Reverses the elements of the array and returns the modified array.
	`> var a = [1, 2, 3];`
	`> a.reverse();`
	[3, 2, 1]
	`> a;`
	[3, 2, 1]

Property/method	Description

`shift()`	Like `pop()` but removes the first element, not the last.
	`> var a = [1, 2, 3];`
	`> a.shift();`
	1
	`> a;`
	[2, 3]

`slice(start_index, end_index)`	Extracts a piece of the array and returns it as a new array, without modifying the source array.
	`> var a = ['apple', 'banana', 'js', 'css', 'orange'];`
	`> a.slice(2,4);`
	["js", "css"]
	`> a;`
	["apple", "banana", "js", "css", "orange"]

`sort(callback)`	Sorts an array. Optionally accepts a callback function for custom sorting. The callback function receives two array elements as arguments and should return `0` if they are equal, a positive number if the first is greater and a negative number if the second is greater.
	An example of a custom sorting function that does a proper *numeric* sort (since the default is *character* sorting):
	`function customSort(a, b) {`
	`  if (a > b) return 1;`
	`  if (a < b) return -1;`
	`  return 0;`
	`}`
	`Example use of sort():`
	`> var a = [101, 99, 1, 5];`
	`> a.sort();`
	[1, 101, 5, 99]
	`> a.sort(customSort);`
	[1, 5, 99, 101]
	`> [7, 6, 5, 9].sort(customSort);`
	[5, 6, 7, 9]

Property/method	Description

`splice(start, delete_count, i1, i2, i3,...)`	Removes and adds elements at the same time. The first parameter is where to start removing, the second is how many items to remove and the rest of the parameters are new elements to be inserted in the place of the removed ones.
	`> var a = ['apple', 'banana', 'js', 'css', 'orange'];`
	`> a.splice(2, 2, 'pear', 'pineapple');`
	["js", "css"]
	`> a;`
	["apple", "banana", "pear", "pineapple", "orange"]

`unshift(i1, i2, i3,...)`	Like `push()` but adds the elements at the beginning of the array as opposed to the end. Returns the length of the modified array.
	`> var a = [1, 2, 3];`
	`> a.unshift('one', 'two');`
	5
	`> a;`
	["one", "two", 1, 2, 3]

ECMAScript 5 additions to Array

Property/method	Description

`Array.isArray(obj)`	Tells if an object is an array because `typeof` is not good enough:
	`> var arraylike = {0: 101, length: 1};`
	`> typeof arraylike;`
	"object"
	`> typeof [];`
	"object"
	Neither is duck-typing (if it walks like a duck and quacks like a duck, it must be a duck):
	`typeof arraylike.length;`
	"number"
	In ES3 you need the verbose:
	`> Object.prototype.toString.call([]) === "[object Array]";`
	true
	`> Object.prototype.toString.call (arraylike) === "[object Array]";`
	false
	In ES5 you get the shorter:
	`Array.isArray([]);`
	true
	`Array.isArray(arraylike);`
	false

`Array.prototype.indexOf(needle, idx)`	Searches the array and returns the index of the first match. Returns `-1` if there's no match. Optionally can search starting from a specified index.
	`> var ar = ['one', 'two', 'one', 'two'];`
	`> ar.indexOf('two');`
	1
	`> ar.indexOf('two', 2);`
	3
	`> ar.indexOf('toot');`
	-1

Property/method	Description

`Array.prototype.lastIndexOf(needle, idx)`	Like `indexOf()` only searches from the end.
	`> var ar = ['one', 'two', 'one', 'two'];`
	`> ar.lastIndexOf('two');`
	3
	`> ar.lastIndexOf('two', 2);`
	1
	`> ar.indexOf('toot');`
	-1

`Array.prototype.forEach(callback, this_obj)`	An alternative to a `for` loop. You specify a callback function that will be called for each element of the array. The callback function gets the arguments: the element, its index and the whole array.
	`> var log = console.log.bind(console);`
	`> var ar = ['itsy', 'bitsy', 'spider'];`
	`> ar.forEach(log);`
	itsy 0 ["itsy", "bitsy", "spider"]
	bitsy 1 ["itsy", "bitsy", "spider"]
	spider 2 ["itsy", "bitsy", "spider"]
	Optionally, you can specify a second parameter: the object to be bound to this inside the callback function. So this works too:
	`> ar.forEach(console.log, console);`

Property/method	Description

`Array.prototype.every(callback, this_obj)`	You provide a callback function that tests each element of the array. Your callback is given the same arguments as `forEach()` and it must return `true` or `false` depending on whether the given element satisfies your test.
	If all elements satisfy your test, `every()` returns `true`. If at least one doesn't, `every()` returns `false`.
	`> function hasEye(el, idx, ar) {`
	`  return el.indexOf('i') !== -1;`
	`  }`
	`> ['itsy', 'bitsy', 'spider'].`
	`  every(hasEye);`
	true
	`> ['eency', 'weency', 'spider'].`
	`  every(hasEye);`
	false
	If at some point during the loop it becomes clear that the result will be false, the loop stops and returns false.
	`> [1,2,3].every(function (e) {`
	`  console.log(e);`
	`  return false;`
	`  });`
	1
	false

`Array.prototype.some(callback, this_obj)`	Like `every()` only it returns true if at least one element satisfies your test:
	`> ['itsy', 'bitsy', 'spider'].`
	`  some(hasEye);`
	true
	`> ['eency', 'weency', 'spider'].`
	`  some(hasEye);`
	true

`Array.prototype.filter(callback, this_obj)`	Similar to some() and every() but it returns a new array of all elements that satisfy your test:
	`> ['itsy', 'bitsy', 'spider'].`
	`  filter(hasEye);`
	["itsy", "bitsy", "spider"]
	`> ['eency', 'weency', 'spider'].`
	`  filter(hasEye);`
	["spider"]

Property/method	Description

`Array.prototype.map(callback, this_obj)`	Similar to `forEach()` because it executes a callback for each element, but additionally it constructs a new array with the returned values of your callback and returns it. Let's capitalize all strings in an array:
	`> function uc(element, index, array) {`
	`  return element.toUpperCase();`
	`}`
	`> ['eency', 'weency', 'spider'].map(uc);`
	["EENCY", "WEENCY", "SPIDER"]

`Array.prototype.reduce(callback, start)`	Executes your callback for each element of the array. Your callback returns a value. This value is passed back to your callback with the next iteration. The whole array is eventually reduced to a single value.
	`> function sum(res, element, idx, arr) {`
	`  return res + element;`
	`}`
	`> [1, 2, 3].reduce(sum);`
	6
	Optionally, you can pass a start value which will be used by the first callback call:
	`> [1, 2, 3].reduce(sum, 100);`
	106

`Array.prototype.reduceRight(callback, start)`	Like `reduce()` but loops from the end of the array.
	`> function concat(result_so_far, el) {`
	`  return "" + result_so_far + el;`
	`}`
	`> [1, 2, 3].reduce(concat);`
	"123"
	`> [1, 2, 3].reduceRight(concat);`
	"321"

Function

JavaScript functions are objects. They can be defined using the `Function` constructor, like so:

```
var sum = new Function('a', 'b', 'return a + b;');
```

This is a (generally not recommended) alternative to the function literal (also known as function expression):

```
var sum = function (a, b) {
  return a + b;
};
```

Or, the more common function definition:

```
function sum(a, b) {
  return a + b;
}
```

The Function.prototype members

Property/Method	Description

`apply(this_obj, params_array)`	Allows you to call another function while overwriting the other function's this value. The first parameter that `apply()` accepts is the object to be bound to this inside the function and the second is an array of arguments to be send to the function being called.
	`function whatIsIt(){`
	`  return this.toString();`
	`}`
	`> var myObj = {};`
	`> whatIsIt.apply(myObj);`
	"[object Object]"
	`> whatIsIt.apply(window);`
	"[object Window]"

`call(this_obj, p1, p2, p3, ...)`	The same as `apply()` but accepts arguments one by one, as opposed to as one array.

`length`	The number of parameters the function expects.
	`> parseInt.length;`
	2
	If you forget the difference between call() and apply():
	`> Function.prototype.call.length;`
	1
	`> Function.prototype.apply.length;`
	2
	The call() property's length is 1 because all arguments except the first one are optional.

ECMAScript 5 additions to a function

Property/method	Description
`Function.prototype.bind()`	When you want to call a function that uses this internally and you want to define what this is. The methods `call()` and `apply()` invoke the function while `bind()` returns a new function. Useful when you provide a method as a callback to a method of another object and and you want this to be an object of your choice. `> whatIsIt.apply(window);` **"[object Window]"**

Boolean

The `Boolean` constructor creates Boolean objects (not to be confused with Boolean primitives). The Boolean objects are not that useful and are listed here for the sake of completeness.

```
> var b = new Boolean();
> b.valueOf();
false

> b.toString();
"false"
```

A Boolean object is not the same as a Boolean primitive value. As you know, all objects are truthy:

```
> b === false;
false

> typeof b;
"object"
```

Boolean objects don't have any properties other than the ones inherited from `Object`.

Number

This creates number objects:

```
> var n = new Number(101);
> typeof n;
"object"

> n.valueOf();
101
```

The `Number` objects are not primitive objects, but if you use any `Number.prototype` method on a primitive number, the primitive will be converted to a `Number` object behind the scenes and the code will work.

```
> var n = 123;
> typeof n;
"number"

> n.toString();
"123"
```

Used without `new`, the `Number` constructor returns a primitive number.

```
> Number("101");
101

> typeof Number("101");
"number"

> typeof new Number("101");
"object"
```

Members of the Number constructor

Property/method	Description
`Number.MAX_VALUE`	A constant property (cannot be changed) that contains the maximum allowed number. `> Number.MAX_VALUE;` **1.7976931348623157e+308**
`Number.MIN_VALUE`	The smallest number you can work with in JavaScript. `> Number.MIN_VALUE;` **5e-324**

`Number.NaN`	Contains the Not A Number number. The same as the global NaN.
	`> Number.NaN;`
	NaN
	NaN is not equal to anything including itself.
	`> Number.NaN === Number.NaN;`
	false

`Number.POSITIVE_INFINITY`	The same as the global `Infinity` number.
`Number.NEGATIVE_INFINITY`	The same as `-Infinity`.

The Number.prototype members

Property/method	Description

`toFixed(fractionDigits)`	Returns a string with the fixed-point representation of the number. Rounds the returned value.
	`> var n = new Number(Math.PI);`
	`> n.valueOf();`
	3.141592653589793
	`> n.toFixed(3);`
	"3.142"

`toExponential (fractionDigits)`	Returns a string with exponential notation representation of the number object. Rounds the returned value.
	`> var n = new Number(56789);`
	`> n.toExponential(2);`
	"5.68e+4"

`toPrecision(precision)`	String representation of a number object, either exponential or fixed-point, depending on the number object.
	`> var n = new Number(56789);`
	`> n.toPrecision(2);`
	"5.7e+4"
	`> n.toPrecision(5);`
	"56789"
	`> n.toPrecision(4);`
	"5.679e+4"
	`> var n = new Number(Math.PI);`
	`> n.toPrecision(4);`
	"3.142"

String

The `String()` constructor creates string objects. Primitive strings are turned into objects behind the scenes if you call a method on them as if they were objects. Omitting `new` gives you primitive strings.

Creating a string object and a string primitive:

```
> var s_obj = new String('potatoes');
> var s_prim = 'potatoes';
> typeof s_obj;
"object"
```

```
> typeof s_prim;
"string"
```

The object and the primitive are not equal when compared by type with `===`, but they are when compared with `==` which does type coercion:

```
> s_obj === s_prim;
false

> s_obj == s_prim;
true
```

`length` is a property of the string objects:

```
> s_obj.length;
8
```

If you access `length` on a primitive string, the primitive is converted to an object behind the scenes and the operation is successful:

```
> s_prim.length;
8
```

String literals work fine too:

```
> "giraffe".length;
7
```

Members of the String constructor

Property/method	Description
`String.fromCharCode (code1, code2, code3, ...)`	Returns a string created using the Unicode values of the input: `> String.fromCharCode(115, 99, 114, 105, 112, 116);` **"script"**

The String.prototype members

Property/method	Description
`length`	The number of characters in the string. `> new String('four').length;` **4**

`charAt(position)`	Returns the character at the specified position. Positions start at 0.
	`> "script".charAt(0);`
	"s"
	Since ES5, it's also possible to use array notation for the same purpose. (This feature has been long supported in many browsers before ES5, but not IE)
	`> "script"[0];`
	"s"

`charCodeAt(position)`	Returns the numeric code (Unicode) of the character at the specified position. `> "script".charCodeAt(0);` **115**
`concat(str1, str2, ....)`	Return a new string glued from the input pieces. `> "".concat('zig', '-', 'zag');` **"zig-zag"**

`indexOf(needle, start)`	If the needle matches a part of the string, the position of the match is returned. The optional second parameter defines where the search should start from. Returns `-1` if no match is found.
	`> "javascript".indexOf('scr');`
	4
	`> "javascript".indexOf('scr', 5);`
	-1

`lastIndexOf(needle, start)`	Same as `indexOf()` but starts the search from the end of the string. The last occurrence of `a`: `> "javascript".lastIndexOf('a');` **3**

Property/method	Description

`localeCompare (needle)`	Compares two strings in the current locale. Returns `0` if the two strings are equal, `1` if the needle gets sorted before the string object, `-1` otherwise.
	`> "script".localeCompare('crypt');`
	1
	`> "script".localeCompare('sscript');`
	-1
	`> "script".localeCompare('script');`
	0

`match(regexp)`	Accepts a regular expression object and returns an array of matches. `> "R2-D2 and C-3PO".match(/[0-9]/g);` **["2", "2", "3"]**

`replace(needle, replacement)`	Allows you to replace the matching results of a regexp pattern. The replacement can also be a callback function. Capturing groups are available as `$1, $2,...$9`.
	`> "R2-D2".replace(/2/g, '-two');`
	"R-two-D-two"
	`> "R2-D2".replace(/(2)/g, '$1$1');`
	"R22-D22"

`search(regexp)`	Returns the position of the first regular expression match. `> "C-3PO".search(/[0-9]/);` **2**

`slice(start, end)`	Returns the part of a string identified by the start and end positions. If `start` is negative, the start position is `length + start`, similarly if the `end` parameter is negative, the end position is length + end.
	`> "R2-D2 and C-3PO".slice(4, 13);`
	"2 and C-3"
	`> "R2-D2 and C-3PO".slice(4, -1);`
	"2 and C-3P"

`split(separator, limit)`	Turns a string into an array. The second parameter, limit, is optional. As with `replace()`, `search()`, and `match()`, the separator is a regular expression but can also be a string.
	`> "1,2,3,4".split(/,/);`
	["1", "2", "3", "4"]
	`> "1,2,3,4".split(',', 2);`
	["1", "2"]

Property/method	Description

`substring(start, end)`	Similar to `slice()`. When start or end are negative or invalid, they are considered 0. If they are greater than the string length, they are considered to be the length. If `end` is greater than `start`, their values are swapped.
	`> "R2-D2 and C-3PO".substring(4, 13);`
	"2 and C-3"
	`> "R2-D2 and C-3PO".substring(13, 4);`
	"2 and C-3"

`toLowerCase()` `toLocaleLowerCase()`	Transforms the string to lowercase. `> "Java".toLowerCase();` **"java"**
`toUpperCase()` `toLocaleUpperCase()`	Transforms the string to uppercase. `> "Script".toUpperCase();` **"SCRIPT"**

ECMAScript 5 additions to String

Property/method	Description

`String.prototype.trim()`	Instead of using a regular expression to remove whitespace before and after a string (as in ES3), you have a `trim()` method in ES5.
	`> " \t beard \n".trim();`
	"beard"
	`Or in ES3:`
	`> " \t beard \n".replace(/\s/g, "");`
	"beard"

Date

The `Date` constructor can be used with several types of input:

You can pass values for year, month, date of the month, hour, minute, second, and millisecond, like so:

```
> new Date(2015, 0, 1, 13, 30, 35, 505);
```
Thu Jan 01 2015 13:30:35 GMT-0800 (PST)

- You can skip any of the input parameters, in which case they are assumed to be 0. Note that month values are from 0 (January) to 11 (December), hours are from 0 to 23, minutes and seconds 0 to 59, and milliseconds 0 to 999.

- You can pass a timestamp:

  ```
  > new Date(1420147835505);
  ```

  Thu Jan 01 2015 13:30:35 GMT-0800 (PST)

- If you don't pass anything, the current date/time is assumed:

  ```
  > new Date();
  ```

  Fri Jan 11 2013 12:20:45 GMT-0800 (PST)

- If you pass a string, it's parsed in an attempt to extract a possible date value:

  ```
  > new Date('May 4, 2015');
  ```

  Mon May 04 2015 00:00:00 GMT-0700 (PDT)

Omitting `new` gives you a string version of the current date:

```
> Date() === new Date().toString();
```

true

Members of the Date constructor

Property/method	Description

`Date.parse(string)`	Similar to passing a string to new `Date()` constructor, this method parses the input string in an attempt to extract a valid date value. Returns a timestamp on success, `NaN` on failure:
	`> Date.parse('May 5, 2015');`
	1430809200000
	`> Date.parse('4th');`
	NaN

`Date.UTC(year, month, date, hours, minutes, seconds, ms)`	Returns a timestamp but in UTC (Coordinated Universal Time), not in local time. `> Date.UTC (2015, 0, 1, 13, 30, 35, 505);` **1420119035505**

The Date.prototype members

Property/method	Description/example

`toUTCString()`	Same as `toString()` but in universal time. Here's how Pacific Standard (PST) local time differs from UTC:
	`> var d = new Date(2015, 0, 1);`
	`> d.toString();`
	"Thu Jan 01 2015 00:00:00 GMT-0800 (PST)"
	`> d.toUTCString();`
	"Thu, 01 Jan 2015 08:00:00 GMT"

`toDateString()`	Returns only the date portion of `toString()`: `> new Date(2015, 0, 1).toDateString();` **"Thu Jan 01 2010"**
`toTimeString()`	Returns only the time portion of `toString()`: `> new Date(2015, 0, 1).toTimeString();` **"00:00:00 GMT-0800 (PST)"**

`toLocaleString()`
`toLocaleDateString()`
`toLocaleTimeString()`
	Equivalent to `toString()`, `toDateString()`, and `toTimeString()` respectively, but in a friendlier format, according to the current user's locale.
	`> new Date(2015, 0, 1).toString();`
	"Thu Jan 01 2015 00:00:00 GMT-0800 (PST)"
	`> new Date(2015, 0, 1).toLocaleString();`
	"1/1/2015 12:00:00 AM"

`getTime()` `setTime(time)`	Get or set the time (using a timestamp) of a date object. The following example creates a date and moves it one day forward: **> var d = new Date(2015, 0, 1);** **> d.getTime();** **1420099200000** **> d.setTime(d.getTime()** **+ 1000 * 60 * 60 * 24);** **1420185600000** **> d.toLocaleString();** **"Fri Jan 02 2015 00:00:00 GMT-0800 (PST)"**

Property/method	Description/example

`getFullYear()`
`getUTCFullYear()`
`setFullYear(year, month, date)`
`setUTCFullYear(year, month, date)`
	Get or set a full year using local or UTC time. There is also `getYear()` but it is not Y2K compliant, so use `getFullYear()` instead.
	`> var d = new Date(2015, 0, 1);`
	`> d.getYear();`
	115
	`> d.getFullYear();`
	2015
	`> d.setFullYear(2020);`
	1577865600000
	`> d;`
	Wed Jan 01 2020 00:00:00 GMT-0800 (PST)

`getMonth()`
`getUTCMonth()`
`setMonth(month, date)`
`setUTCMonth(month, date)`
	Get or set the month, starting from 0 (January):
	`> var d = new Date(2015, 0, 1);`
	`> d.getMonth();`
	0
	`> d.setMonth(11);`
	1448956800000
	`> d.toLocaleDateString();`
	"12/1/2015"

`getDate()`
`getUTCDate()`
`setDate(date)`
`setUTCDate(date)`
	Get or set the date of the month.
	`> var d = new Date(2015, 0, 1);`
	`> d.toLocaleDateString();`
	"1/1/2015"
	`> d.getDate();`
	1
	`> d.setDate(31);`
	1422691200000
	`> d.toLocaleDateString();`
	"1/31/2015"

Property/method	Description/example

`getHours()`
`getUTCHours()`
`setHours(hour, min, sec, ms)`
`setUTCHours(hour, min, sec, ms)`
`getMinutes()`
`getUTCMinutes()`
`setMinutes(min, sec, ms)`
`setUTCMinutes(min, sec, ms)`
`getSeconds()`
`getUTCSeconds()`
`setSeconds(sec, ms)`
`setUTCSeconds(sec, ms)`
`getMilliseconds()`
`getUTCMilliseconds()`
`setMilliseconds(ms)`
`setUTCMilliseconds(ms)`
	Get or set the hour, minutes, seconds, milliseconds, all starting from 0.
	`> var d = new Date(2015, 0, 1);`
	`> d.getHours() + ':' + d.getMinutes();`
	"0:0"
	`> d.setMinutes(59);`
	1420102740000
	`> d.getHours() + ':' + d.getMinutes();`
	"0:59"

`getTimezoneOffset()`	Returns the difference between local and universal (UTC) time, measured in minutes. For example, the difference between PST (Pacific Standard Time) and UTC:
	`> new Date().getTimezoneOffset();`
	480
	`> 420 / 60; // hours`
	8

Property/method	Description/example

`getDay()`
`getUTCDay()`
	Returns the day of the week, starting from 0 (Sunday):
	`> var d = new Date(2015, 0, 1);`
	`> d.toDateString();`
	"Thu Jan 01 2015"
	`> d.getDay();`
	4
	`> var d = new Date(2015, 0, 4);`
	`> d.toDateString();`
	"Sat Jan 04 2015"
	`> d.getDay();`
	0

ECMAScript 5 additions to Date

Property/method	Description
`Date.now()`	A convenient way to get the current timestamp: `> Date.now() === new Date().getTime();` **true**

`Date.prototype.toISOString()`	Yet another toString().
	`> var d = new Date(2015, 0, 1);`
	`> d.toString();`
	"Thu Jan 01 2015 00:00:00 GMT-0800 (PST)"
	`> d.toUTCString();`
	"Thu, 01 Jan 2015 08:00:00 GMT"
	`> d.toISOString();`
	"2015-01-01T00:00:00.000Z"

`Date.prototype.toJSON()`	Used by JSON.stringify() (refer to the end of this appendix) and returns the same as toISOString().
	`> var d = new Date();`
	`> d.toJSON() === d.toISOString();`
	true

Math

`Math` is different from the other built-in objects because it cannot be used as a constructor to create objects. It's just a collection of static functions and constants. Some examples to illustrate the differences are as follows:

```
> typeof Date.prototype;
"object"

> typeof Math.prototype;
"undefined"

> typeof String;
"function"

> typeof Math;
"object"
```

Members of the Math object

Property/method	Description

`Math.E`
`Math.LN10`
`Math.LN2`
`Math.LOG2E`
`Math.LOG10E`
`Math.PI`
`Math.SQRT1_2`
`Math.SQRT2`
	These are some useful math constants, all read-only. Here are their values:
	`> Math.E;`
	2.718281828459045
	`> Math.LN10;`
	2.302585092994046
	`> Math.LN2;`
	0.6931471805599453
	`> Math.LOG2E;`
	1.4426950408889634
	`> Math.LOG10E;`
	0.4342944819032518
	`> Math.PI;`
	3.141592653589793
	`> Math.SQRT1_2;`
	0.7071067811865476
	`> Math.SQRT2;`
	1.4142135623730951

Property/method	Description

`Math.acos(x)`
`Math.asin(x)`
`Math.atan(x)`
`Math.atan2(y, x)`
`Math.cos(x)`
`Math.sin(x)`
`Math.tan(x)`
	Trigonometric functions

`Math.round(x)`
`Math.floor(x)`
`Math.ceil(x)`
	`round()` gives you the nearest integer, `ceil()` rounds up, and `floor()` rounds down:
	`> Math.round(5.5);`
	6
	`> Math.floor(5.5);`
	5
	`> Math.ceil(5.1);`
	6

`Math.max(num1, num2, num3, ...)`
`Math.min(num1, num2, num3, ...)`
	`max()` returns the largest and `min()` returns the smallest of the numbers passed to them as arguments. If at least one of the input parameters is `NaN`, the result is also `NaN`.
	`> Math.max(4.5, 101, Math.PI);`
	101
	`> Math.min(4.5, 101, Math.PI);`
	3.141592653589793

`Math.abs(x)`	Absolute value.
	`> Math.abs(-101);`
	101
	`> Math.abs(101);`
	101

`Math.exp(x)`	Exponential function: `Math.E` to the power of `x`. `> Math.exp(1) === Math.E;` **true**
`Math.log(x)`	Natural logarithm of `x`. `> Math.log(10) === Math.LN10;` **true**

Property/method	Description

`Math.sqrt(x)`	Square root of x.
	`> Math.sqrt(9);`
	3
	`> Math.sqrt(2) === Math.SQRT2;`
	true

`Math.pow(x, y)`	x to the power of y. `> Math.pow(3, 2);` **9**

`Math.random()`	Random number between 0 and 1 (including 0).
	`> Math.random();`
	0.8279076443185321
	`For an random integer in a range, say between 10 and 100:`
	`> Math.round(Math.random() * 90 + 10);`
	79

RegExp

You can create a regular expression object using the `RegExp()` constructor. You pass the expression pattern as the first parameter and the pattern modifiers as the second.

```
> var re = new RegExp('[dn]o+dle', 'gmi');
```

This matches "noodle", "doodle", "doooodle", and so on. It's equivalent to using the regular expression literal:

```
> var re = ('/[dn]o+dle/gmi'); // recommended
```

Chapter 4, Objects and *Appendix D, Regular Expressions* contains more information on regular expressions and patterns.

The RegExp.prototype members

Property/method	Description
`global`	Read-only. `true` if the `g` modifier was set when creating the regexp object.
`ignoreCase`	Read-only. `true` if the `i` modifier was set when creating the regexp object.
`multiline`	Read-only. `true` if the `m` modifier was set when creating the regexp object

Property/method	Description

`lastIndex`	Contains the position in the string where the next match should start. `test()` and `exec()` set this position after a successful match. Only relevant when the `g` (global) modifier was used.
	`> var re = /[dn]o+dle/g;`
	`> re.lastIndex;`
	0
	`> re.exec("noodle doodle");`
	["noodle"]
	`> re.lastIndex;`
	6
	`> re.exec("noodle doodle");`
	["doodle"]
	`> re.lastIndex;`
	13
	`> re.exec("noodle doodle");`
	null
	`> re.lastIndex;`
	0

`source`	Read-only. Returns the regular expression pattern (without the modifiers).
	`> var re = /[nd]o+dle/gmi;`
	`> re.source;`
	"[nd]o+dle"

`exec(string)`	Matches the input string with the regular expression. A successful match returns an array containing the match and any capturing groups. With the `g` modifier, it matches the first occurrence and sets the `lastIndex` property. Returns `null` when there's no match.
	`> var re = /([dn])(o+)dle/g;`
	`> re.exec("noodle doodle");`
	["noodle", "n", "oo"]
	`> re.exec("noodle doodle");`
	["doodle", "d", "oo"]
	The arrays returned by exec() have two additional properties: index (of the match) and input (the input string being searched).

`test(string)`	Same as `exec()` but only returns true or false.
	`> /noo/.test('Noodle');`
	false
	`> /noo/i.test('Noodle');`
	true

Error objects

Error objects are created either by the environment (the browser) or by your code.

```
> var e = new Error('jaavcsritp is _not_ how you spell it');
> typeof e;
"object"
```

Other than the `Error` constructor, six additional ones exist and they all inherit `Error`:

- `EvalError`
- `RangeError`
- `ReferenceError`
- `SyntaxError`
- `TypeError`
- `URIError`

The Error.prototype members

Property	Description

`name`	The name of the error constructor used to create the object:
	`> var e = new EvalError('Oops');`
	`> e.name;`
	"EvalError"

`message`	Additional error information:
	`> var e = new Error('Oops... again');`
	`> e.message;`
	"Oops... again"

JSON

The JSON object is new to ES5. It's not a constructor (similarly to `Math`) and has only two methods: `parse()` and `stringify()`. For ES3 browsers that don't support JSON natively, you can use the "shim" from `http://json.org`.

JSON stands for **JavaScript Object Notation**. It's a lightweight data interchange format. It's a subset of JavaScript that only supports primitives, object literals, and array literals.

Members of the JSON object

Method	Description

`parse(text, callback)`	Takes a JSON-encoded string and returns an object:
	`> var data = '{"hello": 1, "hi": [1, 2, 3]}';`
	`> var o = JSON.parse(data);`
	`> o.hello;`
	1
	`> o.hi;`
	[1, 2, 3]
	The optional callback lets you provide your own function that can inspect and modify the result. The callback takes `key` and `value` arguments and can modify the `value` or delete it (by returning `undefined`).
	`> function callback(key, value) {`
	`console.log(key, value);`
	`if (key === 'hello') {`
	`return 'bonjour';`
	`}`
	`if (key === 'hi') {`
	`return undefined;`
	`}`
	`return value;`
	`}`
	
	`> var o = JSON.parse(data, callback);`
	hello 1
	0 1
	1 2
	2 3
	hi [1, 2, 3]
	Object {hello: "bonjour"}
	> o.hello;
	"bonjour"
	`> 'hi' in o;`
	false

Method	Description

`stringify (value, callback, white)`	Takes any value (most commonly an object or an array) and encodes it to a JSON string.
	`> var o = {`
	`  hello: 1,`
	`  hi: 2,`
	`  when: new Date(2015, 0, 1)`
	`  };`
	
	`> JSON.stringify(o);`
	"{"hello":1,"hi":2,"when":"2015-01-01T08:00:00.000Z"}"
	The second parameter lets you provide a callback (or a whitelist array) to customize the return value. The whitelist contains the keys you're interested in:
	`JSON.stringify(o, ['hello', 'hi']);`
	"{"hello":1,"hi":2}"
	The last parameter helps you get a human-readable version. You specify the number of spaces as a string or a number.
	`> JSON.stringify(o, null, 4);`
	"{
	"hello": 1,
	"hi": 2,
	"when": "2015-01-01T08:00:00.000Z"
	}"

D
Regular Expressions

When you use regular expressions (discussed in *Chapter 4, Objects*), you can match literal strings, for example:

```
> "some text".match(/me/);
```
["me"]

But, the true power of regular expressions comes from matching patterns, not literal strings. The following table describes the different syntax you can use in your patterns, and provides some examples of their use:

Pattern	Description
[abc]	Matches a class of characters. `> "some text".match(/[otx]/g);` **["o", "t", "x", "t"]**

[a-z]	A class of characters defined as a range. For example, [a-d] is the same as [abcd], [a-z] matches all lowercase characters, [a-zA-Z0-9_] matches all characters, numbers, and the underscore character.
	`> "Some Text".match(/[a-z]/g);`
	["o", "m", "e", "e", "x", "t"]
	`> "Some Text".match(/[a-zA-Z]/g);`
	["S", "o", "m", "e", "T", "e", "x", "t"]

[^abc]	Matches everything that is not matched by the class of characters. `> "Some Text".match(/[^a-z]/g);` **["S", " ", "T"]**

Pattern	Description

a|b	Matches a or b. The pipe character means OR, and it can be used more than once.
	`> "Some Text".match(/t|T/g);`
	["T", "t"]
	`> "Some Text".match(/t|T|Some/g);`
	["Some", "T", "t"]

a(?=b)	Matches a only if followed by b.
	`> "Some Text".match(/Some(?=Tex)/g);`
	null
	`> "Some Text".match(/Some(?= Tex)/g);`
	["Some"]

a(?!b)	Matches a only when not followed by b.
	`> "Some Text".match(/Some(?! Tex)/g);`
	null
	`> "Some Text".match(/Some(?!Tex)/g);`
	["Some"]

\	Escape character used to help you match the special characters used in patterns as literals.
	`> "R2-D2".match(/[2-3]/g);`
	["2", "2"]
	`> "R2-D2".match(/[2\-3]/g);`
	["2", "-", "2"]

\n	New line
\r	Carriage return
\f	Form feed
\t	Tab
\v	Vertical tab
\s	White space, or any of the previous five escape sequences. `> "R2\n D2".match(/\s/g);` **["\n", " "]**
\S	Opposite of the above; matches everything but white space. Same as [^\s]: `> "R2\n D2".match(/\S/g);` **["R", "2", "D", "2"]**
\w	Any letter, number, or underscore. Same as [A-Za-z0-9_]. `> "S0m3 text!".match(/\w/g);` **["S", "0", "m", "3", "t", "e", "x", "t"]**

Pattern	Description
`\W`	Opposite of `\w`. `> "S0m3 text!".match(/\W/g);` **[" ", "!"]**
`\d`	Matches a number, same as [0-9]. `> "R2-D2 and C-3PO".match(/\d/g);` **["2", "2", "3"]**
`\D`	Opposite of `\d`; matches non-numbers, same as [^0-9] or [^\d]. `> "R2-D2 and C-3PO".match(/\D/g);` **["R", "-", "D", " ", "a", "n", "d", " ", "C", "-", "P", "O"]**

`\b`	Matches a word boundary such as space or punctuation.
	Matching R or D followed by 2:
	`> "R2D2 and C-3PO".match(/[RD]2/g);`
	["R2", "D2"]
	Same as above but only at the end of a word:
	`> "R2D2 and C-3PO".match(/[RD]2\b/g);`
	["D2"]
	Same pattern but the input has a dash, which is also an end of a word:
	`> "R2-D2 and C-3PO".match(/[RD]2\b/g);`
	["R2", "D2"]

`\B`	The opposite of `\b`.
	`> "R2-D2 and C-3PO".match(/[RD]2\B/g);`
	null
	`> "R2D2 and C-3PO".match(/[RD]2\B/g);`
	["R2"]

`[\b]`	Matches the backspace character.
`\0`	The null character.
`\u0000`	Matches a Unicode character, represented by a four-digit hexadecimal number. `> "стоян".match(/\u0441\u0442\u043E/);` **["сто"]**

`\x00`	Matches a character code represented by a two-digit hexadecimal number.
	`> "\x64";`
	`"d"`
	`> "dude".match(/\x64/g);`
	`["d", "d"]`

Pattern	Description

^	The beginning of the string to be matched. If you set the m modifier (multi-line), it matches the beginning of each line.
	`> "regular\nregular\nexpression".match(/r/g);`
	["r", "r", "r", "r", "r"]
	`> "regular\nregular\nexpression".match(/^r/g);`
	["r"]
	`> "regular\nregular\nexpression".match(/^r/mg);`
	["r", "r"]

$	Matches the end of the input or, when using the multiline modifier, the end of each line.
	`> "regular\nregular\nexpression".match(/r$/g);`
	null
	`> "regular\nregular\nexpression".match(/r$/mg);`
	["r", "r"]

.	Matches any single character except for the new line and the line feed.
	`> "regular".match(/r./g);`
	["re"]
	`> "regular".match(/r.../g);`
	["regu"]

*	Matches the preceding pattern if it occurs zero or more times. For example, `/.*/` will match anything including nothing (an empty input).
	`> "".match(/.*/);`
	[""]
	`> "anything".match(/.*/);`
	["anything"]
	`> "anything".match(/n.*h/);`
	["nyth"]
	Keep in mind that the pattern is "greedy", meaning it will match as much as possible:
	`> "anything within".match(/n.*h/g);`
	["nything with"]

?	Matches the preceding pattern if it occurs zero or one times. `> "anything".match(/ny?/g);` **["ny", "n"]**

Pattern	Description

+	Matches the preceding pattern if it occurs at least once (or more times).
	`> "anything".match(/ny+/g);`
	["ny"]
	`> "R2-D2 and C-3PO".match(/[a-z]/gi);`
	["R", "D", "a", "n", "d", "C", "P", "O"]
	`> "R2-D2 and C-3PO".match(/[a-z]+/gi);`
	["R", "D", "and", "C", "PO"]

{n}	Matches the preceding pattern if it occurs exactly n times.
	`> "regular expression".match(/s/g);`
	["s", "s"]
	`> "regular expression".match(/s{2}/g);`
	["ss"]
	`> "regular expression".match(/\b\w{3}/g);`
	["reg", "exp"]

{min,max}	Matches the preceding pattern if it occurs between a min and max number of times. You can omit max, which will mean no maximum, but only a minimum. You cannot omit min.
	An example where the input is "doodle" with the "o" repeated 10 times:
	`> "doooooooooodle".match(/o/g);`
	["o", "o", "o", "o", "o", "o", "o", "o", "o", "o"]
	`> "doooooooooodle".match(/o/g).length;`
	10
	`> "doooooooooodle".match(/o{2}/g);`
	["oo", "oo", "oo", "oo", "oo"]
	`> "doooooooooodle".match(/o{2,}/g);`
	["oooooooooo"]
	`> "doooooooooodle".match(/o{2,6}/g);`
	["oooooo", "oooo"]

(pattern)	When the pattern is in parentheses, it is remembered so that it can be used for replacements. These are also known as capturing patterns.
	The captured matches are available as $1, $2,... $9
	Matching all "r" occurrences and repeating them:
	`> "regular expression".replace(/(r)/g, '$1$1');`
	"rregularr exprression"
	Matching "re" and turning it to "er":
	`> "regular expression".replace(/(r)(e)/g, '$2$1');`
	"ergular experssion"

Pattern	Description
(?:pattern)	Non-capturing pattern, not remembered and not available in $1, $2... Here's an example of how "re" is matched, but the "r" is not remembered and the second pattern becomes $1: `> "regular expression".replace(/(?:r)(e)/g, '$1$1');` **"eegular expeession"**

Make sure you pay attention when a special character can have two meanings, as is the case with `^`, `?`, and `\b`.

Index

Symbols

^ 350
!= 42
!== 42
? 350
. 350
(?: pattern) 352
* 350
\ 348
\\ 35
+ 351
< 42
<= 42
== 41
=== 41
> 42
>= 42
\0 349
$ 350
$ character 22
[^abc] 347
[abc] 347
[a-z] 347
[\b] 349
\b 349
\B 349
\d 349
\D 349
\f 348
{min,max} 351
{n} 351
\n 36, 348
--, operators 26
-, operators 25
*, operators 25
/, operators 25
%, operators 25
+, operators 25
++, operators 26
(pattern) 351
\r 36, 348
\s 348
\S 348
\u 36
\u0000 349
\v 348
\w 348
\W 349
\x00 349

A

a(?!b) 348
a(?=b) 348
a|b 348
accessor descriptors 313
actualWork() function 84
addEventListener/attachEvent methods 273
addEventListener() method 258
addListener() method 279
addSubscriber() method 297
Ajax 260
anonymous function 76
array
  about 97-99, 114-116
  methods 117
Array constructor
  about 318
  Array.prototype members 319
  ECMAScript 5 additions to Array 322
array literal notation 99

array methods
about 117
join() method 117
push() method 117
slice() method 118
sort() method 117
splice() method 118
Array.prototype members
concat(i1, i2, i3,...) 319
join(separator) 319
length 319
pop() 319
push(i1, i2, i3,...) 319
reverse() 319
shift() 320
slice(start_index, end_index) 320
sort(callback) 320
splice(start, de-lete_count, i1, i2, i3,...) 321
unshift(i1, i2, i3,...) 321
arrays
about 45
array content 47, 48
elements, adding 46
elements, deleting 47
elements, updating 46
Asynchronous JavaScript and XML. *See* **Ajax**
Asynchronous JavaScript loading 275
attributes 313
attributes, DOM nodes 234

B

best practice 73
black box function 67
BOM
about 9, 213, 215
cheat sheet console 217
overview 214
window.alert() 223
window.confirm() 223
window.document 226
window.frames 219, 220
window.history 218, 219
window.location 217, 218
window.moveTo() 222
window.navigator 216
window object, revisiting 215
window.open()/close() 222
window.prompt() 223, 224
window.resizeTo() 223
window.screen 221
window.setInterval() 225, 226
window.setTimeout() 225, 226
boolean 125
Boolean constructor 327
Boolean() function 125
Booleans 36
break 301
Browser Object Model. *See* **BOM**
built-in Functions
about 305, 306
decodeURI() 307
decodeURIComponent() 307
encodeURI() 307
encodeURIComponent() 306
eval() 307
isFinite() 306
isNaN() 305
parseFloat() 305
parseInt() 305
built-in objects
array 114
Array constructor 318
augmenting 164, 165
boolean 125
Boolean constructor 327
data wrapper objects 113
date 134, 135
Date constructor 333
error objects 113, 343
function 118
Function constructor 325
JSON 343
math 132
Math constructor 339
number 126, 127
Number constructor 328
object 113
object constructor 309
prototype gotchas 166, 168
RegExp 138
RegExp constructor 341
string 127, 128

String constructor 329
utility objects 113

C

callback function
about 77, 78
examples 78, 79
Cascading Style Sheets (CSS) 273
case 301
catch 301
chaining pattern 287
child nodes 233
child object
parent, accessing 181, 182
classes 13
closures
about 85
closure #1 88
closure #2 88
closure #3 89
getter/setter 92, 93
in loop 90, 92
iterator 93
scope chain 85
used, for chain breaking 86, 87
code blocks
about 50, 51
alternative if syntax 53
variable existence, checking 51, 52
coding patterns
about 272
chaining pattern 287
configuration object 280, 281
immediate functions 285
init-time branching 278, 279
JSON 288, 289
lazy definition pattern 279
modules 286
namespaces 275
private functions, as public methods 284
private properties 282, 283
privileged methods 283
web page, building blocks 272
comments 61
comparison
about 41
null 43, 44
Operator symbols 41, 42
Undefined 43
compound operators 27
conditions
about 48
else clause 49, 50
if condition 49
Console tab 18
constructor
borrowing 198, 199
prototype, copying 200
constructor functions 104, 105
constructor property 107, 168
continue 301
core DOM 229, 230
Core ECMAScript objects 214
createTextNode() method 242

D

data. *See* **functions**
data descriptors 313
Date() 134, 135
Date constructor
about 333, 334
Date.prototype members 335
ECMAScript 5 additions 338
members 334
date objects
working with, methods 136-138
date objects methods
getMonth() 136
setHours() 136
setMonth() 136
Date.prototype members
getDate() 336
getDay() 338
getFullYear() 336
getHours() 337
getMilliseconds() 337
getMinutes() 337
getMonth() 336
getSeconds() 337
getTime() 335
getTimezoneOffset() 337
getUTCDate() 336

getUTCDay() 338
getUTCFullYear() 336
getUTCHours() 337
getUTCMilliseconds() 337
getUTCMinutes() 337
getUTCSeconds() 337
setDate(date) 336
setFullYear(year, month, date) 336
setHours(hour, min, sec, ms) 337
setMilliseconds(ms) 337
setMinutes(min, sec, ms) 337
setMonth(month, date) 336
setSeconds(sec, ms) 337
setTime(time) 335
setUTCDate(date) 336
setUTCFullYear(year, month, date) 336
setUTCHours(hour, min, sec, ms) 337
setUTCMillise-conds(ms) 337
setUTCMinutes(min, sec, ms) 337
setUTCMonth(month, date) 336
setUTCSeconds(sec, ms) 337
toDateString() 335
toLocaleDateString() 335
toLocaleString() 335
toLocaleTimeString() 335
toTimeString() 335
toUTCString() 335
debugger 301
decodeURI() 307
decodeURIComponent() 306
decorate() method 296
decorator
about 294
Christmas tree, decorating 295
deep copy 190-192
default 301
delete 301
design patterns
about 289
decorator 294
factory 292, 293
observer 296-299
singleton 290
singleton 2 290
do 302
documentElement 232
document node 231, 232
Document Object Model. *See* **DOM**
DOM
about 8, 213, 227, 228
core DOM 229
HTML DOM 229
overview 214
tree, walking through 239
DOM event listeners 252
DOM nodes
accessing 230
access shortcuts 235, 236
attributes 234
child nodes 233
documentElement 232
document node 231, 232
firstChild 238
forms 240, 241
internal tag content, accessing 234, 235
lastChild 238
modifying 239
new nodes, creating 242
nextSibling 237
previousSibling 237
styles, modifying 240
doSomething() method 294
do-while loops 57

E

ECMA 8
ECMAScript. *See* **ES**
ECMAScript 5. *See* **ES**
ECMAScript 5 additions to Array
Array.isArray(obj) 322
Ar-ray.prototype.every(callback, this_obj) 324
Ar-ray.prototype.filter(callback, this_obj) 324
Ar-ray.prototype.forEach(callback, this_obj) 323
Ar-ray.prototype.indexOf(needle, idx) 322
Ar-ray.prototype.lastIndexOf(needle, idx) 323
Ar-ray.prototype.map(callback, this_obj) 325
Ar-ray.prototype.reduce(callback, start) 325

Ar-ray.prototype.reduceRight(callback, start) 325
Ar-ray.prototype.some(callback, this_obj) 324
elements 99
else clause 49
encapsulation 14
encodeURI() 307
encodeURIComponent() 306
enumerable 160
enumerated array 100
error objects
about 343
Error.prototype members 343
Error.prototype members
message 343
name 343
ES
about 12, 309
OOP 12
European Computer Manufacturers Association. *See* **ECMA**
eval()
about 71, 307
alert() function 71, 72
drawbacks, performance 71
drawbacks, security 71
events
about 250
bubbling 253, 254
capturing 253, 254
cross-browser listeners 258
default behavior, preventing 257
DOM event listeners 252
element properties 251
inline HTML attributes 251
propagation, stopping 255, 256
types 259
events, types
form 260
keyboard events 259
loading/window events 259
mouse events 259
exercises 211, 212, 268, 269
exponent literals 30
extendCopy() function 190
extend() function 182

F

factory() function 108, 109
factory() method 294
finally 302
firstname property 101
foo() function 154
Function() constructor
about 118, 119, 326
arguments 123
Function.prototype members 326
function objects, methods 121
object types, inferring 124
properties 120
prototype property 120, 121
function expression 75
function literal notation 75
function N() 89
function objects, methods
apply() 122, 123
call() 122
say() method 122
Func-tion.prototype.bind() property 327
Function.prototype members
apply(this_obj, params_array) 326
call(this_obj, p1, p2, p3, ...) 326
ECMAScript 5 additions to a function 327
length 326
functions
about 64, 75, 76
anonymous functions 76
callback functions 77
calling 64
components 64
immediate functions 80, 81
inner(private) 81
inner(private), benefits 82
parameters 65, 66
predefined functions 66
replacing 83, 84
returning values 82
future reserved words 302, 303

G

Gadget() constructor 155
getArea() method 196
getAttribute() method 234

getDecorator() method 295
getElementByClassName() method 237
getInfo() method 155
getter function 92
getValue() 93
global object 105-107
global property 139

H

hash 100
hasOwnProperty() method 158, 160
hexadecimal numbers 29
hoisting 74
HTML DOM 229, 230
HTML-only DOM objects
about 247
accessing, primitive ways 247, 248
cookies 249
document.write() 248, 249
domain 249, 250
referrer 249
title 249
HTML page
JavaScript, including 213, 214

I

if condition 49
ignoreCase property 139
immediate functions 285
inArray() method 164
indexed array 100
indexOf() method 141
infinity
about 31, 32
NaN 32
inheritance 171
inheritance part
isolating, into function 182, 183
init-time branching 278
inline HTML attributes 251
inner (private) function 81, 82
instanceof operator 108, 174
isFinite() function 70, 306
isNaN() function 69, 70, 306
isPrototypeOf() method 162
iterator functionality 93

J

JavaScript
about 7
BOM 9
Browser Wars 10
DOM 8
ECMAScript 8
future 11
history 8
including, in HTML page 213, 214
uses 10, 11
JavaScript Object Notation. *See* **JSON**
join() method 117
JSON
about 288, 343
members 344

K

keywords, ES5
break 301
case 301
catch 301
continue 301
debugger 301
default 301
delete 301
do 302
else 302
finally 302
for 302
function 302
if 302
ifn 302
instanceof 302
new 302
return 302
switch 302
this 302
throw 302
try 302
typeof 302
var 302
void 302
while 302
with 302

L

lastIndexOf() method 141
lastIndex property 139, 342
lazy definition pattern 279
logical operators
about 37
lazy evaluation 40, 41
operator precedence 39
possible operations 38, 39
loops
about 48, 56
for-in loops 60
for loops 57, 59
infinite loop 56
while loops 56

M

make() method 297
match() method 141
Math 132, 133
Math constructor
about 339
members 339
maybeExists() function 147
members, Date constructor
Date.parse(string) 334
Date.UTC(year, month, date, hours, minutes, seconds, ms) 334
members, JSON
parse(text, call-back) 344
stringi-fy(value, callback, white) 345
members, Math constructor
Math.abs(x) 340
Math.acos(x) 340
Math.E 339
Math.exp(x) 340
Math.LN2 339
Math.LN10 339
Math.LOG2E 339
Math.LOG10E 339
Math.log(x) 340
Math.max(num1, num2, num3, ...) 340
Math.PI 339
Math.pow(x, y) 341
Math.random() 341
Math.round(x) 340
Math.SQRT1_2 339
Math.SQRT2 339
Math.sqrt(x) 341
members, Number constructor
Number.MAX_VALUE 328
Number.MIN_VALUE 328
Number.NaN 328
Number.NEGATIVE_INFINITY 328
Number.POSITIVE_INFINITY 328
members, String() constructor
String.fromCharCode (code1, code2, code3, ...) 330
methods 99
modules 286
multi() function 195
multiline property 139
multiple inheritance
about 195, 196
mixins 197

N

named function expression. *See* **NFE**
namespace() method 277
namespaces
constructors 276
namespace() method 277, 278
object 275
NaN 32
new F() 179, 180
new nodes
cloneNode() 243
creating 242
DOM-only method 243
insertBefore() 244
new operator 108
newtoy.toString() 157
next() function 93
NFE 75
nodes
removing 245, 246
now() method 137
number 126, 127
Number constructor
about 328
members 328
Number.prototype members 329

Number() function 126
Number.prototype members
toExponential(fractionDigits) 329
toFixed(fractionDigits) 329
toPrecision(precision) 329

O

object constructor
about 309
ECMAScript 5 additions 312-317
memebers 310
Object.prototype 310
Object.prototype members 311, 312
Object.create(obj, descr) property 315
Ob-ject.defineProperties(obj, descriptors) property 316
Ob-ject.defineProperty(obj, descriptor) property 315
Object.freeze(obj) property 317
object() function 192, 193, 197
Ob-ject.getOwnPropertyDescriptor(obj, property) property 315
Ob-ject.getOwnPropertyNames(obj) property 315
Ob-ject.getPrototypeOf(obj) property 314
Ob-ject.isExtensible(obj) property 316
Object.keys(obj) property 317
object literal notation 99
object-oriented programming. *See* **OOP**
Ob-ject.preventExtensions(obj) property 316
Object.prototype members
constructor 310
hasOwnProper-ty(prop) 312
isPrototypeOf(obj) 312
propertyIsEnumera-ble(prop) 312
toLocaleString() 311
toString(radix) 310
valueOf() 311
objects
about 13
comparing 110
global object 107
inheriting, from objects 188, 190
passing 109, 110
Object.seal(obj) property 317
object's methods
altering 102, 103
calling 102
object's properties
accessing 100
calling 102, 103
objects, WebKit console
about 111
console.log 112
observer pattern 296-299
octal number 29
OOP
about 12
aggregation 15
classes 13
encapsulation 14
features 16
inheritance 15
objects 13
polymorphism 16
summary 16
operation 38
operators
- 25
-- 26
* 25
/ 25
% 25
+ 25
++ 26
about 24
overriding 15

P

parasitic inheritance 197, 198
parseFloat() function 68, 69, 305
parseInt() function 67, 68, 305
polyfills 166
polymorphism 16
predefined functions
about 66
eval() 71
isFinite() 70
isNaN() 69, 70
parseFloat() 68, 69
parseInt() 67, 68

preventDefault() method 257, 258
previously reserved words 303
primitive data types
about 28, 44
exponent literals 30
hexadecimal numbers 30
infinity 31
in JavaScript 44
numbers 29
octal numbers 29
typeof operator 28
privileged methods 283
properties
about 99
copying 184, 185
property descriptors 312
propertyIsEnumerable() method 160
prototypal inheritance 193
prototypal inheritance and copy property combination
using 193-195
prototype
inheriting 177, 178
new F() 179, 180
prototype chaining
about 171, 172
example 172-175
shared properties, moving 175-177
prototype's methods
own properties 156, 157
prototype properties 156
using 155, 156
prototype's property
about 154
enumerating 159-161
isPrototypeOf() method 162
overwriting, with own property 157, 158
secret __proto__ link 163
used, for method adding 154, 155
used, for property adding 154, 155
publish() method 298
push() method 117

Q

querySelectorAll() method 237
querySelector() method 237, 241

R

radix 67
random() function 133
rating property 157
readystatechange event 262
readyState property 262
Rectangle constructor 209
RegExp
about 139
accepting, as parameters 141
callbacks, replacing 142, 143
error objects 145-147
match()method 141
methods 140
properties 139
replace() method 142
search() method 141
split() method 144
string, passing 144
RegExp constructor
about 341
RegExp.prototype members 341
RegExp properties
global 139
ignoreCase 139
lastIndex 139
multiline 139
source 139, 140
RegExp.prototype members
exec(string) 342
global 341
ignoreCase 341
lastIndex 342
multiline 341
source 342
test(string) 342
regular expression. *See* **also RegExp**
regular expression
^ 350
? 350
. 350
(?: pattern) 352
* 350
\ 348
+ 351
\0 349

$ 350
a(?!b) 348
a(?=b) 348
a|b 348
[^abc] 347
[abc] 347
about 347
[a-z] 347
[\b] 349
\b 349
\B 349
\d 349
\f 348
{min,max} 351
{n} 351
\n 348
(pattern) 351
\r 348
\S 348
\u0000 349
\w 348
\W 349
\x00 349
removeSubscriber() method 297
replaceChild() method 245
replace() method 142
responseText property 264, 288
return 302
reverse() method 165

S

sayName() method 104
Script tab 20
search() method 141
secret __proto__ link 163
secret variable 92
setter function 92
setup() function 94
setValue() 93
shapes
analyzing 205
drawing 205
implementation 206-209
testing 210
shims 166
simple assignment operator 26
Singleton 290
Singleton 2
about 290
Constructor property 291
global variable 291
in private property 292
slice() method 118
someSetup() function 84
sort() method 117
source property 139
splice() method 118
split() method 131, 144
stopPropagation() method 255, 258
string
about 127-129
methods 129
String() constructor
about 329, 330
ECMAScript 5 additions to String 333
members 330
String.prototype members 331
string methods
about 127, 128, 129
charAt() 130
indexOf() 130
lastIndexOf() 130
slice() 131
split() method 131
substring() 131
toLowerCase() 129
String.prototype members
charAt(position) 331
charCodeAt(position) 331
indexOf(needle, start) 331
length 331
localeCompare(needle) 332
match(regexp) 332
replace(needle, re-placement) 332
search(regexp) 332
slice(start, end) 332
split(separator, limit) 332
substring(start, end) 333
toLocaleLowerCase() 333
toLocaleUpperCase() 333
toLowerCase() 333
toUpperCase() 333
String.prototype.trim() property 333

strings
about 33
conversions 34
special strings 35, 36
sum() function 66
Switch 54, 55

T

this value
using 104
toString() method 127, 157, 158, 173
training environment setup
about 17
consoles 19, 20
JavaScriptCore 18
WebKit's web inspector 17, 18
Triangle constructor 176
typeof operator 28, 75

U

uber property 181, 182
Uniform Resource Identifier. *See* **URI**
Uniform Resource Locator. *See* **URL**
URI 70
URL 70

V

valueOf() method 125
variables
$ character 22
about 21, 22
case sensitive 23, 24
hoisting 74
scope 72, 73

W

W3C 8, 214
WebKit console
objects 111
WebKit'sWeb Inspector 17
web page, building blocks
Asynchronous JavaScript loading 275
behavior 273
behavior separation, example 274
content 272
presentation 273
while loops
about 56
do-while loops 57
window.alert() 223
window.confirm() 223
window.document 226
window.frames 219, 220
window.history 218, 219
window.location 217, 218
window.moveTo() 222
window.navigator 216
window.open()/close() 222
window.prompt() 223, 224
window.resizeTo() 222
window.screen 221
window.setInterval() 225, 226
window.setTimeout() 225, 226
World Wide Web Consortium. *See* **W3C**

X

XMLHttpRequest
about 260
Asynchronous 264
example 265, 266
request, sending 261
response, processing 262
steps 261
XML 264
XMLHttpRequest objects, creating in IE 263
XMLHttpRequest object 10

[PACKT] PUBLISHING

Thank you for buying Object Oriented JavaScript *Second Edition*

About Packt Publishing

Packt, pronounced 'packed', published its first book "*Mastering phpMyAdmin for Effective MySQL Management*" in April 2004 and subsequently continued to specialize in publishing highly focused books on specific technologies and solutions.

Our books and publications share the experiences of your fellow IT professionals in adapting and customizing today's systems, applications, and frameworks. Our solution based books give you the knowledge and power to customize the software and technologies you're using to get the job done. Packt books are more specific and less general than the IT books you have seen in the past. Our unique business model allows us to bring you more focused information, giving you more of what you need to know, and less of what you don't.

Packt is a modern, yet unique publishing company, which focuses on producing quality, cutting-edge books for communities of developers, administrators, and newbies alike. For more information, please visit our website: `www.packtpub.com`.

Writing for Packt

We welcome all inquiries from people who are interested in authoring. Book proposals should be sent to `author@packtpub.com`. If your book idea is still at an early stage and you would like to discuss it first before writing a formal book proposal, contact us; one of our commissioning editors will get in touch with you.

We're not just looking for published authors; if you have strong technical skills but no writing experience, our experienced editors can help you develop a writing career, or simply get some additional reward for your expertise.

[PACKT]
PUBLISHING

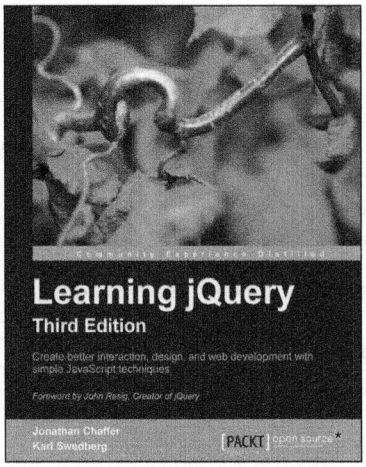

Learning jQuery Third Edition

ISBN: 978-1-84951-654-9 Paperback: 428 pages

Create better interaction, design, and web development with simple JavaScript techniques

1. An introduction to jQuery that requires minimal programming experience
2. Detailed solutions to specific client-side problems
3. Revised and updated version of this popular jQuery book

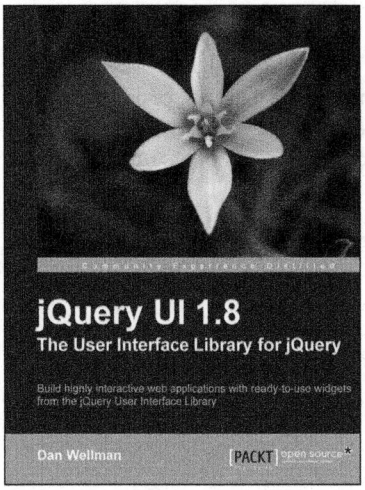

jQuery UI 1.8: The User Interface Library for jQuery

ISBN: 9781-8-4951-652-5 Paperback: 424 pages

Build highly interactive web applications with ready-to-use widgets from the jQuery User Interface Library

1. Packed with examples and clear explanations of how to easily design elegant and powerful front-end interfaces for your web applications
2. A section covering the widget factory including an in-depth example on how to build a custom jQuery UI widget
3. Updated code with significant changes and fixes to the previous edition

Please check **www.PacktPub.com** for information on our titles

[PACKT]
PUBLISHING

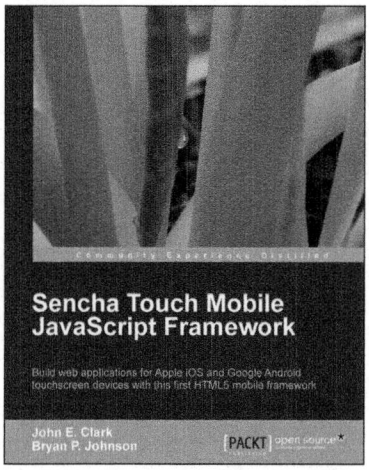

Sencha Touch Mobile JavaScript Framework

ISBN: 978-1-84951-510-8 Paperback: 316 pages

Build web applications for Apple iOS and Google Android touchscreen devices with this first HTML5 mobile framework

1. Learn to develop web applications that look and feel native on Apple iOS and Google Android touchscreen devices using Sencha Touch through examples
2. Design resolution-independent and graphical representations like buttons, icons, and tabs of unparalleled flexibility
3. Add custom events like tap, double tap, swipe, tap and hold, pinch, and rotate

---

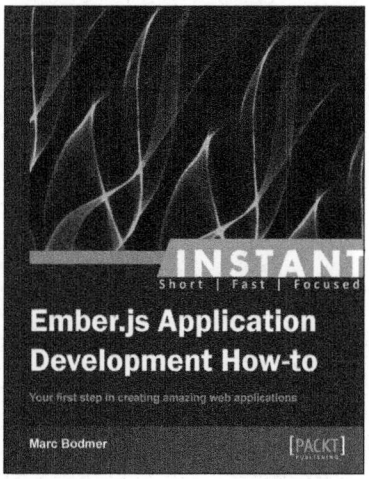

Instant Ember.js Application Development How-to

ISBN: 978-1-78216-338-1 Paperback: 48 pages

Your first step in creating amazing web applications

1. Learn something new in an Instant! A short, fast, focused guide delivering immediate results
2. Create semantic HTML templates using Handlebars
3. Lay the foundation for large web applications using the latest version of Ember.js in an easy to follow format
4. Follow clear and concise examples to build up a fully working application

Please check **www.PacktPub.com** for information on our titles

CPSIA information can be obtained
at www.ICGtesting.com
Printed in the USA
LVOW03s0730071216
516151LV00004B/54/P